"Sosnowski's fascinating account of how Napa and Sonoma winemakers struggled to survive during the national insanity known as Prohibition fills a giant hole in the history of American wine. Wine lovers everywhere should thank her for tracking down survivors, many now in their nineties, who provided rich accounts of what it was like to live through that terrible nightmare. A tale well told, Sosnowski has a fine touch."
— George M. Taber, bestselling author of *Judgment of Paris*

"Rich, moving and evocative, Sosnowski's exquisite writing brings to life a chapter of American history that has largely been forgotten. Anyone who enjoys California's legendary wines will absolutely adore *When the Rivers Ran Red*. A book to be savored, word by word. Were this a great bottle of wine, it would deserve 5 stars out of 4."
— Don and Petie Kladstrup, bestselling authors of
Wine & War: The French, the Nazis and the
Battle for France's Greatest Treasure and
Champagne: How the World's Most Glamorous
Wine Triumphed Over War and Hard Times

"Sosnowski's *When the Rivers Ran Red* will defeat the misconception that fine California wine represents a recent phenomenon. This fast paced, crisply written account of California winemakers' battle to survive Prohibition breathes new life into this precious American tradition and shows in gripping detail how deep these vines' roots run in the soils of lovely Napa and Sonoma Valleys."
— William Echikson, author of
Noble Rot: A Bordeaux Wine Revolution

"Intensely moving, fast-paced, horrifying and inspiring in turns, *When the Rivers Ran Red* is a beautifully written, deeply researched story of liberty and tyranny, the love of life and the sickness of its enemies. I shall remember it every time I visit California wine country."
— Hugh Johnson, bestselling author of
The World Atlas of Wine, *The Story of Wine*
and the *Pocket Wine Book* series.

"The tentacles of the Volstead Act were powerful and far-reaching. In telling what happened in California's valleys during the difficult years of Prohibition, Vivienne Sosnowski puts a human face on the misery and desperation, but shows the courage and ingenuity that has ultimately led to the triumph of the state's wine growers."
— Gerald Asher, *Gourmet* magazine, and author of
The Pleasures of Wine and *Vineyard Tales*

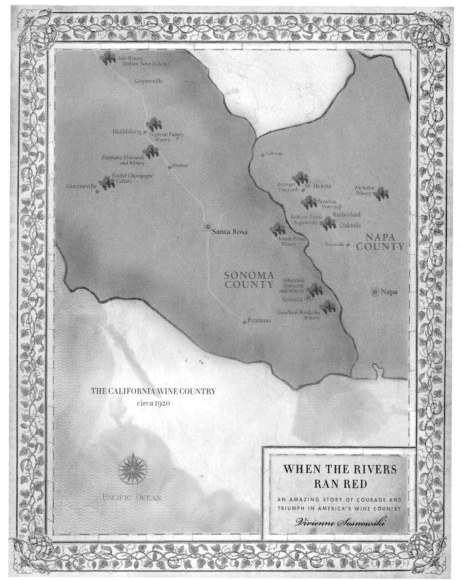

THE CALIFORNIA WINE COUNTRY
circa 1920

Asti Winery
(Italian Swiss Colony)

Geyserville

Healdsburg
Seghesio Family
Winery

Foppiano Vineyards
and Winery

Windsor

Korbel Champagne
Cellars

Guerneville

Calistoga

Beringer
Vineyards
St. Helena

Nichelini
Winery

Beaulieu
Vineyard

Santa Rosa

Rubicon Estate
(Inglenook)
Rutherford
Oakville

Kunde Estate
Winery

Yountville

NAPA
COUNTY

SONOMA
COUNTY

Sebastiani
Vineyards
and Winery

Sonoma

Napa

Gundlach Bundschu
Winery

Petaluma

PACIFIC OCEAN

**WHEN THE RIVERS
RAN RED**

AN AMAZING STORY OF COURAGE AND
TRIUMPH IN AMERICA'S WINE COUNTRY

Vivienne Sosnowski

Credit: Terry Forte, HR Hegnauer.

When the
Rivers Ran Red

To Joanne:
On the occasion of the 90th
anniversary of the beginning of
Prohibition — 1920/2010. Enjoy!

When the Rivers Ran Red

An Amazing Story of Courage and Triumph in America's Wine Country

Vivienne Sosnowski

palgrave
macmillan

ISBN: 978–0–230–60574–9

Library of Congress Cataloging-in-Publication Data is available from the Library
of Congress.

A catalogue record of the book is available from the British Library.

Design by Letra Libre

First edition: June 2009
10 9 8 7 6 5 4 3 2 1
Printed in the United States of America.

Contents

To my Mum,

Doreen Betty Martin Sosnowski,

who really knew how to tell a story

Acknowledgments

There have been so many people instrumental to the birth of this book to whom I offer my warmest and most sincere thanks.

A most grateful thank you goes to the inventive Gina Riner, who first introduced me to the pioneers who became the subject of the Enduring Spirit exhibition, now hanging in Healdsburg's city hall. Those wonderful survivors—including the late "Barney" Barnard, Angelo "Kelly" Micheli, Elsie Nardi Passalacqua, Rose Ferrari Demostene Benson, Evelyn Day Iversen, Maurice Wilcox, George Greeott (all but one in their nineties—Barney was over 100 years old) shared their rich experiences from years past as Gina and I prepared that exhibition. It was some of their recollections, some heart-warming, some sad, many inspiring, that led directly to the idea of this book. I thank them all. Very special thanks go to the amazing Louis J. Foppiano, a man who has so far experienced 84 grape harvests since his father passed away. First he helped his mother, then became a grape grower, winemaker, and winery owner in his own right. I recently enjoyed a champagne toast with Lou on his 98th birthday. Lou generously allowed me to spend memorable hours and hours with him over the past three years. Many thanks also to the much-missed Gene Cuneo and to E. Walter Murray who always made time to share his superb stories.

Deepest thanks to Bob Swofford, he kindly, patiently and quietly did what seems like a million things to make this book happen.

Especially warm thanks to my book agent, Robert Shepard—I count my blessings daily for having had him to guide me. He helped enormously, day after day, month after month.

To my editor, Alessandra Bastagli at Palgrave Macmillan, so many thanks for her most important direction, contributions, enthusiasm, and wisdom—all deeply valued. To Yasmin Mathew, the production editor, sincerest appreciation for all her excellent work.

Thanks to Rachel Ann Seghesio, whose graciousness so exemplifies the generosity and community spirit that is so evident at the Seghesio Family Winery. Thanks to Toni Nichelini-Irwin at the Nichelini winery, who not only fed me great sandwiches and pickles, she shared endless fascinating family stories over a few months of visits. I appreciate the time she gave me so unselfishly. Many thanks, too, to Harry Bosworth of the Bosworth and Son general store in Geyserville for his impressive knowledge of the history of that special place and the surrounding beautiful countryside. He was so generous and welcoming to the stranger I was when I started to call on him.

Thanks also to these wonderful and kind Wine Country people to whom I am deeply indebted: Lou Colombano, Bob Meyer, Harvey Rose, Joe and Ray Pelanconi, Mary Decia, David Cooper at Yoakim Bridge Winery, Keith Power. Thanks to the impressive librarians at every library I visited, all of whom were solicitous, and encouraging and immensely helpful help. Thanks especially to Bo Simons at the Sonoma County Wine Library who has built a global treasure chest of wine research and who could find the answer to every question I ever asked; to Charles Miller at NARA, the National Archives and Records Administration Pacific Region (San Francisco); to John Skarstad, at Special Collections at UC Davis; to Dr. Jeffrey Burns at the Archives of the Archdiocese of San Francisco, to the warm staff at the Library of Congress in Washington. And to the generous Jane Firstenfeld at Wines & Vines,

To my two inspiring colleagues at the *Washington Examiner:* Stephen Smith, executive editor, and Mark Tapscott, editorial page editor, who generously shared their deep understanding of government and Washington which helped me immeasurably: thank you.

Many special thanks to Holly Hoods, research curator at the Healdsburg Museum: a scholar of strength and intelligence who offered her insight, enthusiasm and encouragement. So many hours of her time, so much appreciated.

Thanks to all the authors of fine books on wine and history in California: Gilman Ostrander, Charles Sullivan, Ernest Peninou, Jack Florence, William Heintz, Kevin Starr, Thomas Pinney, and Rod Smith whose knowledge and learning made researching this book so illuminating.

To A. Kath, U. John and A. Rube—whose love over the years changed everything.

To my sister Anna, whose cheerful, indomitable spirit was a loving support to me during the long gestation of the book.

And to my adored children, James and Anna Maria and Merrin and Waverly, who make everything worthwhile. Thanks to you all.

Vivienne Sosnowski
Healdsburg, 2009.

Prologue

A trickle of dark liquid began to flow, slowly at first; hesitating a little, and then with a deep-throated roar it became a torrent so mighty it was if the heavens themselves had been ripped open. When the deluge hit the ground, the red liquid roiled into a fast-moving wave that churned up an angry froth. The small crowd of men, women, and children who stood watching was stunned into silence. Then their eyebrows lifted in astonishment as thousands upon thousands of gallons of liquid began to stream past their feet into a great ditch that ran alongside the Foppiano's vineyard. Moments later the crowd gasped as the flood bubbling around them grew deeper and wilder. Instinctively they yelled in terror and, in one huge convulsion, charged backwards, fathers and mothers pulling children almost out of their shirts as they dragged them out of harm's way. They turned to look back only when they felt they were far enough to gaze at the terrifying spectacle in safety.

As the ruby waves kept rolling, the vast dark stain spread wider and wider. It soon filled the great ditch and began to run every which way into the road, then across it. A makeshift dam was hurriedly constructed in an effort to contain it. The small puddle soon grew into a red lake in places two and three feet deep. Before the deluge was over, it had poured for almost two days. But this first day was the one that took everyone by surprise.

As the flood finally settled to a steady flow, the crowd started to surge back toward it. They walked up to the edge of the red lake that now stretched out before them and stared down. None of them had ever contemplated such a sight. One of the men knelt, leaned into the lake, and tentatively stuck his fingers into it. Gingerly he brought them to his lips, sucked, swallowed, and turned to the others.

"What? What?" they called.

He smiled and chuckled, and the others stepped forward to taste the liquid, too. The wine had been aging—like all wines, there were years when this wine had been at its prime, then it would naturally sour and rapidly become undrinkable—and the crowd had been expecting the worst. But from the first taste, good news—it had not turned too noticeably on the tongue. The wine was still drinkable. Yes, eminently so. In seconds, everyone was shouting for help from the children, who ran as fast as their legs could carry them to bring the bottles, jugs, and pans they had carried from home for this moment. Now they began to fill every container they could find: jam jars that ordinarily contained homemade preserves, milk bottles from the town's dairies that had been scrubbed out in happy anticipation, olive oil containers, and more. Soon they were all filled and placed carefully in baby carriages, or hand-wagons, or in the pockets of jackets and shirts. They were even nestled in the backseats of the many cars now surrounding the site.

The crowd was jubilant. This was better than a vacation. Before them, after all, was a reservoir of free wine. Soon, up to 140,000 gallons of wine, made in the traditional Italian style at the renowned Foppiano family vineyard, would run from the hoses into the public ditches and beyond. The Foppianos had made their reds from Zinfandel, Petite Sirah, and Carignane grapes—when they were put in barrels and sold, they were named Burgundy or Barberone. "The difference was strictly in the color," explained Louis J. Foppiano in a 1996 interview with Richard Paul Hinkle that appeared in *Wines & Vines* as he recalled his family history. "If it was heavy and dark, it was Barberone."[1] In the days before Prohibition, he continued, consumers saw little distinction among the reds—that came later with better labeling and marketing, and the development of consumers' wine tastes.

Had it made the trip to market, the wine that ended up in a lake in 1926 would mostly have been sold in barrels directly to dealers and then resold to grocery and general stores across the nation. In most places, if you wanted wine, you brought your own jug or bottle. In San Francisco, you could buy an empty jug for filling for 25 cents and, as Lou Foppiano remembered, "The wines had to be dark and have a lot of body to sell."[2]

The Foppianos' vineyard stretched across 50 acres through the gentle green splendor of Sonoma County, 60 miles north of San Francisco and even closer to the craggy Pacific coast. The family lived just off the dusty, winding highway to the city and only steps away from their winery, with its huge redwood barrels. Usually their wines ended up in the homes and restaurants of San Francisco,

Chicago, New York, and New Orleans, and made a fine living for the family. On a day still described with horror in their community 80 years later, many years of hard work was suddenly worth nothing at all.

That momentous day did not spell bad luck for everyone. For neighbors who made the 15-minute trek south from the tiny farming community of Healdsburg, it turned into a riotous holiday. For the Foppianos, the day had been a cruel trial. Mathilda, the proud head of the family, a beautiful and composed young widow whose husband had died from a heart attack only two years earlier, had gained the admiration of her neighbors for her composure throughout the disasters of the previous few years. She had shown great strength in taking on the responsibility for an entire winery and grape ranch. As she walked on this tough day into the morning sunshine with her three children, Rosalind, Norma, and her youngest, Louis, she crossed defiantly to where a line of huge redwood tanks held the fruits of several growing seasons. The Foppianos had been making wine on this fertile Russian River Valley flatland since 1896, and none of them ever dreamed that one day they would be watched by federal agents, permits in hand and revolvers tucked into their waistbands, as they turned a spigot to a hose connected to the bottom of their huge wine tanks, destroying what had taken this small family so much exhausting work to produce.

As the wine spilled out over the countryside, the two federal agents hung back from the crowd. At first they were subjected to a barrage of nasty catcalls and even sharper cuss words, but as the wine continued to flow, fewer in the crowd took notice of the silent officials. As the wine ebbed, the men scribbled notations on their official papers, happy to have survived the morning without being pelted by eggs or tomatoes, as they had been on so many similar occasions. The Foppianos watched the destruction, horrified as the results of so many years of perseverance—pruning, harvesting, crushing, and aging the wine as it slowly developed to drinkability—were wiped out in one cruel stroke.

The revelers were soon joined by carloads of sightseers; one newspaper declared that "thousands" of the thirsty and curious showed up.[3] The story of a reporter from another paper, the *Healdsburg Tribune*, appeared the next day under the headline "River of Wine Runs on Sunday: Many Take Drink." The article continued: "Impromptu Charlestons and songs of festivity were staged on the highway in celebration of the waste of jazz fluid, as the volunteer sponges began to get a 'kick' from the fermented product of the vine."[4] The breakneck dancing slowed considerably as the day warmed to nearly 100 degrees and the drinking progressed. By suppertime, most of the mothers and children who had settled in soft, deep grasses, protected from the searing sun by the leafy umbrellas of prune trees, started to rouse themselves back into action. They packed away the last remnants of their picnics of bread and cheese and homemade pastries, wrapped up their babies and gathered together their tired toddlers. Then they bumped their baby carriages across the Russian River's narrow truss bridge and disappeared into their homes on the dozen or so now-misty streets of Healdsburg, festooned at that time of year with billows of watercolor pink and yellow roses and the softest mauve crape myrtle.

By dusk, fathers and sons slowed by the alcohol followed the women down the main road. A few men remained behind: when they could no longer stand, they had fallen asleep under the trees, and they slept on for some hours. One local who had been enjoying the event with perhaps too much enthusiasm was hit by a car near the scene. After being taken to the local hospital to be treated for painful cuts and bruises, he was arrested and given 30 days in the county jail.[5]

Much later, hoboes—victims of the harsh boom-or-bust nature of California's resource and agricultural industries—wandered back through the darkening evening to the railroad tracks just west of the Foppiano vineyard, some awaiting the puffing of a steam locomotive that meant another ride north or south, others making their way to the Russian River to spend the night under the bridge. Thought to be last to abandon the much-shrunken lake of wine was the prescient local farmer who had brought a sleeping bag to the revelries and who had spent the day drinking wine, napping, and then drinking wine again all afternoon. There in the dark blue valley, where the summer fog had just rolled off the Pacific to blanket the stars and the moon, he folded up his sleeping bag, slung it over his shoulders, and headed home.[6]

As the stragglers left, the singing and laughing quieted down, and before long the little town of 2,500 slept as silently as it did every other night. The day had been one long party for everyone but the Foppianos. And now Healdsburg's citizens headed to bed as they always did in recent times: uneasy, and still struggling to comprehend how Prohibition was changing their town, their economy, and their lives.

Chapter One

The Land was Sacred to These Families

Everyone involved in the northern California's wine industry knew well the precise date on which their lives had changed. Seven years before the Foppiano calamity, on Wednesday October 29, 1919, the people of Sonoma and Napa awoke to a deceptively perfect autumn day and many read an astonishing headline. "BONE DRY AMERICA AT ONCE EFFECTIVE BY SENATE'S VOTE" shrieked the *Santa Rosa Press Democrat*'s front page in a bold, entirely capitalized headline.[1] The influential newspaper in the Sonoma County seat reported the Volstead Act's successful passage in Washington the day before. That law had been hurriedly crafted to complement and enforce the Eighteenth Amendment to the Constitution, banning the making, sale, transportation, and importing and exporting of alcoholic beverages, a historic piece of legislation passed in December 1917 that had then taken its sweet time to achieve ratification across the nation in January 1919.

The news from the nation's capital rocked the wine communities like a shock wave from the San Andreas Fault only a few miles to the southwest. For the winemakers and grape growers in the two counties, nestled up against the rugged Mayacamas Mountains, wine was both a pleasure and livelihood, and had been for almost a century. For decades before Prohibition, alcohol was as much a part of the daily routine for many Americans as feeding the chickens or milking the family cow. But unlike most other imbibers across the country, for whom beer and whiskey ruled, in Napa and Sonoma it was the homegrown hearty wines and rich, fruity brandies that many locals drank with the most pleasure and pride. Wine-makers of Sonoma and Napa might start their day with coffee and a small brandy (distilled in their own woodsheds or barns from the family wines). Then they would pour the day's first glass of wine at midmorning, followed by another at lunch, one in the late afternoon, and finally a glass or two at dinner to stimulate the appetite and to relax them after a day's backbreaking work in the vineyards. Wine was the natural and expected accompaniment to every part of the day, and to many who lived in California, it seemed to have always been that way.[2]

But as important as wine was to the counties' lifestyle, for decades it had been another important linchpin of a bustling farm economy. Long before Prohibition, green and fertile Sonoma County was renowned as the breadbasket of San Francisco for its wheat, potatoes, oats, barley, butter, cheese, pears, peaches, and cherries. Many families still owed their solid homes and pleasant lives to those splendid crops, especially to the massive local prune harvest—gathered from plum trees and dried in the sun or in mechanical dryers—and exported as far away as Germany. Hops were sold nationwide to a vast U.S. beer industry that expanded daily, as were many delicious varieties of apples from the region that owed their flavor and crunch, it was said, to the ocean fogs that drifted through the county on so many summer nights. The U.S. military was an important apple consumer; its orders were for a dried version to be stored for use by American men in uniform around the world.

By the late decades of the 1800s, it was the wine, already sold across the country and increasingly to Europe, that was becoming not just a trademark but also one of the irreplaceable centerpieces of the economy. By 1919, Californians had planted vast tracts of land with dozens of wine varietals: Some of the 400,000 tons of wine grapes produced that year had been turned into dry and sweet wines, notwithstanding Prohibition, perhaps in the belief of winemakers that it was better to act while the grapes were ripe and deal with the consequences later.[3]

The central San Joaquin Valley still produced the bulk of the state's total grape output, but by 1900, long before Prohibition, vineyards in Napa and Sonoma boasted cellars filled with barrels of good reds and whites and hundreds of thousands of bottles of sparkling wine. By the early 1900s, thrifty and hardworking families like the Beringers, Seghesios, Bundschus, Simis, Passalacquas, and

Foppianos were cultivating some of the most successful vineyards and grape ranches in the two counties and their operations supported their families in often unaccustomed comfort. By Prohibition many of them were able to add cars, gramophones, and spacious homes to their greatest asset: their invaluable and much-loved acres of fertile land.

The land was sacred to these families, and it meant much more to them than comfortable lives. Many of the winemakers could recall their immigrant fathers' stories about the early years: how they used meager savings to buy property; how they cut down huge trees and wrenched giant stumps out of the ground with chains and horses or struggled with mules and plows on raw, arid land buzzing with rattlesnakes; and how they built their first homes with their own hands, often with lumber they had cut themselves.

Among the increasingly notable Sonoma clans, the Foppianos were typical: a small, tight-knit family who labored shoulder to shoulder, day after day. Their patriarch, Giovanni, had established his lush vineyard just before the end of the nineteenth century. The land he bought had a dramatic history even before the state of California was established. The Foppiano property and the surrounding hills, valleys, and mountains had been part of the vast Sotoyome Rancho when Mexico still ruled this land. The 48,800-acre rancho had been a lavish grant by the Mexican government to a clever sea captain and astute businessman named Henry Delano Fitch, a native of New Bedford, Massachusetts, who had sailed his ship into San Diego harbor in 1826 and had promptly fallen deeply in love with Josefa Carrillo, the teenage daughter of a well-connected Mexican soldier. The couple married after a risky elopement to South America. Fitch acquired a general store in San Diego, surveyed and mapped land, and became a public figure: first a town attorney, then justice of the peace, and then *alcade,* the chief executive of San Diego, all the while continuing his trading by ship.[4] Fitch had a charmed life, but one of the most fortuitous parts of it was that one of Josefa's sisters, Francisca Benecia, married General Mariano Vallejo, the most powerful man in California. This family relationship smoothed the way for Fitch's massive land grant. Over time, the land Fitch amassed was broken into much smaller parcels, including the land where the Foppianos worked their vines.

Like tens of thousands of his countrymen from Italy in the last half of the 1800s, Giovanni Foppiano had come to California in 1864 in search of gold. And like many of the others, he too left his hometown apprehensive about the long journey to reach the gold fields, although he did not know enough to realize that when he set off he would take one of the more complicated routes possible in search of his dream. After sailing from Europe to Panama, family lore says he walked across the isthmus, and although there had been a railroad built there by 1855 mainly for travelers headed to the Gold Rush that crossed a 47-mile sliver of land from the Atlantic to the Pacific, it is likely Giovanni traveled through the isthmus' jungle, rivers, and lakes by road and by boat like many others. Then he would have boarded yet another sailing ship for the last leg up the coast to San Francisco.[5] This courageous young man from Genoa was also resilient and inventive.

For everyone who made it big in the gold fields, hundreds, perhaps thousands, of others left empty-handed, aghast at the isolation, daily violence, armed robberies, drunkenness, and starvation on the remote rivers that rushed down from the soaring peaks of the Sierra Nevada. Giovanni, like others, must have looked around one day at the mining life he had embarked on and asked himself if another calling could offer more to a man with more practical expectations. Soon other immigrants from southern Europe, including many Italians, ran prosperous market gardens throughout California. Setting themselves up with a handful of simple tools and a few acres of land, they grew and sold vegetables to housewives. Grapevines were almost an afterthought to business, often planted to provide wine so the farmers and their families could enjoy a glass with dinner, as had been their tradition back home. But many of them, Giovanni Foppiano included, also brought an unerring instinct for business to their agricultural endeavors; if they could grow grapes to make wine for themselves, they could also turn winemaking into another kind of enterprise. By 1896, Giovanni had amassed enough capital to build a winery.

Giovanni's neighbors were cut from the same cloth: industrious, entrepreneurial, independent. Just a few miles over a bridge, then through a dusty town plaza, a tiny square of parkland, in the little city of Healdsburg and onward north just a few short miles, Edoardo Seghesio, another Italian immigrant, had already purchased land in this county and had begun to plant his own vineyard. By that time, Seghesio had plenty of experience with grapes and wine. Edoardo had first labored in the winery and fields at Sonoma County's huge Italian Swiss Agricultural Colony winery near Asti, about 80 miles north of San Francisco at the invitation of the great winemaker Pietro Carlo Rossi. Seghesio had worked for the Rossi family back in Italy and had impressed family members there.[6] Andrea Sbarboro, who had traveled in steerage to a still-wild San Francisco many years before when he was 13, had launched the Italian Swiss Agricultural Colony in 1881.

He had arrived in the port city a year before a young Levi Strauss and his legendary bolts of denim cloth had landed by boat from New York under circumstances just as physically uncomfortable.[7] The Colony began with nearly 1,500 acres of land at Asti, just south of Cloverdale, purchased for $25,000, $10,000 of which was the downpayment.[8] Just after the turn of the twentieth century, it operated a wine vault in San Francisco on the corner of Battery and Greenwich streets that could store two million gallons of wine. [9]

During his years at the Swiss Colony, Edoardo had been able to save a lump sum on which to build his future. By 1895 he had married the very intelligent and pretty Angela Vasconi, equally industrious as he, and the daughter of his Asti boss. Edoardo used his savings to buy his first plot of land. Sturdy and still in his middle years, he, too, was unafraid of hard work and the uncertainties of living so far from his family roots in the Piedmontese village of Dogliani, not far from the original Asti.

As his tiny ranch began to prosper, Seghesio looked for more grape-growing land that he could afford. By 1910, the family's new home in the Alexander Valley was surrounded by Zinfandel grapes that would turn into the great spicy red wines with their fruity and peppery finish, so dear to the heart of Californians. And soon new parcels too, would be planted to hearty varietals, some from his homeland, including Sangiovese and Trebbiano. By 1918, Edoardo was making 100,000 gallons of wine a year, remembered his son Eugene many years later. He cleared $4,000 a year and had $80,000 in the bank. He was to risk everything and lose a great deal not long after that.[10]

Just as hardworking as the Seghesio family were the Cuneos. The family's main asset was fertile land in the Dry Creek Valley, some parts sloping, some parts pancake flat, a few short miles by road from the vineyards of the Foppianos and Seghesios. The Cuneo family produced some wine but were also important grape growers in the district. John Cuneo, who abandoned his baptismal name of Giovanni when he arrived in San Francisco as a 17-year-old, left Liguria in 1900 with $5 in his pocket and the knowledge that he would soon be eligible for the draft if he stayed. A farm laborer at first, he soon became a cooper and then bought a share in a garbage-hauling business in San Francisco.

Like many of his countrymen, John depended on family connections to get him established, starting a grape farm with his brother-in-law and asking his mother to send a wife from his home village of Chiavari, outside Genoa. The tall and enchanting Maria, who spoke no English, arrived on one of the derisively nicknamed "macaroni boats" with the words "San Francisco" printed on a sign tied with a ribbon around her neck. In 1919, John Cuneo still ran the original ranch with his four children—and all of them, especially their only son, Eugene— were vital participants in every part of the ranch operations. The Cuneos considered themselves lucky to have such hardworking children; they could hire fewer ranch hands.[11]

Frank Passalacqua, another neighbor and winemaker, had arrived in the United States from Italy by way of New York in 1865 when he was 18. One of six sons of a family that lived about 12 miles from Genoa and completely unschooled, Passalacqua had started work at age six picking olives. He had saved enough money by the time he was 13 to buy his first pair of shoes. After some of his teenage years spent selling fish in France, he set out for America. Frank was yet another lionhearted refugee who originally tested his fortunes unsuccessfully in California's cruel gold country. Nearly 20 years after he arrived in California, he was settled in Healdsburg in Sonoma County. Thanks to Healdsburg's salubrious climate he raised crops throughout the year. On one three-quarter acre parcel "he picked 1,000 to 1,200 baskets of strawberries a week."[12] By 1889, Frank had 20 acres in vines that produced 25 tons of Zinfandel.[13]

Although many Italian families were well established in the 1900s, the wine industry in Sonoma and Napa had been born long before. California's first grape growers came from an unlikely place: Russia, whose czar sent colonists to develop a trading base on California's North Coast in the spring of 1812.[14] The Russian-American Company's attempt to cultivate grapes was a victim of the climate on the blustery, misty cliffs of Sonoma County's coast. The endless bone-chilling damp of that raw exposed seacoast was in stark contrast to the mild winters and torrid summer days that blessed Napa and Sonoma only a few dozen miles inland, both tucked behind the protecting embrace of a ripple of coastal mountains.

Another beginning for the wine industry came during the mild winter of 1823, in a tiny clearing among the oak trees that would later become the pretty wine village of Sonoma. Here, a tough Franciscan priest planted 3,000 grapevines to provide wine for the sacrament of mass as well as for enjoyment.[15] Mission priests had green thumbs, along with the time and the help in the fields to make the most of them. They planted flowers: lilies, roses, jasmine, and lavender. They gathered their own nuts and fruits year round: oranges, limes, peaches, pears, pomegranates, and almonds. They were able to cook hearty meals from the rice, wheat, maize, lentils, and garbanzos they grew, and they spiced those meals with home-grown spices and flavorings: tamarind, anise, and cumin. The mission priests cultivated many other necessities of life, including cotton, flax, hemp, and tobacco.[16] And they planted grapes. You could reach from a window and almost touch the vines planted just a few feet outside the newly completed mud walls of the Mission San Francisco Solano de Sonoma, the most northerly of 21 religious outposts on the Camino Real, the Spanish royal trail from San Diego to Sonoma. Then controlled by the Catholic Church, the missions were soon to be secularized by Mexico, abandoned, and then swallowed up by that brand-new creation, the state of California. But the legacy of that tiny vineyard was momentous: It was the first to be carved out of a valley that would one day evolve into Sonoma's rich quilt of vineyards.

In 1917, the granddaughter of early Napa Valley settler George C. Yount (for whom the town of Yountville was named) related her memories of winemaking in the 1840s. Mrs. George J. Bucknall's grandfather, thanks to his friendship with General Vallejo, once the commanding general of Alta California for the Mexican government, had acquired a "lordly domain of more than twenty square miles extending across the heart of the [Napa] valley and reaching from ridge to ridge of the mountains." Yount soon secured cuttings of Mission grape vines and was one of the first winemakers in the state. "I remember well the primitive manner in which I first saw the pressing out of the grape juice," Mrs. Bucknell related. "A huge ox skin cleansed and stretched was firmly fastened to four stout stakes driven securely into the ground," and two or more stalwart Native Americans "trampled out the vintage in truly pastoral style. Later troughs were used, the Indians crushing the grapes with their feet. The juice was run into vats and after fermenting was put in casks."[17]

As the nineteenth century wore on, still more immigrants destined to become winemakers continued to arrive on ships from Europe, most still braving the long journey around Cape Horn to San Francisco. After 1869, the journey got easier—it was now possible to cross the Atlantic to New York and then head to California via the new transcontinental railroad. At first, there was no hearty welcome for what little California wine was produced for sale. America was a nation of confirmed beer drinkers who developed a whiskey habit once the growth of Midwestern grain fields made hard liquor production cheap. What wine Americans coveted came from Europe; even Californians preferred French wines to those produced nearby. In San Francisco, where the gold frenzy had made men rich enough to build stately homes on the top of Nob Hill and to be entertained in grand hotels and private clubs, the city's savvy wine agents wrote out orders for wine from France's most renowned wine-making areas. In the past, wines from Bordeaux were sent as ballast, the ships returning home with grain. Later, as Californian fortunes grew, other much finer wines along with champagne and brandy, arrived in the holds of clipper ships after passages as long as six months at sea. The cost of such long journeys was one of the reasons French wine sold at a terrific premium. The French ship *Aurelie,* which arrived in the port of San Francisco on March 29, 1851, was typical. It had sailed from Le Havre 152 days before, carrying only seven passengers but 1,000 "packages" of Champagne and 2,557 cases of wine.[18]

However felicitous consumers found imported wine, interest in developing fine wines in California continued to grow. In an effort to improve the state's industry, Agoston Haraszthy, a Hungarian immigrant who has sometimes been called the father of California's wine industry, brought numerous wine cuttings of many varietals back to Sonoma from elsewhere, though it is not clear, says Charles Sullivan in his *Companion to California Wine,* exactly what effect they really had on the future of California wine.[19] An oft-repeated, perhaps apocryphal story relates that Haraszthy's life ended in tragedy. It is said he died at age 57 while traveling on business in Venezuela, after slipping off a log bridge and dying in the jaws of an alligator.

By the middle of the 1860s California could boast an estimated 25 million vines of hundreds of grape varietals in cultivation. Already harvests were skyrocketing, and it was possible to grow enough wine not only for household needs but for retail and wholesale customers too. The wines were getting better, prices were more affordable, and consumers were beginning to notice. Eastern markets were also taking notice. And California was already exporting hock, Champagne, port and claret, along with Muscatel and Angelica which had brandy added to them for fortification.[20]

By 1883, California winemakers had become a community which included wineries in Los Angeles, El Dorado, Placer, San Joaquin, Santa Clara, Napa, and Sonoma counties, among others: "140,000 acres of grapes were under cultivation and 8,500,000 gallons of wine produced."[21] By 1879, one winemaker in Sonoma made 114,000 gallons on his 40 acres of vines;[22] and Joshua Chauvert produced 9,000 gallons on 30 acres.[23]

Beginning in Sonoma in 1873 and 1874, however, the dreaded insect phylloxera had invaded northern California vineyards, spreading to Napa and becoming a widespread epidemic in the 1880s and 1890s. Writing in March 1887, Ben Truman of the *New York Times* reported that entire vineyards had suffered in the two counties.[24] A phylloxera infestation stunts, even kills grapevines by feeding on the sap in their roots, and the insect was in its glory in the heavy clay soils of the two wine counties. Many vineyard owners had to rip out their vines and replant with resistant stock.

The cost of replacing vines was a hardship not only for those who were still struggling to establish their businesses but also for those vineyards that had started to gain some success across the nation and in Europe. Waiting the three years necessary for new vines to reach full bearing—or for the five years some winemakers believe a new vine needs before it produces grapes that truly resonate their full personality derived from soil and the climate—meant reduced harvests for a few years that put them at a decided disadvantage with competitors and the drinking public everywhere.

Truman spent the week reporting from the two valleys, and his articles gave a rare insight into the surprisingly developed state of the wine business in the late 1880s. He noted that Napa Valley already shipped 50,000 gallons of wine a year to eastern markets and that the reputation of Napa and Sonoma as producers of the best red and white wines in the state was growing.

The two wine counties, Napa and Sonoma, were small change compared to the biggest vine-growing areas of the state located farther south and east, in Los Angeles and in Fresno counties in the middle of the hot, dry Central Valley where irrigation was essential.

Napa County spanned 505,000 acres, 13,852 of which were in vines: 1,547 were 1-year vines, 2,396 were 2-year vines, 2,396 were 3-year vines, 2,256 were 4 years old, and 4,697 were 5 years old and more. In comparison, Sonoma County encompassed 905,000 acres, 18,183 of them in vines with an astounding 6,046 of those vines from 5 to 30 years old already. Sonoma County had produced almost 3,000,000 gallons of wine and brandy in 1886, reported Truman, with Napa making about 5,000,000 gallons, he said.

The vineyards of Napa had first been planted on the valley floor often with Zinfandel. As growers became more experienced, they had started to plant on the hills and benchlands of the valley. While that land produced fewer grapes per vine, it made for fruit that turned into wine of much higher quality. Zinfandel was now considered a second-class grape in Napa, said Truman, and it was expected that Cabernet Sauvignon, Cabernet Franc, Merlot, Verdot, and Malbec de Bordeaux—from which French superstars like Château Lafitte and Château Margaux were produced—would soon be taking its place.

Truman met with some winemakers in the state—Henry. W. Crabb, Major William Scheffler, the Honorable Morris Estee, Captain Hamden W. McIntyre, and Jacob Schram—and he said they considered Napa to have the combination of soil and atmosphere most similar to the grandest of French vineyards in Bordeaux. What was needed to make Napa wine as good as the best of France was expertise in blending, although he noted that some of the county's best vineyards had already brought cellar men from famed French vineyards. As these wines were released to the public, Truman expected a revolution in America's wine habit.

In all, Truman said there were 132 winecellars in Napa County and 108 wineries in Sonoma, plus approximately 100 stills for making brandy. Among Napa's most distinguished properties already was one that remains well known to Wine Country travelers today: the Niebaum family's Inglenook Vineyard (now part of movie director Francis Ford Coppola's considerable winemaking holdings), which Truman deemed "one of the finest and completest in any country." Niebaum's wines were already established in New York, where the Wines and Spirit Traders' Society had commended them. Niebaum had already opened offices on New York's Vesey Street and on London's Mincing Lane in order to help sell his wine, which in his winery he could store 250,000 gallons at a time.

Jacob Schram had already been making wine for more than 20 years, another notable winemaker who stored his wines in cellars carved out of the mountains near Calistoga, said Truman. Although his white wines were commendable, he probably did not sell any wine outside California because demand in the state was so high.

Truman described an ideal winery of the time that belonged to Morris Estee, a lawyer and state politician. Named Hedgeside, it was located about three and a half miles outside Napa. Its approach was through a drive of tall cedars, waving palms, and dark-green leafed orange trees. Estee had 425 acres of grapes planted with some of the best red and white varietals from Germany and France and an immaculate winery with a capacity of 300,000 gallons.[25]

At the Chicago Exposition of 1893, 63 exhibitors from California displayed 301 varieties of wine, including 143 varieties of white wine, 120 red, and many varieties of sweet wine including Malaga, Muscatel, port, Sherry, and Tokay. The state exhibit also showed off 5 varieties of sparkling wine and 44 of grape brandy. A few vineyards displayed their own products, including Vina Vineyard of the Leland Stanford Estate—the former governor of California Stanford had also founded Stanford University—which topped its exhibit with two jaw-dropping fountains, one of which spewed forth "a jet of sparkling wine," the other a cascade of red wine.[26]

On April 18, 1906, San Francisco's Great Earthquake and fire damaged millions of gallons of wines in San Francisco, the second great disaster to strike California winemakers. The once-beautiful city, full of immense mansions and glamorous hotels, hundreds of restaurants and busy shopping thoroughfares, and thousands of ordinary workplaces and homes, was devastated by a quake that lasted less than two minutes and a resulting firestorm that did even more damage. In the initial tremblor, which began after 5 A.M., buildings wavered and collapsed, chimneys toppled and roofs fell in. Roads tore in two. Everywhere was the sound of breaking glass and panic-stricken inhabitants rushed from their homes to the streets. A massive fire storm consumed the city for days and finished off what the earthquake had not. Among the city's decimated businesses were hundreds of wine dealers and stores. Although the wineries of Napa and Sonoma avoided great damage, many lost wine stocks held in San Francisco.

"Half of the wines stored in California—were licked [as] if by the greedy flames," the *California Grape Grower* reported on the earthquake's twentieth anniversary. "The California Wine Association's wonderful collection of aged wines, which they had hoped to put out in bottle form, was completely wiped out and so were the valuable stocks of twenty other firms whose vintages had won recognition at home and abroad."[27]

Some of the devastated firms had exhibited in the Paris International Universal Exposition in 1900 and were hoping that export sales would grow exponentially after that.[28] They included Vista Wines (wine dealers in the grand Palace Hotel, which had survived the flames longer than most other buildings thanks to a state-of-the-art water system); wine merchants Ciocca & Lombardi, who were part owners of Sonoma County's Geyser Peak Winery; and the Cresta Blanca Wine Company owned by Charles Wetmore, who originated the idea of the state's first viticultural commissioner. The venerable Gundlach Bundschu wine company, which had begun operations more than 40 years earlier by Jacob Gundlach and partners and whose 400-acres of prime vineyards were tucked into the gentle hills east of Sonoma, lost its city premises on Bryant Street along with a million gallons of wine. There were many others. A rare survivor was the Italian Swiss Colony's salesroom and vault operation near the city's waterfront. In the months after the earthquake, the *Grower* recalled, it was able to supply its customers the Colony's Sonoma County wines "just as though nothing had happened."

Wine reportedly had a beneficial effect on one neighborhood even during the conflagration, as the *Grower* reported: "A cluster of homes on Telegraph Hill were saved by desperate Italians who poured their stores of wine on their burning roofs when the city's water supply was cut off by the destructive upheaval caused by the earthquake."[29]

Other wineries in Napa and Sonoma benefited as well. At the time of the earthquake, dry wine was selling for about 11 and 12 cents a gallon wholesale, remembered Antonio Perelli-Minetti, who had come to the Italian Swiss Colony in the early 1900s and who eventually owned a huge winery in the Central Valley. After the quake "the only wine that was left was in the country," and prices in Wine Country shot up to 28 cents a gallon.

Perelli-Minetti declared that the earthquake had changed the weather in Wine Country: "Before the earthquake, in Healdsburg, it would snow in the valley: some four or five inches would fall." Afterward that no longer happened, he declared in a 1969 interview with Ruth Teiser for the Regional Wine History Office of The Bancroft Library. And after the earthquake, winters got colder. "You couldn't sit in the plaza in Healdsburg without an overcoat, it was so cold. The fog—you couldn't see yourself from here to over there. Before you could go anyplace, to San Francisco, to Eureka and you'd seldom see a speck of fog in the winter. Now it's so foggy that it kills."

As northern California slowly picked itself up from the earthquake, wineries started to fight their way back. The mighty California Wine Association, which lost its huge collection of aged wines, said Peretti-Minelli, "maybe a couple of million gallons,"[30] built a vast and earthquake-proof plant called Winehaven on San Francisco Bay. California's wine industry, which had survived a major infestation and the destruction of an epic earthquake and fire, however, was no match for the next disaster that started in earnest too soon after the quake.

Although the clamor for temperance grew throughout the first decades of the 1900s, grape growers and winery owners felt far removed from that conversation.

In so many ways, life seemed to unfold as usual for the population of the two counties. These were people of a philosophical and patient nature, like most whose lives are built on agriculture. They were used to standing fast under the arbitrary whims of nature and the shifting tastes and fortunes of their customers. And so Napa and Sonoma did what they always did every harvest. Not much more than a decade after the big earthquake: 1919, the year before absolute Prohibition, was no exception. Winemakers there continued as always to transform the year's splendid harvest into wine. By Thanksgiving of that year, most of the vintage from that bumper crop was already tucked into wineries, starting on its tranquil journey and growing richer and more complex each day. Local churches celebrated the annual harvest with song and prayer and displays of the bounty of the land: spaces around fonts and lecterns were stacked with sheaves of bronze wheat, bundles of golden sunflowers, piles of pumpkins and squash, baskets of apples and tomatoes and peppers. During every mass, golden marigolds and the last of the pale summer roses sat in big jugs on altars and were tied with big bows of ribbons around pulpits. Churchgoers agreed there had been much to be thankful for; they felt humbled again by the grace of God for the blessings of nature and the opportunity to toil diligently and in dignity on one's own land.

The year in Wine Country had began, as ever, with early spring rains that fell in soft, windblown curtains across the sparkling Navarro, Russian, and Napa rivers and the Mark West and Dry creeks. Reaching the sea full to their banks, the flow of the largest rivers was the first sign that the summer's irrigation, so necessary to sustain millions of grapevines, would run reliably. The rivers gurgled through lush grasslands then rolled under woodlands of oak and pine and forests of firs and redwoods. Steelhead and Chinook salmon fought the currents to find warm shallows to lay their eggs. Mink, muskrats, and gray fox loped across the near blue hills while bears, mountain lions, and gaggles of wild turkeys raised new families in the wilderness that lay beyond the hills. Rattlesnakes stirred underground. And above all that were the sounds of ducks, great blue herons, red-tailed hawks, turkey vultures, and white egrets heading to their nesting grounds.

As it still does some 90 years later, spring burst out as if in a dance: Thousands of prune trees with pale blossoms looked like so many ballerinas twirling in frothy tulle. Golden mustard flowers glowed among chocolate brown vines still to leaf. All summer, the hot afternoon air helped the green grapes swell to juicier sweetness each day: even the red wine grapes start green only turning to red as they ripen. Many evenings, vast Pacific fogs poured quietly over rippling ridges into the two valleys and the surrounding flatlands. Once settled, the fog's soft embrace cooled the winemaking families and the grapes they depended on; the moist night air gave rest to the fruit, slowing the ripening and allowing it more time to engorge and develop richer, fuller flavors. Summer gardens were picked early before the day's heat set in: Kitchen tables overflowed before breakfast with sweet, fat tomatoes and even sweeter corn, and salad makings of lettuce and beets and cucumbers. Juicy stone fruits—peaches, nectarines, apricots, and cherries—were set on platters next to strawberries, raspberries, blueberries, watermelons, and a rainbow of plums in shades of yellow and green and red and purple. Before long, canning cupboards were full of berry jams and sweet pickles and row after row of vegetables in jars in almost every color of the spectrum. Vines overhung gates and fences: Small but sweet table grapes jostled for the sun alongside purple morning glories and climbing roses in white and red. Tiny, potent jasmine blossoms scented the air.

By fall, deep red peppers, gleaming purple eggplants and huge rippled pumpkins glowed in every garden. Baskets of walnuts were collected and the last dark ripe figs of the year laid gently into kitchen towels. It was hard to keep count of the many varieties of apples that had been picked and stored away in barns and attics. Hunting season was done. Ducks, geese, and deer and the fierce wild pigs of both counties had been cleaned and butchered and ready for company. And as the mild warm winter began, the last of the vegetables would be dug up and the final bales of oats, alfalfa, and wild hay stood alongside boxes of horse corn and sacks of walnuts.

And now it was time to rest: The party resorts of Sonoma, Russian River, and Napa Valleys imported top bands from San Francisco, even New Orleans; and couples drove out of town for soirees, with energetic dancing. Soon the ranch families would sweep out their prune barns—the strong straight floors were considered the best dancing surfaces in the valleys. They would wrestle a barrel of their best red wine into the corner, and they would gather up their neighbors and families and hire their favorite accordion players to play popular and familiar songs: "Lady of Spain" and "Beer Barrel Polka." Everyone would dance and at midnight, a supper would be served, a substantial meal that would last through many more hours of dancing. The women would wrap their arms around huge bowls of steaming pasta topped with the fruity tomato sauce made with their homegrown vegetables and herbs and set them down gently on long trestle tables groaning with the weight of huge loaves of bread from local ovens, plates of homemade salamis and sausages, jugs of wine, and bowls of pickles and nuts and crackers. Always a favorite on the party menu, especially as the autumn evenings grew chillier, were vast platters of warm polenta that the cooks stirred with lashings of local cheese and lumps of butter the size of eggs. Often they topped it off with ladles full of rich meat stews that had bubbled in ovens for hours. Next came the sweet course: pies stuffed high with peaches and strawberries, blackberries and apples, and before everyone had the chance to ladle on cream so thick you could stand spoons in it, trays with glasses filled to the top with homemade brandy made the rounds.[31] In 1919, during an especially glorious autumn before Prohibition, the world was still full of promise for all the wine and ranching families in the valleys. But that promise, along with their faith in their country, would soon be brutally broken.

Chapter Two

No Nation is Drunken where Wine is Cheap

*I*n the deepest part of the winter in early 1920, in the dark hills above Napa Valley, Caterina and Antone Nichelini gazed across a huge dinner table at their family of boisterous children and beloved grandchildren, who had been able to make it back to the homestead for the weekly family meal. Although all of them anticipated the hearty servings of the old-country dishes Caterina would serve, there must have been a somber undercurrent to the evening's cheer.

Caterina, Antone, and their 12 children had long depended on their small winery to provide a living. The close-knit family, used to braving tough times, was well aware of—and anxious about—the perilous and uncharted future. Fortunately, Antone, who had left Switzerland's Italian-speaking Ticino canton at the age of 19, had other skills besides winemaking. He was a talented stonemason who, as a boy, had apprenticed for many years in France and was also an able and seasoned mining engineer—a valuable skill at a time when Napa County's magnesite and quicksilver (mercury) mines were an integral part of its economy. But it was the family's 40-acre vineyard that was most essential to the clan's well-being.

The last few years had been worrisome. William, at 28 the oldest son, had lost his young wife to influenza a year before, just days after she gave birth to twins; the infant boy and girl joined a sister 18 months older. The couple had only just

saved enough to leave the bustling Nichelini homestead in Chiles Valley and settle at the north end of Napa Valley, where William was the proprietor of a garage
in the tiny historic hot-springs resort town of Calistoga. And then, only months
after losing his wife, William lost his baby daughter to what a contemporary account called getting "the phlegm in her throat"—probably the flu or pneumonia.

Antone and Caterina had arrived in Chiles Valley 30 years earlier, possessing
little but strong characters, good health, and intelligence. In three decades of backbreaking work they had turned a forested wilderness of bluffs, ridges, and steep
slopes into expansive gardens, orchards, and the profitable vineyard. Their comfortable farmhouse was perched on the crest of a sharp valley overlooking pristine
Sage Creek, a tiny, sparkling watershed that tumbled over rocks and waterfalls
some eight miles down from Chiles Valley into Napa Valley. Salmon still battled
against the current all the way up the creek from the coast each fall, much to the
delight of the family.

If Antone Nichelini's rise had been rapid, he also had some advantages other
Napa families lacked. His father, Francisco, had preceded him to California, sending money home for the rest of the family; in 1919, Francisco was still making
wine on Napa County's Mount Veeder. Antone's sister had married and lived in
the valley too, and their brother was the proprietor of the hardware store on the
square in Sonoma; his buckboard delivery wagon with the words "F. Nichelini"
painted on the side was well known throughout the area. An uncle was a baker, and
the skills Antone learned from him and passed on to Caterina would eventually
prove invaluable to the young couple.

When the 22-year-old Antone, fresh from an apprenticeship with the winemaking Chauvet family of Sonoma, chose Chiles Valley for the site of his homestead and vineyard, it was because he could not afford land in the flat, fertile heart
of the Napa Valley around Rutherford, even with all of his advantages. All the
most arable spots were spoken for; the valley provided the fruit and wheat for the
booming city of San Francisco and beef for markets throughout California and beyond. Tens of thousands of grapevines were producing wines that sold around the
world and made fortunes for their owners.

Today the Rutherford Viticultural area of Napa Valley with its lush vineyards,
a mere six square miles of deep gravel, sand and loam, is a high-class temple for
red wine lovers that draws fastidious connoisseurs from around the globe to taste
its wines. The countryside around the tiny hamlet of Rutherford is just as prized
by its inhabitants as the Bordeaux region in France, and is home to some of the

most coveted wines of the New World. In 1884, Antone Nichelini drove through this real estate already too expensive for him and urged his horse up a lonely, winding trail. Where the pine woods give way to the dry, stiff, and distinctively stubby chaparral of lonely Chiles Valley, about 1,000 feet above the valley floor, Antone found a spring—crucial in these dry hills—and decided to lay out his homestead. His 160-acre spread would come free of charge, as long as he made improvements for each of five years.

Antone married Caterina in 1890 after a whirlwind courtship in San Francisco, where she worked as a hotel chambermaid. She had come to America alone, after a love affair gone bad. When she had asked her father for the ticket to America, he had sent her one way, pleased to be rid of his disappointed daughter. Only weeks after arriving, she met and married Antone, who had grown up just a few miles from her home in Switzerland. Now she joined him on the Chiles Valley property he had owned for six years. Just a handful of other winemaking families lived in the splendid but remote sliver of a valley named for one of California's great adventurers, Colonel J. B. Chiles, a Kentuckian who had arrived in the 1840s and had planted some grape vines on a Mexican land grant.

Antone's first work had been to ready 40 of his 160 acres for planting, clearing off trees and their stumps, plowing and turning the soil, and clearing a flatland for the house and garden. He built the couple's first home out of the durable redwood of California's coastal forests, cutting the roof shakes himself. It was in this one-room cabin, a mere 12 square feet complete with a big metal stove for cooking and heating, that Caterina gave birth to the couple's four children. The wood stove made the cabin even hotter in summer, when the temperatures hovered between 80 to 100 degrees: but that could be forgotten during the long damp months of winter. Though the valley's midwinter gales could be daunting, Chiles Valley was perfect grape-growing territory, with long, hot cloudless summers whose occasional cooling fogs slowed the ripening process a little and enabled the Nichelini grapes to reach the perfect balance of flavors to make fine wine.

Antone had dreamed of planting Zinfandel. He had seen the success of that grape in this climate while he worked for the Chauvets, and in a few years, hundreds of the varietal's vines stretched deep into his land. He constructed a true hillside vineyard with no terraces, just as he had learned to do in his Swiss hometown of Verscio, where his family had grown Merlot for their own household. In 1896, Antone constructed a new and larger farmhouse atop a substantial cellar that he carved from the valley stone himself, filling it with their precious wines.

Hugely social, the Nichelinis had accumulated friends as well as vines, and when they dedicated the new house that September, more than 100 attended a party that lasted long into the night. Antone and Caterina hired a popular local band, Miller and Payne's Orchestra, and Caterina and her girls spent days preparing a generous supper, with plenty of Caterina's famous desserts and Antone's wine—and likely his grappa, a high-octane brandy made from the pulpy residue left over from the pressing of wine grapes. The dancing started early. Then the party was fed—Caterina and her daughters had to reset the tables four times to accommodate all the guests. After the meal, the dancing and the orchestra started up again. Only after many hours did the tired but happy partygoers set off in wagon caravans through the dark hills to their own valleys.

Through good times and bad, one thing the Nichelinis never had to worry about was feeding children and grandchildren. Like any mother and housewife in rural California, Caterina had carved a substantial garden out of the partly forested property, and she tended it faithfully throughout the long, mild growing season. Her most important crop was tomatoes, the plants as tall and broad as a man: They would produce a welcome crop of fruit to be simmered for hours and then canned for a year's worth of sauces. Caterina also planted beans and eggplants and peppers and an assortment of root and leafy crops. A little farther down the slopes, she nurtured a noble grove of walnut trees—English walnuts she and Antone had grafted onto American black walnuts. She had planted tall grapefruit and orange trees with their dark and shiny leaves, apples, pears, almonds, and Mission figs, whose fat, black fruits arrived early in the summer and had to be picked promptly—not only to make sure they were ripe but because they were favorites of the valley's birds, who could peck through a ripe fig in a matter of minutes. Olive trees rustled in the wind near the Nichelini barn. Wild blackberries ranged throughout the property, along with wild plum trees.

What the Nichelinis did not grow, they could buy from neighbors and from itinerant goatherds or hunt. In the hills were quail, deer, ducks, doves, even robins for stews. If money was tight and they ran out of bullets, they snared rabbits—but not in summer, when jackrabbits were thought to suffer from boils. And what the family produced but could not eat, it could sell to others. Caterina sold chickens, eggs, walnuts, and almonds for extra money to buy dry goods from town. Travelers passing on the road in front of their homestead were eager to buy from such a tidy farmhouse. Caterina also supplied dozens of loaves of bread a day to the cookhouses of the valley's mining camps, baking them in a big stone outdoor oven Antone had built into the hill just below her kitchen. The family also sold wine to the mining camps: Barrels of Nichelini Zinfandel were stacked in cookhouses throughout the valley. The miners, many of whom were Italian, would take their mugs to those communal barrels when they wanted a wine with breakfast or any other meal.[1]

The Nichelinis had spent little time talking about Prohibition before the act was passed. Like so many other wine families, they had not delved too deeply into how it might affect them. Political chatter about Prohibition, looming like a black cloud on a far-off horizon, and what it might mean to the lives and fortunes of the winemakers of northern California had been part of the background noise in Napa and Sonoma for so many years that the citizens of America's two premier wine counties might be forgiven for putting it aside to concentrate on their families and their land, to focus on the running of their vineyards and wineries.

So casual had some in the wine industry become about the subject that just a month before Prohibition came into full effect, the editor of the *California Grape Grower,* Horatio F. Stoll, wrote with frustration of his efforts to get the industry, winemakers, and grape growers alike, to take the whole matter seriously. The lack of preparation, he wrote, "amazed" him.[2]

To eliminate wine from daily life would have been unthinkable for many living in the two counties in the early years of the twentieth century, and those sentiments had lulled many in the wine industry into a comfortable stupor. In 2007, the 97-year-old veteran winemaker Louis J. Foppiano, looking back at those times, said: "Prohibition? Back then no one ever thought it would happen." Foppiano had always had a strong head for business and an ability to make connections around the country to sell the family's wine. He had been a leader among winemakers, jump-starting California's interest in Petite Sirah by calling it "noble" and making sure others saw it the same way. He remembered that many in the wine industry thought Prohibition "might last a few months, if ever, and then things would get back to normal. It was nothing we took really seriously."[3] However, for many years before its implementation, Prohibition had been a subject of increasingly impassioned debate across the United States.

By the time Sonoma and Napa developed their vineyards, anti-alcohol sentiment had become deeply entrenched throughout the country. Calls for temperance had been made since the country's inception: During the Revolution, military leaders had demanded moderate drinking from their troops, and by the middle of the 1800s, nascent temperance movements—driven by concerned citizens soon to be called Drys—were holding meetings at which they made clear their point of view: Americans drank too much. Drys thought alcohol encouraged vice, crime, family violence, and poverty, and aimed their vitriol most specifically at the working men's saloon as a center of all that threatened the American way of life. Saloons were, in effect, affordable working men's clubs. Was the Drys' anger against them well founded? A report prepared during 1910 and 1911 by the Chicago Vice Commission "counted 928 prostitutes in the back rooms of 236 saloons on a single night." Yet another commission in that city reported that more than 3,000 of the city's more than 7,000 bars were connected to hotel and sleeping rooms.[4]

Beyond their distress about prostitution, Drys believed too many family paychecks were being squandered in saloons, that the enticements of the saloon sent men home late at night and drunk to their virtually abandoned families, and left men unable to make it to work the next day because of hangovers—a devastating practice when so many were paid by the hour with no benefits for sickness or vacation. The saloon damaged the economic and moral fabric of the United States, the Drys said. The Dry solution was to legislate temperance. Their opponents—the Wets—believed that Americans should make their own choices about whether to drink or not, and if they drank too much, public education was the only solution. They believed the imposition of anti-drinking legislation would be counterproductive and unenforceable.

As the Prohibition movement gathered strength around the country, it met surprisingly little combined resistance from the three industries that supplied the nation with alcohol: breweries centered in Milwaukee, St. Louis, and Cincinnati; the great distillers of Kentucky; and wine producers located overwhelmingly in California. Each industry had its own anti-Prohibition propaganda and trade organizations, and they never learned to cooperate. Instead, they distrusted each other's intentions, believing that each would sacrifice the others if necessary. The bitter rivalries that grew among them made a powerful, united opposition to Prohibition forces impossible. "The brewers and distillers were hopelessly and bitterly divided," says author Richard Hamm in his book, *Shaping the 18th Amendment.*[5]

Standing still further alone, the winemakers of California believed that their industry was on an entirely different moral plane than whiskey and beer purveyors. In 1907, Andrea Sbarboro of the Italian Swiss Colony wrote a pamphlet entitled "The Fight for True Temperance." Sbarboro's own theory—shared by many others in northern California's wine growing areas especially, was that America's drunkenness would cease if drinkers would only switch from whiskey to wine. Wrote Sbarboro: "No nation is drunken where wine is cheap; and none sober, where the dearness of wine substitutes ardent spirits as the common beverage. It is, in truth, the only antidote to the bane of whiskey."[6]

California with its nascent wine industry had long had its own state Prohibition movement. It had, no doubt, gathered strength during the Gold Rush years of the late 1840s till the late 1850s, when citizens in the state heard dreadful tales of lonely, disillusioned miners embarking on drunken binges for days and terrified communities lived in constant fear of the shoot-'em ups and moral depravity that ensued.

While some Americans had always drunk wine—mostly those who had come to the United States from countries where wine had been made for centuries, such as France and Italy, it had never been anywhere near as popular as other alcoholic drinks. Whiskey and beer had long drawn the ire of American Prohibitionists— the drinks of the abhorred saloon. But California wine was becoming slowly better and better known to consumers, and Americans were downing increasing amounts of domestic wine as the industry developed. Thus the issue had been gradually creeping closer to Napa and Sonoma, even if many people there had not had the time or the prescience to take notice.

The success of California wines slowly drew the state and its winemakers fully into the nation's long battle over temperance. In 1850, Americans had poured 6 million gallons of wine from Europe but only 221,000 gallons of domestic wine. The situation had reversed dramatically by 1896, the year Giovanni Foppiano established his vineyard in Sonoma; by then, U.S. consumers were enjoying 14.5 million gallons of domestic wine compared to only 4.1 million gallons from abroad, a huge increase in U.S. wine drinking overall and a shift in preference to domestic wines.[7] The winemakers of Sonoma and Napa realized that they had tapped into a burgeoning market for alcoholic drinks, and soon they were turning all the raw land they could afford into vineyards. The proximity of San Francisco and its legendary nightlife was another boon to them.

Emotions were running high over Prohibition for some time in California. The wine industry had never been drawn into prohibition discussions as much as had the beer and whiskey industries. The debate in California, as elsewhere, often revolved around the saloon and its role—good or bad—in society, as evidenced by a 1911 debate in the California Legislature over whether or not prohibition legislation could be enacted at city and county, or township level. The California Beer Bottlers State Board of Trade had funded the most visible pro-saloon literature, while on the other side of the argument, president of Stanford University, David Starr Jordan, had written a letter to the Legislature outlining his position on the debate that included these tough words: "Enough beer destroys a boy's will. It may lead to the whisky habit, and that habit to destruction . . . Most young men who frequent saloons sooner or later find themselves in the brothel . . . the saloon as we know it, is everywhere a menace and a curse."[8]

Another early salvo in the California Prohibition battle had come from Dry forces; they took advantage of California's three-year-old initiative process that allowed single issues to be decided by the state's voters instead of leaving decision making up to the legislative body alone. In 1914, a statewide Prohibition initiative lost by only a few votes in Los Angeles but by five to one in San Francisco. One of its main provisions gave startling evidence of the passion behind the Dry strategy: An alcohol ban would have been enforced a mere five days after passage, a flabbergasting speed that encouraged frantic opposition from Wets.[9] Even though that initiative went down to defeat, both the Wet and Dry forces continued to raise money and engage both volunteers and paid employees to run their campaigns.

The Drys' volunteer resources and donations came from churches and those businessmen who thought Prohibition would be advantageous to themselves or to labor. The Drys had an "almost unlimited corps of volunteer labor," of which the Women's Christian Temperance Union was "probably the best organized and the most effective." The national Anti-Saloon League also contributed resources of all kinds in California.[10] The league's leader, Wayne Wheeler, was said in an effusive tribute by his former publicity secretary to have

> controlled six Congresses, dictated to two presidents of the United States, directed legislation in most of the states of the Union, picked the candidates for the more important elective state and federal offices, held the balance of power in

both Republican and Democratic parties, distributed more patronage than any dozen other men, supervised a federal bureau from outside without official authority, and was recognized by friend and foe alike as the most masterful and powerful single individual in the United States.[11]

He was a mighty foe whenever Wets fought Drys across the country.

The Wets raised money in California, too. Organizers included the members of a state-wide Wet organization, United California Industries, along with, "the Importers & Wholesale Liquor Merchants Association, the San Francisco Brewers' Protective Association and the Bottlers' Protective Association." And every saloon in the state was thought to have had to donate the equivalent of one month's rent to the cause, raising an estimated $2 million for the Wets' cause.[12]

As the Drys' campaigns grew more and more intense, the wine industry of Sonoma and Napa decided to join the fray, and to support the Wets. More importantly for them and much more pragmatically, they were defending their own industry.

In January 1916, four years before Prohibition would become law, more than 100 wine men and grape growers, members of the Napa County Grape Protective Association, decided to devote more energy to a pushback campaign against the incessant Dry propaganda. Their target was two Dry amendments on the November ballot that they hoped to neutralize as quickly and fully as possible.[13]

That fall voters would be asked to vote "yes" to the first Prohibition amendment if they believed that no wine, or other alcohol for that matter, should be made or sold or brought into California after January 1, 1920, for use by the general public. After that date, alcohol could be used only for medicinal, sacramental, or scientific purposes. On the same ballot, voters would also be asked to vote on an alternate amendment that would permit the making of alcohol but prohibit its sale in California—although it could be sold elsewhere. Californians alone would have to order alcohol for delivery to their homes in quantities of more than two gallons—a decided challenge for many people who would have lived from paycheck to paycheck. This was clearly an effort to discourage a workingman from having a glass of wine, or a drink of any other liquor, as he might not be able to afford to purchase it in volume.

The wine industry believed that both amendments had little chance of passing because California's voters had shown a tendency for tolerating drinking for many years. And the first amendment was so draconian it was held to have no chance of succeeding. But the second, because it was less punitive, was more worrisome. To make it quite clear what voters would be agreeing or disagreeing with, the California Grape Protective Association spelled out carefully in advertisements that while Proposition 1 was an insult, Proposition 2 would wipe out practically every legitimate avenue for the distribution of California wine and would prevent Californians from buying a glass of wine with meals outside their own town or in a hotel or restaurant. No one would be able to serve wine at a banquet, or at a summer resort, or use wine or liquor to make cakes or sauces. And no customers could roll up to a winery and buy a bottle or barrel of the winery's products.[14]

There was a multiplicity of voices on the side of the "wine men." Former president William Howard Taft appeared in pro-wine literature sponsored by the United California Industries, the pro-business association, saying: "Nothing is more foolish, nothing more utterly at variance with sound public policy than to enact a law which, by reasons of the conditions surrounding the community in which it is declared to be law is incapable of enforcement."[15]

Rallied by seemingly good support for their cause, that group of about 100 Napa wine men drove out from their vineyards and wineries and funneled into a theater in St. Helena. There they calculated that if 10 cents per ton was levied on the approximately 20,000 tons of grapes produced in their valley, they could build up a substantial war chest to defeat both those unacceptable ballot measures.[16] Other groups met to debate the same amendments. The Napa County Taxpayers' Association, organized to "systematically" fight the prohibition movement filled the Odd Fellows Hall in April, promising to organize efforts in every voting precinct in that county.[17] At a Home Industry meeting in San Francisco that same month, Horatio F. Stoll, at that time a member of the State Viticultural Commission, encouraged listeners to action with a dire prediction that "the passage of the proposed amendments would wipe out the wine industry of the State."

Stoll pointed out something that was not fully understood by many businessmen or, for that matter, voters in the state, especially those in central and southern California. It was not only the wine counties of northern California that would be devastated by the two amendments; the ripples of Prohibition would damage much more than the state's premier winegrowing areas. The grape growers of California were inextricably linked by common economic interests.

"Not only would the wine grape growers be ruined," Stoll continued, "but the table and raisin grape growers" of central California "would suffer financial ruin. During a normal year 100,000 tons of second crop Muscat and table grape culls are used by the wineries and this output represents a considerable portion of the profits of the table and raisin grape growers."[18]

The damage to the secondary grape crop of the San Joaquin Valley in addition to the ravaging of Napa and Sonoma would rock the state's economy. John Fox, Napa Horticultural Commissioner wrote in the newspaper of St. Helena, then a dusty town in the center of Napa's rich Wine Country, that: "The vine industry of California is its pride and its boast. 330,000 acres of her land is devoted to grapes and every acre, whether wine, table or raisin grape, is dependent on the wine industry for its continuance. When the table grape market has been satisfied the balance of these grapes is sent to the wineries."[19]

If wine was banned, there would be a tough economic landing, not only in Napa and Sonoma but also for thousands of other farm families across the state. The 1910 census showed that 145 million grape vines were planted in California, which would have been the backbone of a fine living to many in 1916. Napa County had 8.5 million vines, Sonoma County, 17.9 million. Even those great wine-producing counties paled by comparison to Fresno, in the state's Central Valley, with more than 40 million vines that mostly produced raisins and table grapes. And Alameda, Contra Costa, Kings, Sacramento, and Tulare counties—even still-rural Los Angeles—each had more than 2 million vines. From Shasta to San Diego, a staggering 39 of the state's 58 counties were planted with grapes. It was a crop of immense importance to California's economy. Surely it could not be jeopardized by voters or legislators anywhere.[20]

As it became more clear that Prohibition was a serious threat, the wine men of Sonoma and Napa started to push for some assurance that either the state or federal government would take some responsibility for decisions regarding the now long-established wine industry: They asked for compensation from either or both levels of government if a shutdown of their industry ever happened.

There was an eerie silence on this issue wherever it was broached.

Bismarck Bruck, the popular assemblyman who represented Napa and Lake counties in the state assembly in Sacramento, had already proposed an amendment asking for the payment of compensation if any law resulted result in damage to any "vineyard, wine cellar, hop field, brewery, distillery, or other property used in producing, growing, or raising grapes or hops, or in manufacturing wine, beer, malt or distilled liquors." Bruck had proposed his amendment, "primarily as a protection for wine growers." He lost by an exasperating three votes.[21] Bruck understood the wine counties like few Sacramento politicians. He was just the man for the valley—because he was a man *of* the valley. He superintended a large Napa vineyard and had also been a municipal, then county politician. He knew everyone in the valley and he knew everyone's vines, vineyards, and wines. Horticultural commissioner John H. Fox agreed with Bruck on the crucial issue of compensation. In his report entitled "What Prohibition Really Means to the Wine Industry," which ran in the *St. Helena Star* he wrote:

> The man who does not know thinks a vineyardist can simply hook out his vines and replant something equally profitable in a few years. A greater fallacy never existed. Viticulture as a science is vast and absorbing. Thousands of men spend their whole lives in its study. . . . It would be just as easy to take a lawyer and tell him he would have to make a go of it as a doctor.
>
> Imagine a poor man who has spent his best working years carving an estate out of the wilderness and making it profitable being told in middle life or old age that his living has been confiscated and he must learn a new method of making out.

Fox railed against those Prohibitionists who deluged the vineyard owners of the two wine counties with advice on what to grow instead of grapes. He derided their suggestions to try walnuts, corn, potatoes, or even rice, reminding readers that much of the land they were talking about had only 18 inches or less of soil, "land that would not average one-half ton of hay to the acre—not even enough to pay for seed." He added, "Such suggestions to a man who knows, are not only an insult to his intelligence but they are a crude mockery."[22]

Bruck and winemakers and grape growers of Napa and Sonoma were gravely worried about the outcome of the two ballot amendments that voters would vote on in November.

Judge D. D. Bowman of San Francisco, speaking to a crowd of 200 at St. Helena's Liberty Theater, "called especial attention to the awful ruin that would be wrought by the amendment in the destruction of our vineyards and wineries." He continued on with the information that the state had "$150,000,000 invested in the business and from it we get an annual revenue of $30,000,000."

Some of the claims challenged rationality, or worse. Bowman ridiculed the popular charge that wine's alcohol content was deleterious; after all, he noted, wine had little effect on the "Belgians, Germans, French, Italians, and others who used it properly." In fact, Bowman argued, wine actually decreased and, in fact, almost eradicated drunkenness. More to the point, close to 300,000 Californians would be thrown out of work and into an already overcrowded labor market if the amendments passed. "Who would give them work?" he asked. "Would the prohibitionists?"

The fact that a judge from the bench of a major city where many Prohibition cases might eventually be tried was speaking so passionately about the benefits of the wine, beer, and liquor industries was astonishing. One could only surmise that sentences applied in the future by him and his fellow judges in San Francisco to recalcitrant wine drinkers and sellers might not be meted out with a neutrality befitting the bench.[23]

Before the autumn vote of 1916 on the Dry amendments, there was a grape season to oversee. The news was no more cheering there. To add further disquiet to the lives of the grape growers in the valleys, a frost early in the year had hurt the harvest. A disastrous frost had hit many vineyards in May, said the *St. Helena Star,* causing widespread damage to the vines. By the time the sun had risen that day, the scene was heartbreaking. Hundreds of acres of vineyards across the valley bottom and reaching onto the hills that only hours before had been "green and beautiful" were now "black and withered." And as the sun warmed, the frozen leaves turned into slime. Grape growers thought it the worst frost in more than 40 years.[24]

Late frosts in spring and early rain in fall are the most feared occurrences in the calendar of a grape grower. Both can damage the crop dramatically. Spring frost damage is at its worst when buds have already emerged. Grape growers debated whether to strip the vines of the dead foliage or leave them as they were, in the hope they might heal themselves. One grower, W. F. Bornhorst—who farmed 50 acres in the valley—had waited anxiously through the night to check his vines at dawn and found half of them frosted and black. He decided to strip some of the vines and cut back others. Later in the season, he reported that he had stripped off his vines including his Petite Syrah and pruned back close to the frozen shoots and believed that he would eventually get 50 percent of his crop. The vines he had cut back were doing better than those he had cut back.[25]

Smudge pots—small oil stoves with tall chimneys that belched a thick black smoke from crude oil—had saved much fruit that otherwise would have been damaged. Once lit in early morning when frost threatened, they created a smoke ceiling above the vines that kept more heat from escaping, in much the way that a night with low clouds may be warmer than a perfectly clear one.

Still, the losses were horrific. By the summer of 1916, it was clear many of the vines were not going to recover. The heaviest damage had occurred in the Napa Valley's heart, around the town of Rutherford and all the way to Calistoga, the spa town at the valley's northern end. In Napa, it was conservatively estimated that the previous year's four million gallons of wine production would be halved. Sonoma fared a bit better, but it was estimated that production would fall by a quarter. The bad news hit both counties just as the true danger of Prohibition was beginning to sink in.[26]

Fortunately, September brought a glimmer of hope: Word from the vineyards was that the harvest, while light, was of excellent quality. At the Beaulieu Vineyards, proprietor George de Latour was pleased with the grapes and the wine that was being made from them. After he had 160,000 gallons of new dry wines settling in his tanks, he started manufacturing sweet wine. His vines, too, had suffered terribly from the May frosts, but he had put an army of men to work immediately cropping or stripping the injured vines. As a result, Latour harvested a fair crop: 627 tons of grapes from his two vineyards.[27]

As November's Election Day neared, interest in the amendments was high. Napa's electoral officials announced that the country had the largest voter registration ever: The wine folk left their cellars and vineyards in droves to mark their ballots for all levels of government.

On November 10, 1916, Woodrow Wilson, who had campaigned on a platform of continued neutrality in the war that had engulfed Europe, was reelected president of the United States, beating Charles Evans Hughes, a Republican who had resigned his Supreme Court seat to run for office. Wilson won by fewer than 600,000 popular votes and 23 seats in the Electoral College, and California had played a significant role, providing him with 13 electors. Locally, Napa had given Hughes a slight edge, 3,907 votes to 3,406, but across the state, Hughes lost by 4,000 votes. He had crossed a picket line during the campaign in California and had lost the state's powerful union vote, which is especially important to a politician in San Francisco and Los Angeles.[28]

Bismarck Bruck won a more convincing victory in Napa's state assembly race. But best of all results for Napa and Sonoma was that the state's Prohibition amendments took a drubbing: The amendment on total Prohibition was defeated by 100,000 votes as 55.2 percent of California voters said no versus 44.8 percent of voters who said yes, though the second, less stringent amendment lost by only 45,000 votes.

"The prohibitionists in this state have received another good sound trouncing," declared an editorial in the *St. Helena Star.*[29] But there was to be little breathing space for the winemakers and grape growers of California. Before the industry had time to settle its nerves after the worries of the 1916 initiatives, Prohibition forces were at it again. Even though they had just been defeated in the election, they were pounding at the state's politicians. Would there ever be a let-up in their push for a Dry state? Completely ignoring the voice of the state's voters, they continued to press forward in hopes they would reach their goal: total Prohibition.

Sensitive to the fact that not only California had voted against Prohibition but that the nation's voters had recently reelected an anti-Prohibition president, the Dry forces chose, for a time, to support less draconian measures. They now turned to restricting the free sale of alcohol rather than promoting a wholesale ban. It was hoped the so-called Rominger bill, that would ban distilled liquor but would allow beer and wine with alcohol contents of less than 14 percent along with sales of fortified sweet wine for drinking at home and the manufacture of brandy for export, would show voters that "wherever restrictions were placed on the liquor traffic the resulting improvement in conditions encouraged the people to demand new restrictions and so (would lead) inevitably to prohibition." Ultimately it was defeated because while the Wets hated it, many Drys distrusted it, too. Supporters vowed to put it back on the 1918 ballot.[30]

While Californians wrestled with ballot measures and Sacramento's politicians debated limited bans on alcohol, an equally volatile war of attrition was under way in Washington. The first session of the Sixty-fourth Congress, which ran from December 1915 to September 1916, saw debates on more than 40 petitions, amendments, bills, opinions, and resolutions on the subject of Alcoholic Liquor Traffic—the catch-all designation for all legislation related to the prohibition, sale, licensing, transportation, and manufacture of all alcoholic beverages.

By 1917, yet another great legislative battle between the Wets and the Drys that would affect the winemakers of Napa and Sonoma was starting to play out in Congress. The draconian Eighteenth Amendment, which would ban the selling and transportation in or out of the country of all alcoholic beverages with more than an almost imperceptible 0.5 percent alcohol content eventually passed Congress just before Christmas of 1917, in the middle of the country's mobilization for the Great War in Europe. From its genesis, it was touted by proponents as a practical step by which to safeguard the nation's supply of grain for the production of foodstuffs rather than see it distilled into alcohol: a precautionary measure in case the German blockade on the Atlantic disrupted national food imports and exports in any significant way. Anti-Saloon League supporters argued that the nation should consider its devotion to the pleasures of drink unacceptable at a time when "our boys" in uniform were suffering unimaginable cruelties on Europe's military fronts.

To its opponents, however, the league's pressure during the mobilization for war amounted to nothing more than opportunism. Many suggested there were racist overtones to Prohibition rhetoric, since the largest breweries, with their German American names such as Anheuser-Busch and Schlitz, were easy targets. It was not hard to drum up populist reasons why these firms should not continue to thrive when across the Atlantic soldiers with similar names were fighting against the United States.

In this battle, California was completely outgunned, with only 11 elected representatives, not all of whom would vote against liquor control. Compared to the highly populated states of the East Coast, California was still the frontier; its 1910 population of 2.3 million lagged far behind that of New York State's 9.1 million citizens (and 43 representatives) and Pennsylvania's 7.6 million citizens (and 36 representatives). Cut off from the rest of the country by long railroad journeys and primitive highways, the value of the state seemed insignificant, its promise unperceived, its legislative firepower weak. Writer H. L. Mencken blamed Prohibition on "primitive inhabitants of the 'cow states', who resented the fact that they had to swill raw corn liquor while the men in the big cities could enjoy good whiskeys and vintage wines,"[31] although the reality was that California's strength in the House was inconsequential—a little more than 2 percent of the total.

The amendment would now go to the states. If and when 36 of the then 48 states agreed with it, the amendment would be ratified and become part of the nation's Constitution.

Even with that huge threat—or promise, depending on one's politics—hanging over the heads of the nation's voters, still more legislation, campaigning, and fundraising was ahead. In 1918, California voters prepared yet again to vote on Prohibition in the state. But now the nation was at war.

Dozens of young men had cheerfully set off from both Napa and Sonoma counties to fight in Europe. To manage the wartime economy, the government took over not only the railroads and the country's fuel supply but also the supply of grain and wheat flour. The supply and price of sugar were also of grave concern, and newly controlled to prevent price gouging and hoarding. Federal food commissioner Ralph P. Merritt explained the new wheat controls in communications across the country at the same time ordering households to not use more than a pound and a half of wheat per person in any form. He warned that if consumers worked through that much, then their ration would be exhausted and the consumption of any more wheat products in any shape or form would not be permitted.[32]

The misuse of one's sugar allotment was equally serious. Housewives were informed that while the necessary sugar was allowed for home canning and preserving, the supply for that purpose was permitted only after an official signed statement had been made to that effect. In northern California, those statements about sugar use were to be immediately forwarded to the U.S. Food Administration at San Francisco. Abuses were serious. If sugar bought by a woman for canning was eventually, but even advertently, used for cooking or baking, or even to sweeten a cup of coffee or baby's formula, she could be vigorously prosecuted.

Amid this atmosphere of tightly controlled foodstuff, it was not a long reach for legislators to strengthen regulations about wine, beer, and other alcoholic beverages. After all, the winemaking, brewing, and distilling industries made use of basic food products too, including sugar. Was wine a foodstuff that needed to be controlled by the government?

On Capitol Hill, Congressman Julius Kahn, a Republican protector of the interests of the wine counties in Congress and a lawyer from San Francisco, pleaded for the wine industry back home. He told the Senate Agriculture Committee that enactment of Prohibition legislation at this time would bankrupt California wine growers and result in losses totaling millions of dollars.

"Anticipating final ratification of the Federal Constitutional amendment," the *New York Times* reported Kahn saying, "many now are liquidating their property." "I have been told," he added, "that the banks in California have been asked to loan growers $10,000,000 in anticipation of this year's crop. To pass this legislation simply would make every dollar of this investment a total loss, besides making this vintage a total loss."[33]

A month later on a visit to his hometown, San Francisco Democratic senator James Duval Phelan had this daunting opinion: "I think the Prohibition amendment will be adopted in the United States without a doubt and our grape growers will have to carefully consider the future use of their land."

However, Phelan, a Roman Catholic, did not believe that wine or beer would be prohibited during the war because of the thousands of workingmen who drank, beer especially, with their meals, but he thought whiskey and other liquors were doomed. He had no doubt that wine grape growers would be allowed plenty of time to dispose of this year's crop if laws changed as expected.[34]

In Sonoma, the dire issue of wine production and sales took on a new urgency: The added worry of emergency wartime legislation riled the wine counties.

The Italian wine men of Sonoma believed that while wine was nutritious, wine grapes had no value as a table fruit. They were outraged and anxious at developments and saw the sudden appeal of pro-Prohibition forces to patriotic duty as a threat to their business and their way of life. Although badly outnumbered and not completely aware of the scope and tenor of the renewed debate in the nation's capital, they had heard enough to ready themselves for a fight. Their opening salvo was a gathering of the Italian winemakers of Sonoma, held in the Healdsburg Opera House in early August 1918, reported on by the *Tribune*. The meeting was attended by some of the local wine industry heavyweights: Andrea Sbarboro, of the Italian Swiss Colony at Asti; Edmund Rossi, the Colony's longtime head; Antonio Perelli-Minetti, winemaker with Italian Swiss and Simi Winery; winemaker Silvestro Scatena; and Abele Ferrari, who had also worked at the Italian Swiss Colony and who owned the Healdsburg Machine Shop, where presses and machinery for the wine industry were made. A. P. Giannini, the powerful head of San Francisco's Bank of Italy (the future Bank of America) sent a representative, and Horatio F. Stoll, then of the California Grape Growers Association, was secretary.

Father Andriano, a local Roman Catholic priest, shared the stage with winemakers and grape growers and reminded everyone of the generosity with which the Italian residents of Healdsburg, Asti, Cloverdale, and the rest of Sonoma County had supported the war—buying Liberty Bonds, War Savings Stamps, and subscribing to the Red Cross. The *Tribune* reported: "We were in this hall in large numbers at the time of the Liberty Loan campaign and we are here again in equally large numbers to protect our interest in the wine industry. . . . The Italians in America are shedding their blood in defense of America as behooves them as loyal citizens." Father Adriano declared. The percentage of soldiers of Italian ancestry in the American army is large and it would be a serious deprivation to the returning troops to find that Prohibition had destroyed their liberties while they are offering themselves on the altar of the nation in the war for freedom."

The wine folk declared that their protest was not just because they were in the business of producing wine. They believed that as loyal Italian immigrants who had come to the United States and worked hard and diligently to help develop a raw, new state, they had the right to be heard as much as the voices of Americans from anywhere else across the country. Their words about their countrymen were poetic: they "have cleared away the brush from hills and have made vineyards grow on barren spots: they have caused the hillsides to blossom as the rose," but they were firm. And those attending the meeting declared as one that only fanatics who did not understand the concept of liberty on which the nation had been founded would continue the unfair battle for Prohibition. A thousand names were signed on the memorandum prepared at that meeting:

To President Woodrow Wilson,
White House,
Washington, D.C.

The vineyardists and wine-makers of Sonoma Country of Italian birth or descent, loyal citizens of the United States, in mass meeting assembled want . . . to set their plight before the President of the United States.

The memorandum continued on, reminding the president of the generosity of the Italians in Sonoma to war subscriptions.

And in making wine from grapes we are not unpatriotic, for wine moderately used, has an intrinsic food value. And the destruction of wine grapes far from conserving food, will waste it. Wine grapes as such have no food value. They cannot be used as table grapes and are useless for raisins . . .
Therefore, we the undersigned, in mass meeting assembled at Healdsburg, Sonoma County, this 4th day of August, pray you use your influence with Congress to see that we wine-growers of Sonoma county receive proper protection at the hands of Congress, and urge that if the prohibition amendment should be passed by Congress, that you exercise your power of veto.[35]

In early September 1918 came more bad news from Washington: The Senate had passed the $12 million Emergency Agricultural Appropriation Bill that would allow national Prohibition from the following July 1 until the American armies were demobilized after the end of the war. It was another devastating blow to Napa and Sonoma. A fight to postpone wartime Prohibition until December 30, 1919, was defeated.

The deal was no win for Napa and Sonoma: The federal Prohibition clause would stop the sale of all wines on June 30 except for export, medicinal, and sacramental uses and some other industrial uses as for example, in the production of vinegar.[36]

As winemaking began in earnest in Napa and Sonoma in autumn 1918, the harvest was a nerve-wracking experience. The heaviest rainfall in September for many years damaged not only the grapes but also the prune crop of Sonoma and Napa. And while the grape crop, particularly in Napa County, did not suffer as badly as the prunes, the losses would be heavy. In many vineyards, where the end of the long dry summer had shriveled many grapes on the vine, the rain was welcome, but grape varieties with thin skins split in the rain and the damp weather rotted many more.[37]

After that came another blow. California's Republican governor, William Dennison Stephens, the avowed Prohibitionist, was reelected in the general election. He beat out the man the wine industry was rooting for: Theodore Bell, the popular San Francisco attorney, a former congressman for California, and district attorney for Napa for eight years. This was Bell's third unsuccessful attempt to head the state government—he had also run in 1906 and 1910.

In Napa, the hometown candidate outpolled Stephens. Bell received 3,378 votes to Stephens's 1,752. How differently the next years might have played out if Bell had been elected.[38] If California had not ratified the Eighteenth Amendment, other states might have been encouraged to follow suit. Bell's loyalties to the wine industry were fierce—the exact opposite of Stephens, about whom the *St. Helena Star* had declared earlier: "He is certainly in bad in this neck-o'-the-woods, and we presume, equally so in other parts of the State where wine grapes are raised."[39]

Bismarck Bruck, the wine man from Napa, was again elected to the California Assembly, beating his opponent from the Prohibition Party by a margin of 3 to 1.[40]

The state vote, at least, was a little good news. It had, as always, clearly marked the great divide in California. Prohibition was a confrontation between North and South, a war between southern California's Presbyterian-dominated Protestants, who had hailed from Arkansas and Oklahoma, and the multi-ethnic citizens of the Catholic-dominated North, many of whom had come from Italy, France, and Spain, where wine was an integral part of life. The two California state Prohibition initiatives they had voted on in November 1918 were particularly harsh. Proposition 1 was aimed at outlawing saloons. Proposition 22 asked for endless penalties for both makers and sellers of alcohol:

> *Every person, firm or corporation, which manufactures imports or sells intoxicating liquors after December 31, 1918 . . .shall be guilty of a misdemeanor, punishable by a $25 fine and twenty-five days imprisonment for first offense, and by $50 fine and fifty days imprisonment for second offense, and by $100 fine and one hundred days imprisonment for each subsequent offense.*

Both propositions failed. They were too harsh even for southern California. Proposition 1 lost by 342,000 to 257,000 votes. And though the governor, Ohio-born Stephens, had made impassioned pleas in support of the Proposition 22, 306,488 Californians voted no to it compared to the 275,643 who voted yes.[41] Nearly 80,000 of the governor's fellow Los Angeles County voters had voted "yes," while just under 60,000 had voted "no." But in fun-loving, stay-out-all-night San Francisco County, it was no surprise that the vote was reversed: 67,791 nays to 20,531 yeas. In the two wine counties, the votes echoed San Francisco's: Napa's tally was 3,532 nays and 1,290 yeas; Sonoma's, 7,358 nays to 3,590 yeas.[42] It shocked many in Napa and Sonoma that anyone at all voted for Prohibition; winemakers blamed the influence of women and immigrant voters from the nation's South. No hardworking, practical Californian would have voted Dry, they believed.

Again the state's Prohibition amendment went down to defeat, although this time the majority of defeat was smaller than last. But the message was clear: California voters had yet again come down firmly against Prohibition.

Six days after the country had voted in the general election, World War I ended. Americans woke up to the news that the Germans had signed the Armistice. There was a fever of excitement in the little city of Sonoma and the valley surrounding it.

"Immediately upon receipt of the news of the signing of the Armistice, Sonoma Valley was surcharged with the spirit of celebration and rejoicing," reported the

Sonoma Index-Tribune. The whole town came out into the streets to congratulate each other. At night, huge bonfires were lit under the clear sky in the beautiful little Mexican-style plaza that is the center of town, the bells at city hall and at the churches throughout the community pealing time and time again. And the overjoyed citizens made even more noise with bells and whistles and the horns of their cars and trucks.[43]

One hundred and seventeen boys had gone to war from Sonoma and the surrounding area.[44] Surely now all the talk of wartime Prohibition could be dispensed with. Napa and Sonoma could proudly welcome back their boys from the front. And the winemakers and grape growers of the two counties could get back to their vines and wines.

The wine industry held its breath through Christmas and the New Year, hoping against hope that the state legislature would follow the will of the people by refusing to ratify the Eighteenth Amendment on behalf of California.

Chapter Three

These Vines are like Members of My Family

O n January 13, 1919, all eyes in Sonoma and Napa turned to Washington. Even though the citizens of California had voted against Prohibition, California's Dry majority legislature had voted in favor. Against the express wishes of the voters, Sacramento ratified the Eighteenth Amendment. Californians were stunned. On January 16, Wyoming's ratification as the thirty-sixth and final state needed to make the country bone dry from the Atlantic to the Pacific finished off the winemaker's hopes completely.

But the amendment contained no specific instructions as to how the law would be enforced; Congress and the states were simply empowered to "enforce" the amendment by "appropriate legislation."

Now it fell to Congress to pass a further act to explain Prohibition's rules and regulations. The prescriptive legislation was introduced and named for teetotaler Andrew Volstead, a Republican lawyer and the congressman for Granite Falls, Minnesota, a tiny smudge of a town that was a great distance geographically and spiritually from the warm, green hills and vales of California's lush wine counties. Volstead's ascetic face, with its piercing eyes, seemed the very embodiment of Dry sentiment, though it was decorated with a mustache so luxuriant that it looked like a thatched roof attached to his lips.

The son of Norwegian parents, Volstead presided over the powerful House Judiciary Committee, and it was he who shepherded the mechanics of Prohibition through the corridors of Congress. But word was in Washington that the legislation had, in fact, been dictated by Wayne Wheeler, the massive, bulldog-like "Dry boss" of the country, the bullying legal counsel to the Anti-Saloon League and an influential lobbyist with a reputation for lavishing vast sums of money around Congress.

The Volstead Act was in effect a how-to manual to the Eighteenth Amendment. It established a new Prohibition bureaucracy, including a vast staff of lawyers and legions of enforcement officers, who were immediately to be issued guns and axes.

That anything to do with the Eighteenth Amendment or its enforcement was still up for debate had astonished not only the wine communities of Napa and Sonoma but many Americans across the country, since one essential premise of the amendment had been that the country was at war. The war had come to an end with the Armistice of November 11, 1918, two months before the amendment's ratification. But to Drys in both the House and the Senate—most with deep personal convictions regarding alcohol—and to others tempted perhaps by the seductive benefits of Wheeler's deep pockets—the war still loomed large. The Drys in Congress along with Wheeler insisted that the war had not yet legally ended, since the final peace treaty awaited ratification by the Senate; and the U.S. government agreed with them.

California's Representatives on Capitol Hill added up to a mere eleven voices: six Republicans, four Democrats and the only Prohibition party member in Congress—to represent it when the Sixty-sixth Congress of the United States opened with a dramatic special session in May 1919. The session began with fervent debates about how to manage the ending of the Great War that had killed at least 7.5 million soldiers, including 50,000 Americans, and wounded more than 18 million mostly young men, of whom 205,000 were from the United States.[1]

In the House, emotional arguments between labor and business interests—over workers' pay and working conditions in a financial landscape disrupted by the war—made for tense sessions of heightened rhetoric. With nationwide labor disruptions looming, few Americans, including California winemakers preparing for a bountiful grape harvest, had thought Prohibition deserved much attention. More than 45,000 strikers had already paralyzed Seattle's international port, an action now being monitored by police carrying hand grenades and machine guns.

President Wilson had issued an ultimatum to coal miners, whose United Mine Workers union was demanding a five-day workweek and a raise from $8 to $12 a day, and who had threatened to stop production of the entire nation's soft coal supply on November 1. The Brotherhood of Railroad Trainmen was threatening to strike across the country over a wage demand of not less than $150 a month.

In August, unions threatened a "great steel strike" with more than 270,000 men out: The Ohio National Guard was mobilized in Akron, awaiting orders from the governor to act against rioters in steel plants after 1,000 workers were reported to have beaten company officials. In Chicago, 15,000 carpenters had gone on strike in September; 80,000 others across the country struck in solidarity. The Senate had already initialed a bill that would send in the army to operate both coal mines and railroads should the strikes occur, although everyone knew this would be impossible for soldiers, however obedient, to pull off.[2]

Even without the overwhelming labor troubles, the president was dangerously overextended that summer. The Allied peace treaty with Germany needed to be explained to the American people to help ensure that two-thirds of a prickly Senate would vote in favor, so Wilson set off on September 2, 1919, for an exhausting nationwide tour even though he was so ill aides begged him not to go. After speaking in Pueblo, Colorado, on the afternoon of the 25th towards the end of the arduous trip, "his fortieth speech in twenty-one days," says historian Margaret MacMillan, in her book, *Paris, 1919*, his health finally broke. His wife had rushed to his bedside that night to find him "gasping" and dazed. The official report noted that he had suffered a "nervous collapse" and that he was to be carried back to Washington immediately. "Wilson never spoke in public again," adds MacMillan.[3] Day after day, guarded notices about his condition were released by White House officials, until finally, by October, the talk was everywhere that the president had suffered a massive stroke that had partially paralyzed him. Unease built over Wilson's apparent inability to handle all the legislation that needed his immediate attention.

The Volstead Act had been debated fitfully throughout the summer of the Sixty-sixth Congress, but there was little discussion of the real difficulties that would soon face Napa and Sonoma's wine industry. In one of the infrequent debates, Charles Randall, the representative from Los Angeles and the only Californian ever elected as a Prohibitionist, suggested jauntily that the wine industry abandon winemaking and reinvent itself as a grape juice industry, though it is not clear if he had prepared any research on demand for grape juice. Pennsylvania

Republican J. Hampton Moore, a staunch anti-Prohibitionist, leapt from his seat to retort explosively: "Is it not a fact that the action of Congress having virtually put out of business the grape growers of California, that this is about the only way in which they may be able to continue to develop their industry?" Randall, nonplussed by the question and lacking a prepared reply, managed to stammer that he was sure other products could be made from grapes. Moore shot back: "What would become of their farms if the grapevines should have to be torn up?" The Californian replied breezily that, well, the ranches would just have to "be planted to some other product." Moore, disgusted, spat back that this would mean, "confiscating all the capital that they have now invested."[4] A shiver ran through the Wine Country of northern California.

It was left to Clarence Lea, the 45-year-old Representative from Santa Rosa in Sonoma County, to speak more eloquently than anyone else about the future of the wine industry back home. Born in Lake County, just to the north of Napa, Lea was a lawyer who had become a sympathetic and highly popular district attorney of Sonoma County in 1907. A man of courtesy and conversation, he would eventually be elected to Congress unopposed eight times by enthusiastic voters beginning in 1917 and ending in 1946. During a debate on a steaming summer day in 1919, when flies and a blanket of humidity in the House made enduring an afternoon session a decided challenge, he spoke out with vigor and courage on behalf of his constituents even though he already suspected the worst:

> I believe the war prohibition legislation here proposed is vicious . . . [and] the historian of the future will search the pages of the Congressional Record in vain for a logical or an appealing reason why this Nation, that went through the war without prohibition, should enact "war prohibition" after the war was over. . . . War prohibition presupposes a war.

Lea was just warming up. He then offered up the most impassioned plea ever heard in the House in defense of California's wine industry and his constituents back home whose lives depended on it:

> Today there is hanging on the vines in California, approaching harvest time, perhaps the greatest wine grape crop in the history of California, as reported by the Agricultural Department only three weeks ago. . . . If this purposed "war legislation" shall be continued or go into effect eight months after the war is over, and thereby rob those farmers of California of the fruits of their labor, it will be one of the greatest outrages committed in the legislative history of the United States.

Applause greeted these impassioned words. Later, Lea hammered the same audience:

> Next winter when the Federal prohibition amendment goes into effect the farmers of California expect to begin digging up their vines. Do you want to adopt this sort of precedent in the United States of America with reference to farmers who have given so many years of their lives to the development of the vineyards at great expense?

The chairman of the House, whom Lea suspected to be closely affiliated with the Anti-Saloon League, cut further applause short, forbade Lea to continue, and declared: "The time of the gentleman has expired."[5] It was clear that the people of Napa and Sonoma registered not a whit in the House of Representatives.

Even as the session plowed on, there were few discussions about the wartime premise of the Prohibition legislation. However, no one, especially not Randall, queried how the elected officials of a country "still at war" were passing dozens of acts that donated recently captured German cannons to cities across the United States as a sign of the nation's victory. Even in California, the cannons were being given as gifts up and down the state in a frenzy of national pride. Nearly half the legislation in that session introduced by Representative Hugh Hersman, a bustling Democrat from Gilroy, involved donating captured German cannons to many dusty towns and cities across the center of the state, there to be positioned in permanent concrete settings on civic plazas to celebrate the nation's triumphs in Europe.[6]

Lea did not take the time to donate a cannon to his constituency; instead he used the war to press a further emphatic point on the House:

> Today the sons of some of those grape growers lie sleeping the eternal sleep in the soil of France. It is un-American, it is unworthy of the American Congress today, under the pretense of war prohibition . . .to rob those parents of what their industry has legitimately earned.[7]

So sure were the citizens of northern California that the war was over, that they had been celebrating for some time. In April 1919, when trains bringing California's soldiers home from eastern ports steamed through Sacramento on their way to victory celebrations in San Francisco, thousands of people came out to wave and shout thanks. Girls threw masses of golden poppies, California's state flower, to the overjoyed heroes of the Argonne hanging from the train doors and shouting out the windows in their excitement to be back safely on American soil. Market Street, San Francisco's premier shopping and business thoroughfare, was hung with banners and bunting and flags, wrote the *Examiner,* which added: "the whole city will turn out to pay them tribute and let loose a riot of cheering, songs and noise, the like of which even San Francisco has never known."[8]

Only weeks before the Volstead Act passed, the citizens of Healdsburg had been asked to mark their calendars and plan to take part in a magnificent Armistice celebration in the town streets. Judge Emmet Seawell, a talented local orator, was advertised as the headliner of a lavish midday banquet to follow. The Mexican War Veterans, the Civil War Veterans, and the Spanish War Veterans would follow the town band; schoolchildren, citizens, floats, and decorated cars would bring up the rear.[9]

The war seemed over everywhere but on Capitol Hill.

It was a shock to everyone in Congress when Woodrow Wilson roused himself in his sickbed on the afternoon of October 27, 1919, to write a powerful denunciation of the Prohibition legislation and then deploy his angry veto from his rooms in the White House, two miles down Pennsylvania Avenue. To a flummoxed House of Representatives the president wrote: "I am returning, without my signature . . . an act to prohibit intoxicating beverages . . .[this decision] has to do with the enforcement of an act which was passed by reason of the emergencies of the war."[10]

The arrival of the Wilson missive created an immediate uproar among Representatives, many of whom had been dozing through the turgid passage of an oil leasing bill. Volstead and his allies had expected the ailing president to allow the bill to pass almost by default; after all, there was so much else he had to worry about. Now, unexpectedly, House organizers had to muster votes for an override. Since the veto had arrived without warning on a Monday afternoon, Volstead and his Republican allies, Speaker Frederick Gillett and House Majority Leader Frank Mondell, declared they would wait for the override vote to be called in a timely manner later in the week. Thursday would do just fine, they concurred.

But on closer observation of the House at large, they discovered a huge opportunity: A large number of Wets had skipped the day's session. The Speaker called a vote before the Wets could be alerted to scramble back to the chamber.[11]

All the surprised anti-Prohibition forces could do was make a lame attempt to exclude light wines and beers from the ban, but the noise of both sides shouting at one another was too overwhelming. The Wet amendment went unheard, or perhaps simply ignored.[12] With only about half of the eligible representatives in place to vote, the override cleared the House by a comfortable 176 to 55. Missing the vote were many representatives from two of the most virulently anti-Prohibition states: 31 of New York's 43 members and 24 of Pennsylvania's 36 members were absent.[13] Heartbreaking to the Wet forces was the fact that: If the wet members from the New York and Pennsylvania had been in the House they would have "prevented the passage of the prohibition measure over the President's veto" reported the *New York Times*.[14]

Five of the eleven California representatives were also absent, and the other six split their delegation's vote. Voting against the president were Henry Barbour, a Republican lawyer from Fresno, a city in the richest agricultural region of the world and by then the state's biggest grape-growing county, but most of his constituents' interests lay in table grapes, not grapes that made wine; Henry Osborne, newspaperman, U.S. Marshal, and Republican from Los Angeles, deep in the Prohibitionists' stronghold; and John Raker, a Democrat from Alturas in the northeastern corner of the state—timber country, not wine. Siding with the president were three members of Congress whose constituencies lay nearer to Wine Country: Democrat Hugh Steel Hersman of Gilroy and two Republicans, Charles Curry of Sacramento and John Nolan of San Francisco. The anti-Prohibitionists stormed out of the House as soon as the vote was counted, feeling defrauded by what seemed to them to be an illegitimate and essentially malicious act: They felt like stunned victims of a savage ambush.

The president's veto was then delivered to the Senate. The two California senators, even though both came from San Francisco, voted in opposition to each other. Fifty-three-year-old Republican Hiram Johnson, eventually the longest-serving senator in U.S. history, had been governor of California from 1911 to 1917 and served as Theodore Roosevelt's running mate on the 1912 Progressive ticket; now he voted to override Wilson's veto. Voting with the president was the wealthy and urbane Democratic Senator James Phelan, a banker, businessman, and avid art collector who had been a popular mayor of San Francisco and whose personal donation of one million dollars had helped rebuild the city after the 1906 earthquake and fire. Phelan eventually derided his opposing senators with contemptuous words:

> In the Senate, when the prohibition laws were enacted, I moved that an exception be made in favor of wine and beer . . . and [we] would have spared wine and beer, but the lash of the Anti-Saloon League whipped the manhood out of [the senators], and caused them (through fear of losing their next election) to abandon their judgment and desert their principles. It was a sad spectacle.[15]

The Senate overrode the presidential veto by 65 to 20 votes. The veto was dead.

The Senate immediately repassed the Volstead Act.[16]

Northern California's wine industry reeled from the lethal blow. The act decreed it would come into effect at midnight on January 17, 1920. With three months still to go, Napa and Sonoma held out strong hopes that Prohibition would never happen. After all, Wilson had made a comforting announcement just moments before the Senate vote, duly reported in emphatic capitals in Santa Rosa's *Press Democrat* newspaper: "PRESIDENT WILL LIFT BAN WITH PEACE."[17] Wilson announced that he expected the Senate to rapidly agree to the ratification of the peace treaty, and he believed that within a month the Prohibition legislation would be duly overturned.

It was a massively wrong prediction. Wilson's month of Prohibition turned into 14 long years. But no one in Napa or Sonoma could possibly have foreseen it. Instead, throughout that lovely autumn, they were as obsessed with the art and science—and joy—of picking their grapes and turning some of them into wine, not knowing when or where they would be able to sell it.

There was nothing that the Napa and Sonoma winemakers and grape growers could do but wait in the hopes that sometime very soon the president might declare the peace process complete and make the Volstead Act with its lawmen and its bureaucracy needed to police the nation unnecessary. If he did not, the wine industry believed it might have to be declared officially dead in a few months.

However, a glimmer of hope for the vineyards of northern California arrived most unexpectedly when a demand for fresh wine grapes startled the industry. The juice-grape phenomenon had started slowly, and its origins were unclear. But consumers who found it increasingly difficult to buy jugs of wine were perhaps well disposed to learning the mysteries of making jugs of wine. Recipes available in every public library detailed easy methods that let consumers turn out "drinkable" wine in three to four weeks in their own kitchens and cellars.

Many of the new winemakers came from Europe, where winemaking had taken place at home. They knew that it did not take a chemist to turn grape juice into something that wine lovers would happily quaff.

Instead of selling wine as they normally did at that time of year, some vine-yards and grape growers in California had held back on their "crush"—the an-nual pressing of the grapes to extract the juice and start the wine-making process—and had begun instead to sell wine grapes directly to consumers and dealers across the country. Others were making wine-grape juice for the same category of customers.

Many winemakers were distressed by what looked like a future without wine. In the early summer of 1919, Carl Jungmeyer of the *Los Angeles Record* had stopped at the home of Carl Dresel, a pioneer winemaker of Sonoma. Carl and his father, Julius, had arrived in Sonoma 50 years before Prohibition, after a stint in Texas, where as a Republican newspaper publisher Julius had "fought slavery, se-cession and the Confederacy."[18] Carl was now 70, a father of six, who had long ranched 150 acres and had won medals for his wines. As Prohibition neared, he had already cut back his original production of 175,000 gallons of wine a year to 40,000. He was worried that his ranch and cooperage, once valued at nearly $70,000, were now worth only a little more than $5,500. He discounted the money—"That's the least of it," he told Jungmeyer, adding that he could not con-template having to pull up vines even if they were no longer economic. In his vine-yard, he said, he had gnarled old vines that had grown up with his family: "Some I planted when I married, some when my children were born, some when they—why, my boy, these vines are like members of my family."[19]

Knowing that there might still be hope for some of those vines would be re-lief to old-timers like Dresel.

It was a dramatic development. Only a few months later Horatio F. Stoll, the state's viticultural commissioner and his secretary, E. M. Sheehan, had ad-dressed a gloomy August 1919, meeting of some 30 winemakers and grape growers in Calistoga, telling them that there was hardly any hope for the mak-ing of wine in the two counties for some years. Sheehan said he had already dis-posed of his own cellar and quit the business. And both speakers urged the growers to move as fast as they could to get rid of their grapes by any means.[20] Wine grapes had been shipped from California to points outside the state in the past, but it had not been a significant business, especially in the northern part of the state.

Now winemakers who only months earlier had been contemplating their de-mise were rethinking their plans. The ability of the industry to respond to a fresh business opportunity astounded the Drys, and it would infuriate them for years.

Even more maddening to the Drys was the fact that the possibility of a supernova of sales of grapes that would end up in wine barrels and bottles would be legal.

Soon enquiries from local buyers in northern California would provide the first inkling that grape growers might benefit from Prohibition. And it was not long before grape salesmen from across the country, alerted by demand from their own customers in their home states, began ordering grapes in massive quantities. A trial balloon, as it were, had been sent aloft as early as September 1919, some four months before Prohibition would begin, when Napa dealers Merriam & Cairns shipped a carload of fresh wine grapes east—the first, they declared, ever to be shipped from St. Helena rather than being turned into wine locally. In the weeks to follow, the company boasted, it would ship 16 more carloads from St. Helena and 28 from Rutherford.[21]

Other sales of fresh grapes were soon reported in the wine counties. Charles A. Davis, A. P. Chaix, and F. J. Burden, whose vineyards were also located near Rutherford, sold 400 tons of pooled grapes to a San Francisco buyer for shipment to Boston. The purchaser, they reported, even furnished the shipping crates. Intrigued by the unexpected market bounce for wine grapes, the *New York Times* sent reporter Herbert Thompson to investigate. "When the vineyardists of California asserted that prohibition would mean a loss to them this season of 400,000 tons of grapes, the Drys replied that prohibition would, on the contrary, work out as a 'blessing,'" he wrote. "The Drys were right. Profits from grapes broke all records."

Napa and Sonoma were in shock.

Prices were suddenly booming, Thompson explained, not only because grapes were selling in states that had opposed Prohibition, but also thanks to "large numbers of grape buyers from Dry States—even the bone dry. Their bidding against each other was chiefly responsible for running up the prices."[22] Wets had scored one of the first in a series of victories for their cause. California grape growers did not have to look too hard for interest: Buyers from major and minor markets were frantic to sign up future grape harvests throughout Napa and Sonoma and flocked west.

As the official January 1920 start date of the new national Dry law grew closer, many wine families in Napa and Sonoma began to mutter among themselves that if this was what Prohibition was going to be like, then bring it on.

Chapter Four

It was a Clamoring Mob

The wine people of Napa and Sonoma had waited in vain for Washington to announce the end of the wartime emergency, and an appeal to the Supreme Court had not helped either. In spite of their efforts, at 12:01 A.M. Saturday, January 17, 1920, the country was to become bone-dry. After that moment it would be illegal, to manufacture, sell, barter, transport, import, export, deliver, furnish, or possess alcoholic beverages except for a very few exceptions such as for religious or medicinal purposes.

As the bells from the little churches in St. Helena and Healdsburg rang out the final evening mass before Prohibition, the last barrels of wine were being rushed around the counties. The wineries had made the most of the final hours, selling as much as they could, and wine families were delivering everything time allowed to local customers. Buyers had been overwhelming the wineries for days, carting off as much wine as they could stuff into their own cars. Wineries had needed permits to sell wine farther afield; business ceased as the permits ran out. But that Friday, January 16, in one last frenzy, the traffic in wine continued. The wineries had been warned that they needed to stop selling about 30 minutes before 12 A.M., so all sales would absolutely have ceased by midnight. As the deadline approached, now-empty trucks drove back to the wineries and the last customers carefully carried or rolled their precious cargoes into their homes. Then a terrible quiet slowly enveloped the valleys and hills.

By now, the three vast industries that produced alcoholic drinks in the United States were almost completely shut down. The huge breweries of the Northeast and Midwest had reduced production to just a relative trickle of low alcohol "near beer," much ridiculed and resented by the drinkers in a nation that vastly preferred beer to other alcoholic beverages. Many teams of sweating draft horses that every day had strained to haul heavy beer wagons through the streets of the country's biggest cities were at rest in stables awaiting new orders from new owners. And while the breweries were figuring the losses to their business, cities across the nation, too, planned much-reduced budgets. Tax revenues would slide dramatically after owners shuttered bars and saloons. (The great distilleries of Kentucky were quiet, since the use of grains for alcoholic beverages had been restricted during the First World War, when food production took priority. That law had not been changed, the end awaiting, the president said, full demobilization of Kentucky's usually busy railroad lines which were not so busy anymore) The trains that had carried endless barrels of whiskey from the private sidings of distilleries to the nation's saloons and hotels were still.

Kentucky's vast whiskey stores were particularly problematic to the Dry forces. Uncle Sam would soon be the biggest holder of liquor in the world, announced the *Washington Post*, citing the 60 million gallons of whiskey confiscated by government officials and kept under padlock and chains in bonded warehouses.[1] That it would be a siren call to criminals and a constant source of fury to the legal owners who had produced the whiskey there was no doubt. Already an alarming amount of bottled whiskies in bonded storage had gone missing, even though John F. Kramer, the nation's first Prohibition commissioner, had placed special guards at liquor warehouses across the nation when he could find the staff. The number of employees under his direction in those first days made monitoring all storage facilities impossible and Kramer reckoned 2,500 men would be needed to do that single job properly.[2]

That night before Prohibition, across the country, 236 distilleries, 1,092 breweries, and 177,790 saloons and any other places selling intoxicants shuttered their windows and locked their doors.[3] California's registered 700 wineries, 256 in Sonoma and 120 in Napa, braced themselves for a bumpy road ahead: the *California Grape Grower* reported that only 160 wineries in the state still had permits at the end of Prohibition—it would be a devastating loss to the state's economy.[4] Many of the tens of thousands of men and women who had worked for generations in the three alcoholic beverage industries were already unemployed, their talent and experience of no value to anyone in the new world of Prohibition, more workers would soon join them. Beyond them, a supporting army of bottle and barrel makers, machine shop engineers, delivery boys, malt manufacturers, hop pickers, and wagon drivers, all of whose work was essential to the making of beer, whiskey, and wine, were looking for new work.

In Washington, those charged with enforcing Prohibition law were confident. Said Assistant Commissioner H. M. Gaylord of the Internal Revenue Department, "The Government's organization for the enforcement of national prohibition is already so well organized that there will be no alcoholic refreshment available for the ordinary wayfarer" after January 16—unless, he added, a drinker wished to dally with dangerous substitutes, like concoctions made from wood alcohol.[5]

San Franciscans were a little less sanguine. W. A. Kelly, the West's supervising Prohibition officer, and Frank M. Silva of the local district attorney's office, announced that they had not yet fully completed the organization of their new departments, reported the *San Francisco Chronicle*. Kelly could say only that he planned to have six supervisors managing Prohibition in the states of Washington, Oregon, California, Nevada, and Arizona and that each state would *eventually* have a large number of men, some of whom had already been hired, under the direction of a state Prohibition officer. Locals rolled their eyes at the disorganization this announcement signified—first the government forbids the drinking of alcohol, then it announces that there are no finalized plans for enforcement.[6]

The men eventually hired to cover such a wide swath of territory would face daunting responsibilities. The lavish promises of Prohibition's benefits, especially the claims of the Anti-Saloon League, must have incited many Americans to support the movement. Maryland senator Millard E. Tydings rather sarcastically forecast the supposed benefits of Prohibition awaiting the country as he understood them: First, he had been assured by Dry forces that Prohibition "would end drunkenness. Second, it would practically eliminate deaths from alcoholism. Third, it would decrease crime. Fourth, it would practically empty the jails and penitentiaries." It would also bring on the demise of the alcoholic drink industry, and it would "abolish the saloon," "decrease the number of insane," and would "offer a better example for the young."[7]

While the Prohibition Department readied what forces it could, January 16, 1920, afforded both celebrations and wakes to attend for Drys and Wets, respectively.

Across the nation, hymns were sung by those on one side of the fight and toasts for a quick end of Prohibition were made by the other.

The eastern seaboard had awakened to a blustery winter storm that dumped a thick coat of snow across New York City and Washington. In the capital, the violent storm had deposited a thick white coat across the smoky roofs and cupolas of Capitol Hill. Skating on the Tidal Basin had been canceled due to dangerously deep drifts. Reform groups, in town to celebrate the legislation, held somber prayer meetings, undaunted by the inclement weather. At the First Congregational Church, Wayne B. Wheeler of the Anti-Saloon League, the attorney general, the secretary of the navy, and prominent Dry members of Congress planned to join a crowd of well-wishers in an evening of thanks, the activities culminating in a low-key but victorious moment of silence at midnight, when Prohibition became law.[8]

However, all was not to be thoughtful and uplifting in the country's capital city. Home-brewed liquor manufactured in secret in Washington cellars since wartime Prohibition had been enacted the previous summer would make its appearance in "wakes" planned in private homes.[9] A city used to private gatherings that could often include lashings of alcohol for elected officials and their retinues for lobbying, networking, and just plain chewing over the news of the day from the Capitol, wondered how it would cope with the new reality.

Oddly enough, Chicago—which was later to play such a prominent role in the illegal trafficking of alcohol—did not enjoy as much excess of celebration as other cities: One reason may have been that it had already decided that drinking would probably go on unabated whatever the legislation decreed. Another reason why the night before Prohibition was quieter than might have been expected was that Chicago happened to be in the middle of a serious influenza outbreak and many folks also preferred to avoid large crowds out late on a cold night. On January 16, 4 Chicagoans had died and 390 new cases of the flu had been announced.[10] A day later the death toll had risen by another 10 and 650 more cases had been diagnosed.[11] The *New York Times* reported, "Chicagoans cheered the final moments of a moist United States in a more or less tame celebration in the cafes and restaurants." Though there had been lots of activity around town when anyone who owned or bought liquor rushed to store it in the safety of their own homes before midnight struck: Trucks, automobiles and vans had scurried over the city all day transporting liquor from offices and lockers to homes. And there was one unexpected though slight reprieve when late on Friday afternoon, Major

Dalrymple, head of Prohibition enforcement for the central region of the nation, announced that no arrests or confiscations of liquor would be made, except in the case of sales, until ten days of grace had passed.[12]

Some spectacular robberies marked the early hours of Prohibition in Chicago. In one, reported the Associated Press, six masked men bound the yardmaster and watchman of a railroad, locked six trainmen into a shanty and "took between $75,000 and $100,000 worth of whiskey from two boxcars."[13]

In New York, the stormy weather meant partygoers had to dash from cars and cabs and buses and train stations through the swirling snow and howling winds to get to their celebrations. Seemingly in New York, too, as in Washington, the storm did not dampen all the enthusiasm for these final gatherings of booze; some reports even went as far as to paint pictures of jolly and noisy revelries that put to shame many previous celebrations. Manhattan's restaurants, bars, and hotels were ablaze with lights. "Mourners" came to participate in wakes where mock coffins were carried over the heads of partygoers to the toasts of revelers. Drinkers could pay from 75 cents to a dollar for a drink, though some of the fancier venues were charging $30 for a bottle of wine.[14]

Thousands of New Yorkers gathered in city churches to celebrate the successful outcome of their prayers for Prohibition. William H. Anderson, state superintendent of the Anti-Saloon League of New York, gave an address signed by 1,000 pastors from every one of the 57 counties in New York State outside of New York City, declaring that state, "the danger point in the whole nation," and he continued on to describe the city as the country's "center of nullification and seditious activity."[15]

As midnight approached, the cocktail-imbibing population of New York formed funeral processions. Some of the coffins were carried through the chilly streets on the shoulders of mourners who made wobbly, if not happy, pallbearers.[16]

Prohibition's arrival made for some bizarre decisions. Librarians in Springfield, Massachusetts, and New Haven, Connecticut, announced that they had removed all books from their shelves that contained instructions on how to make alcoholic beverages.[17] In Atlanta, a reporter put a quart of an unnamed liquor into the gas tank of a small plane and soared in a caravan of planes over the city, while a passenger scattered ashes in the form of confetti made of Anti-Saloon League literature onto the city below.[18] From Louisville a correspondent for the *New York Times,* reported that no matter how small the town or village where members of the Women's Christian Temperance Union resided, a wake was held. In every church was a watch party that "raised prayers of praise" for the Dry forces and their success.[19]

In Los Angeles, in keeping with the zeitgeist of the city that housed the nation's nascent film industry, a local dean of restaurateurs had organized another mock funeral where a dummy of "John Barleycorn" (an amusing icon for many centuries for liquor made with cereals, such as wheat) was going to be buried in a garbage can in the middle of the dining-room. At a local cabaret venue, six attractive girls carried a stretcher on which sat a demijohn of liquor. Cafés along the spectacular city beaches planned to make their toasts with customers to another John Barleycorn, and later lower his dummy body into the surf in a seafarer's ritual funeral not far from their back doors.[20]

Transportation had hummed clear across the country as liquor distributors sought to export their holdings before it was too late. Nearly $1 million (more than $10 million today) worth of liquor on dozens of railcars had already headed out of the country on trains through Calexico and Mexicali, causing a traffic jam when customs officers could not keep up with the necessary inspections. Twenty carloads were still waiting.[21] This liquor could be stored by its U.S. owners in Mexico or exported anywhere in the world. It was some insurance for the future. In San Francisco, steamships took advantage of the ebb tide as they rode out through the Golden Gate, their holds packed full with wine and brandy headed to China, Japan, Europe, and South America. Trucks had rushed to train stations with wines destined for domestic consumers located in all points east.

Low-riding ships left Baltimore heavy with whiskey. One, the *Lake Ellerslie*, sailed for Nassau on the last possible day, January 16, with $5.5 million ($55 million in 2008 dollars) worth of whiskey on board.[22]

San Franciscans were determined to stockpile as much liquor and wine as possible, given the time and the cost. A front-page *Chronicle* headline in huge type declared "WINE WASHES OUT WET ERA." Approximately 50,000 gallons of wine headed into private San Francisco cellars on January 16, the newspaper reported. All day long trucks and wagons full of liquor had driven between liquor stores and wine vaults delivering barrels and jugs and cases of wine and liquors to customers in every part of town. All available vehicles had been pressed into service: touring cars, limousines, cars ready for the scrap heap (flivvers, as they were called), delivery trucks for vegetables, furniture, anything that could move did, loaded down with precious cargoes that would see San Franciscans through the long dry days and nights ahead. Said the *Chronicle:*

> Bankers and brokers, shipping men, mining men, real estate men, butchers and bakers and candlestick makers, men of every rank and every degree who could raise the price of the liquor were hurrying to their homes or other people's homes in vehicles piled high with liquors. Fair ladies sat in limousines, behind alluring barricades of cases; businessmen in runabouts had cases on their knees.[23]

Perhaps most of the shoppers were too busy to absorb the latest revelations from Washington, where federal officials had suggested that "nosing committees" might be useful in the fight against booze. These agents assigned to attend social events in the country's large cities were literally to sniff as they closed in on anyone suspected of taking an illegal drink, keep notes on the breath of attendees, and report back to the district attorney's office the next morning.[24]

In the coming months, it was apparent that the northern California agents did not take this suggestion too seriously, but by Sunday, January 18, federal enforcement officers in San Francisco were declaring the city to be as dry as the Mojave Desert.[25]

Sonoma County had never seen a rush at its wineries. The *Sonoma Index-Tribune* waxed poetic: "a host of vintage seekers" had come to town, the paper wrote,

> seeking to possess and cache away all the wine they could carry with them before the dawn of prohibition's dread days.
> Where they came from, where they were going, or whence returning, no one seemed to know, but the fact was apparent that a marvelous procession of motor vehicles passed through town loaded to the gunwales with wine which has made Sonoma Valley famous.

Sonoma wine sold for $1.25 a gallon for white and 75 cents for red. Some rare old vintages from the 1850s were sold at $6.50 a gallon. Wine connoisseurs worried that stocks of the great old wines of Sonoma had been decimated due to the strong demand for any wine at all and the belief of some winemakers that the wine industry had no future; some wanted to empty their cellars while it was still possible.[26] Local wine lovers lamented the possibility that the best aged wines had been sold and were gone from Sonoma—they were saddened at the thought that the likes of it might never be tasted there again.

About 40 hilly miles northwest of the city of Sonoma, near the tiny Russian River town of Guerneville, the final days before Prohibition had been as frantic at the Korbel Winery as at most other wineries in the two counties.

The winery packaged and sent to customers' homes the last orders it might be able to fill for many years, if not longer. Korbel sold its many wines—including port, Sherry, claret, Muscat, Zinfandel, and Burgundy along with many others—to dealers and customers across the United States, in Europe, and in parts of Asia. The company's own Chicago branch office manager sent regular reports to Guerneville that were retained in company files. In some of the correspondence, reported in Patsy Strickland's *Korbel History,* he described the last night before Prohibition:

> Moving vans, coal trucks, automobiles and anything that would run on wheels came for the orders and we did our best. Thursday the fun started and Friday at 8 o'clock we had to close down because we could not stand on our feet as we had been going since six thirty in the morning without a chance for a bite of anything to eat. It got so bad that we had to call six detective sergeants to sprinkle in the crowd. . . . It was a clamoring mob and I may say that none of us ever want to repeat the experience. We filled orders amounting to twenty thousand dollars (more than $200,000 today) Thursday and Friday.

Korbel's success, too soon interrupted, had been a marvelous tale of entrepreneurship. Brothers Francis, Anton, and Joseph Korbel had come to the United States from Bohemia, arriving in San Francisco in the early 1860s. They soon succeeded in a number of ventures, including a cigar box factory, a printing establishment, and a lumber mill in California's northern reaches, where they made, among many other things, redwood tanks for wineries. The brothers bought a sturdy steam schooner, the *North Fork,* to carry their lumber from the Humboldt County mill down to San Francisco. Their wine business was a direct result of the Korbels' success with lumber, since grapes were among the crops they planted after clearing their hilly Guerneville property of mighty redwoods. The pinot noir they planted would eventually be turned into their astonishingly successful sparkling wines. By 1882, their first brandy shipment left their winery, and in May 1898, the brothers recorded their first shipments of sparkling wine.

Now the great firm could only commiserate with that Chicago office manager, sending a memo to him that echoed his description of events in the Windy City.

It was that way here in San Francisco. No one would believe that the people were so anxious to get liquor. There was a stream of all kinds of wagons and trucks carrying wines and liquors. It all went to private families. It was hard to believe that they would stock up so. We were not fortunate in moving so much on account of our cellar being in the country and not having it here in San Francisco. . . . Still we have plenty of it on hand, about 125,000 gallons of red and white wine two or three years old and about 75,000 gallons of last years. There must be about 5,000 cases of champagne including the triage and the tables.

How we can dispose of it will have to be decided in the future.[27]

For the winery owners in Sonoma and Napa, January 17, 1920, dawned like no other day. They could no longer sell wine or even accept visitors at the wineries, and unless they had medicinal or sacramental wine permits, their wine had to remain locked in their cellars. However, their vines were precious and still needed tending, even in rainy January. Pruning and cleanup was in full swing in the larger vineyards. It is lore in the vineyards that a man can manage 15 acres of vines by himself—but in those days, a larger property required more help, from wives, children, and hired hands. From a very early age, children participated in the spring cleaning of a vineyard: The tiniest ones were most useful for gathering up the clippings from the prunings and piling them up for bonfires.

In any other January, the smell of the last drifts of smoke from bonfires signified a good, satisfying day of pruning. The drifts themselves hung like soft white necklaces around the mountains surrounding Napa, Alexander and the Dry Creek valleys. Later gentle breezes slowly wafted the ribbons of smoke away to the sky and out of sight but the smell still hung in the air till late that night. It was a comforting aroma to all those who worked at a grape ranch: it meant that the vineyards were getting ready for another good year and that that the growth of a brand new vintage would soon be under way. This had been an unusually sunny New Year, and the dappled clouds across the hills and mountain ranges had meant good field conditions. In the evening, grape growers and winemakers rested their aching arms and legs beside fireplaces stoked with plentiful logs of old oak, glasses of good wine in their hands, many of them still believing that Prohibition would be short-lived. As they settled in front of their cozy fireplaces, they wondered if it would last a month. Or two.

Chapter Five

To Hell with Prohibition

he grape growers of Napa and Sonoma continued to hustle through the spring of 1920, as they always had, diligently pruning their vines and disking and fertilizing their land row by row. By April, the mystical dawn of a new season was before them as the first new buds began to break out on the dark, sleepy vines. The growers could soon see the sprouting of the very tiny protuberations that would, with prayer and luck, grow into fat, luscious bunches of grapes throughout the coming months. Usually the trees and flowers and vines across the hills and valleys of Napa and Sonoma are washed to sparkling by the final rains of spring, then the skies bring almost no moisture until fall arrives. And as April comes to an end, grape growers pray that the weather has well and truly settled down. Heavy rains, frosts, or great winds from here on in can do the most frightening damage of the year. Their eyes turn to the west morning, noon, and night—for that is where their weather nearly always comes from—and they scour the skies beyond the misty hills hoping that the clear blue skies will stay that way. That year the anguish about Prohibition added to the annual worries about the vagaries of the weather. Along with the general woes about the unknown and about the new regulations that affected everything there was also lively chatter around the vineyards. Contrary to their first awful premonition that financial ruin was imminent, the growers talked about the unexpected opportunity that had arisen in the past few months to make some money that might let them survive a little longer. Now that they had had the time to assess last year's harvest and realize how prices had leapt upward for their fresh wine grapes as the season progressed, hopes rose that this phenomenon might continue. They had never sold fresh wine grapes like this before. It was a revelation that such volume was possible.

Although he probably did not realize it then, a statement in that spring of 1920 by then Prohibition commissioner John F. Kramer focused even more of the growers' attention on the possibilities of extensive nationwide wine-grape markets. In the new language of the Prohibition bureaucracy, Kramer allowed: "The National Prohibition Act does not in itself restrict in any manner the sale or shipment of dried or fresh grapes." The growers were overjoyed there would be no limit on the amount of grapes that could be shipped from any vineyard.

The growers now had to shift their thoughts from producing their own wine, to getting their grapes to markets much farther away than they had ever contemplated. There was a lot to learn before they could participate properly in this nascent opportunity.

There was one further catch, however, continued Kramer: "If the shipper has knowledge that the consignee will use the grapes for illegal purposes and the latter so illegally uses same, both the shipped and the consignee will be liable for conspiracy . . . ."[1] But grape growers merely laughed that comment off. Be liable for wine made in New York and Chicago with the grapes they shipped from their little towns in Napa and Sonoma on the opposite side of the continent? No, sir, they thought. Northern California was such a long way from most of the markets where grapes would be turned into wine, and the growers' connections with anything illegal wine merchants or makers thousands of miles away might involve themselves with would be nebulous at best. Their grapes would be shipped from California vineyards to a second party, a shipper; to be bought by a third party, a wholesale or auction house in New York; thence to be sold to the fourth parties, the consumers, who would turn them into wine or whatever they wished. Grape growers did not need to know any further details, they thought, other than that a shipper had bought the fruit of their vineyard. It would be virtually impossible to trace the wine made by that final purchaser in a New York apartment house cellar or a Chicago kitchen back to a grower in Napa or Sonoma. "We never worried about that," said winemaker and grape grower Lou Foppiano. "You could ship fruit from Healdsburg. We always had; pears, apples, prunes. Grapes, even wine grapes, were just fruit as far as we were concerned."[2]

And so it seemed to be for the authorities as well.

With Kramer's good news ringing in their ears, some grape growers went into high gear, looking for delivery contracts across the country. But they did not have to look too hard for sales: Buyers from major and minor markets across the United States were suddenly frantic to sign up future grape harvests throughout Napa and Sonoma and came searching them out.

The California Grape Growers Exchange had earlier that year fixed a minimum pricing schedule for their members' wine grapes: $50 a ton for "burger" grapes, a white varietal once hugely popular in California; $60 for all other white grapes; $65 to $70 for black and color grapes.[3] Those numbers were now starting to seem wildly conservative; the $15 commanded in years before 1919 was forgotten altogether.[4]

In the summer of 1920, the Internal Revenue Department ruled that "fruit juices, non-intoxicating, in fact" could be made in the home. As everyone knew, fruit juices might be nonintoxicating when they were made, but left to themselves, they would not stay that way for long.

"As if by magic," declared the *California Grape Grower*, during that summer of 1920 "California became the Mecca for grape speculators who swarmed first into San Francisco and then out into the grape districts offering unheard of prices and bidding against each other until prices reached $75, $100, $125, $150 a ton for ordinary wine grapes."[5]

Later in the year, the "non-intoxicating" rule was reaffirmed by San Francisco's Internal Revenue Collector, Justus Wardell, who made the huge promise of the emerging wine-grape market even clearer to the wine industry a few months later when he said: "All persons producing fruit juices other than cider, containing one-half of one per cent or more of alcohol by volume are required to register." However, if they did, said Wardell, "the head of a family, who has properly registered, may have 200 gallons exclusively for family use, without payment of tax thereon. If he makes more than 200 gallons, he must give bond and pay a tax on the excess."[6]

It was a further astonishing invitation to millions of Americans across the country that wished to make their own wine now that Prohibition had arrived. The fact that an American household could legally make up to 200 gallons of wine each year without paying taxes dumbfounded everyone. And that this could happen by merely applying for a permit? Two hundred gallons was, after all, a whopping supply of wine—about 1,000 bottles per year. This homemade wine, it became clear very quickly, would be produced not only to stock the cellars of the private citizens who made it but to spike the bootlegging industry's supply as well. Small businesses were quickly set up under the guise of home operations to make as much wine as possible for the illicit market. Family winemakers could make a little extra money for themselves too, selling excess bottles to friends and contacts throughout small rural communities or in dense urban streetscapes in cities like New York and Philadelphia. All this opened the door to the manufacture of millions of more gallons of wine each year than the Internal Revenue might have suspected—as everyone in California knew well already, that 200 gallons was a revolving supply: As you drank, so you replaced.

The winemakers in Napa and Sonoma practiced "constant replenishment" themselves: It was easy to keep 200 gallons on hand so long as grapes were available. California wine grapes were usually available from August to November. A busy winemaker with a large enough cellar or other hiding place and a willingness to take a chance could turn out many multiples of 200 gallons in that period. And in many markets, when grapes were out of season, there were always raisins. Prohibition provided an unexpectedly large loophole that not only helped the wine-grape growers of northern California survive, but also made life surprisingly better for the surprised raisin-grape growers of the Central Valley.

Consumers, it appeared, wanted to make red wine most of all. Dark red wine. And grape buyers, especially in New York, were paying many times the price they had paid in 1918 for Alicante Bouschet, the most desired grape during Prohibition. The varietal may have evolved from the Aramon crossed with Teinturier du Cher, which resulted in Petit Bouschet. When Petit Bouschet was then crossed with Grenache, it created Alicante Bouschet.[7] The word "teinturier" in the grapes' origins referred to their dyelike properties. That this varietal had become the most valuable and the most profitable surprised Napa and Sonoma grape growers, because to their taste wine pressed from Alicante Bouschet was remarkably undistinguished. Yet that grape's tough skin made it easier to ship than the superior Zinfandel grape, and Alicante Bouschet could be relied on to produce an attractively dark red wine at the hands of even the most unskilled home winemaker.

In just a few months after Prohibition was enforced, New York had blossomed to become Napa and Sonoma's greatest fresh-grape market. By the end of 1920, Stoll, editor of the *California Grape Grower*, was curious about how the vast quantities of wine grapes sent east were used, so he set off to see for himself. He learned that "a lot of the 1,500,000 Jews in New York made wine"; and in Italian neighborhoods, there were "grapes galore in the fruit stores, some piled in high mounds and others tied in clusters along the fronts of their stands."

> "I asked one lady in charge if the Italians had made much wine and she laughed at my ignorance," I deadpanned.
> "Sure," she said, "everybody made vino. We got 600,000 Italians in New York and we use plenty of grapes."
> "But how about Prohibition?" I asked. "Weren't you afraid?"
> "To h—l with Prohibition," she said laughingly. "I'm not afraid. If they arrest me, they have to arrest all my friends—everybody—and they not got enough jails to keep us all."

An Italian barber who gave Stoll a shave told the editor he had purchased enough California Zinfandel and Alicante grapes to make 200 gallons of wine and that he was considering getting some friends together to raise $15,000 or $20,000 with which to start a company to produce wine. He said he could see the promise in buying grapes for cheap and turning a profit with this ersatz home brewing phenomenon.[8]

No one could have been more shocked at the financial supernova that was the fresh-grape market across the country than the grape ranchers of California.

All these grape growers had known tough times before, and like farmers around the world they were used to the whims of nature: the sun, the rain, and the heat. Any variation of these could make them richer or poorer in a matter of hours. They were hardened to changing fortunes. But instead of the worst they might usually have imagined, this was far beyond the best they could have dreamed. Instead of being driven to bankruptcy or, worse, losing their land for nonpayment of mortgage or taxes, some were making more money than ever before. And it was all legal.

Nor was the wholesale shipment of grapes the only financial opportunity available to grape growers and winemakers. Sacramental wine sales were another, seemingly profitable outlet for winemakers already, if they were lucky enough to have been granted the permit necessary to make wine to be used for religious purposes. Sacramental wine for the Catholic Church had to be produced only from grapes. If any additives were added to it, say brandy, to fortify it, that product also had to have as its only origins, grapes.

One Napa County winery owner who had been making sacramental wine for nearly two decades and who had contacts and offices around the country long before Prohibition became law was George de Latour of Beaulieu Vineyard. His large operation was based in Rutherford, at the south end of the Napa Valley. Latour appeared quite nonchalant about Prohibition even as he knew the new Dry laws were coming into effect. Months before Prohibition began, he and his wife, Fernande, completed the building of a grand new home on which the *St. Helena Star* had lavished much praise: "There is no more beautiful place in Napa County than Beaulieu Vineyard near Rutherford and among its greatest charms are the wooded foothills that form the background of a setting for an attractive home." It was there that the Latours had built their new home, the newspaper reported, adding that one of the prominent features of the Latour mansion would be "the many French doors that will open off from a long veranda and through which the spacious living room, dining room, family and guest bed rooms may be entered."[9]

Then the couple set off during the first summer of Prohibition on a vacation to France that was to last a couple of months, touring the Argonne Forest and other regions devastated in World War I. They planned to return to Rutherford halfway through September in the middle of harvest.[10]

Sacramental wine is essential to the Catholic Church. Fulfilling the orders for it from around the country had helped keep Latour's vineyard very busy, as it did other large vineyards with sacramental licenses, such as Mont St. La Salle Christian Brothers in Martinez, across the straits on San Francisco Bay, and Covick wines of Oakville. Their wines were already sold directly to churches, such as the Russia St. Michael Cathedral in Sitka, Alaska, which in one order had asked for a single keg and 10 gallons of port; the Holy Rosary Church, in Portland, Maine, which requested a single barrel of sauterne; and the Catholic church, in Costilla, New Mexico, which wanted 25 gallons of wine. An order from Mother Reparata, the Mother Superior at the Loretto Academy in Pueblo, Colorado, called for two kegs and 10 gallons, each of sweet wine; the Catholic church in Natchitoches, Louisiana, wanted 60 large bottles of wine. Other orders went to Los Angeles and Truckee in California; to Montequt in Louisiana; Forney, Texas; Havre, Montana; and Nada, Texas, which ordered two more barrels of the Beaulieu Special in "small kegs for the missions."[11]

Latour was not the only one doing well with sacramental sales. Other winemakers, such as Louis Kunde from Sonoma's Kenwood area, traveled to the East on sacramental business. Kunde had a large depot and warehouse in Brooklyn to facilitate business there. The paperwork to get the first of his post-Prohibition sacramental wine across the country was so complex that Kunde traveled with the shipment, producing papers to identify himself and his goods at various points along the journey.[12]

Larger vineyards were not the only ones to have sacramental wine licenses; some smaller vineyards received them too. Said Lou Foppiano, "You could get one easily"[13] by applying to the Prohibition Department. After vetting by the church and Prohibition officials, it appears the license was granted. Making the right wine for the sacramental trade was a little more difficult. The church and shippers requested lots of sweet wines—muscatel, angelica, malvoisie, sweet sauterne, Sherry—and not all vineyards had the equipment to or interest in making them. Above all, most of them did not have the contacts to make sales happen, especially the smallest ones.

Latour not only had his own sacramental wine salesmen already on site at Rutherford, he had an eastern beachhead at the Beaulieu Distributing Company on Barclay Street in New York City, backed up with agencies in Cleveland, Omaha, Milwaukee, St. Paul, Chicago, and Cincinnati. By the beginning of Prohibition, author Rod Smith reports in *Private Reserve: Beaulieu Vineyard and the Rise of Napa Valley*, Latour's salary was $20,000 a year,[14] this at a time when you could buy a very nice house in Napa for $3,000. Later in Prohibition, Latour was making $24,000, his wife, the vice-president of the company received $9,000, and their daughter Helene, as secretary, was paid $7,500. Men on Beaulieu's bottling line were paid about $12.50 a week; other workers at the vineyard were paid from 25 to 40 cents an hour.[15]

Latour's lifestyle reflected his successes. He drove a Cadillac. He and his wife were known for their gracious entertainment of local and out-of-town socialites. His daughter married a French count during Prohibition in a lavish wedding at which San Francisco's archbishop officiated.

Latour had been born in France's Périgord region, renowned for its epicurean delights of goose, duck, foie gras, truffles, and Armagnac. He was well educated and a natural entrepreneur yet he believed like so many others that the United States offered more opportunity than his homeland.

It was a tartaric acid company that first brought Latour to Napa and Sonoma. Tartaric acid, a derivative of which is used in cooking and called cream of tartar, can be harvested from the scum that rises to the top of the wine as it ferments. Latour soon made deals with winemakers in the two counties and found himself admiring their lifestyles and the future of California's nascent wine industry. He and Fernande bought property in Napa and as soon as they could they began to increase their grape-growing acreage.

That Latour was a savvy wine businessman, with widespread connections, and was well-known throughout Wine Country, was evident from the size of his bustling business at the beginning of Prohibition; but he had one other great advantage that other wineries in Napa and Sonoma did not. Latour had benefited from a working relationship with the Reverend Father Dennis O. Crowley, who ran a home for destitute boys then called St. Joseph's Agricultural Institute located not far down the road from his own operation.

The Reverend Crowley had been given the responsibility for developing the agricultural institute around the turn of the century. It was to house and educate some of the many destitute boys the church had in its care in San Francisco. A life in the country, surrounded by farms and fresh air, was thought to give young boys a better life than in the city. San Francisco was a tough, hard-living, hard-drinking port city in those days, and the children of its unluckiest citizens could easily become collateral damage from broken lives and broken dreams. The skills they could learn in the fields and gardens of the school's own farm would be a huge advantage. Agriculture was California's greatest industry and there was a fine future there or most anywhere else in the country, the church believed, and rightly so, for young men who were trained to farm.

The Catholic Church had purchased the land, perhaps at the urging of Reverend Dennis Crowley, in 1904—the same year Latour set up Beaulieu. Archbishop Patrick William Riordan, who had been born in Canada and who had studied in Rome, selected the land and had chosen his acres well; they had one of the finest pedigrees in Napa and had originally belonged to George C. Yount, the namesake of tiny Yountville. The agricultural establishment was set up with Father Crowley as director.

Father Crowley was a man of many talents and a great interest in improving the lives of the many disadvantaged youth of the Bay Area. He ran the institute in Napa and was the founding director of the Youths' Directory, another orphanage in San Francisco on 19th Street, where about 60 boys, ages 6 to 15, studied under his tutelage. All would speak, read, and write English before they graduated. Crowley had an artistic nature: Before Prohibition, he arranged as a benefit evening for the Youths' Directory an open-air staging of Verdi's famous opera *Aida* in San Francisco's Ewing

Field. The performance included a chorus of 500 singers, a ballet of 75, an orchestra of 150, a stage band of 50, and 100 people participating in pageantry effects.[16]

When the institute was first established and apparently named the Rutherford Agricultural College, the Xaverian brothers, who had been seconded to run it in 1903 from Mont St. Joseph's College of Baltimore County, Maryland, sent out a promotional letter to other clergy noting they had been "appointed and authorized by His Grace Most Rev. Archbishop Riordan to procure and forward pure wine for Altar purposes to any of the Rev. Clergy applying to us for the same." They were preparing for spring shipments and were soliciting orders. It seems the brothers made little wine in the early days at the institute. They appeared to have bought and sold wines which would have proved easier than managing a winery to men who had come from the East with what must have been limited wine-making talents.

The institute had once received praise for the wines it had delivered and included that endorsement in its promotional missive. The Reverend M. C. Donovan of St. Paul's Church in Philadelphia appeared to be enjoying the wine the institute had sent both at mass and as a personal beverage when he wrote: "I received a barrel of Riesling wine from you and it has given satisfaction both for Altar and table use."[17]

Perhaps the brothers at the institute never did produce much wine from their own premises. They were certainly producing little, if any for some years leading up to and into the first years of Prohibition. A report on the institute made on August 6, 1915, declared one of its vineyards "a bright spot in the farm. It is clean and fine." Another ten acres was cited as "neglected."[18] By the time a further report was commissioned by the institute in 1926, it was revealed that the vineyards were still in rough shape; one was missing thousands of vines, elsewhere wild grapes were scattered throughout what remained of the good vines "making harvesting, (and) pruning difficult and expensive."[19]

The good folk at the institute seemed hard-pressed for resources.

The worlds of Latour and Crowley seemed far apart—Latour was considered to be one of the richest men, if not the richest man, in Napa, and the Reverend Crowley tended to mostly charity cases, orphans or boys from broken homes—but there was a close link between them. The sacramental wine made from the grapes from Latour's vineyard for the institute was produced under the officially ordained supervision of the Reverend Crowley. He had an official statement printed to explain this relationship. To emphasize what must have been its great import to him and to the church, he even had it notarized:

> By virtue of the appointment of his Grace, the Archbishop of San Francisco, I have continuously since 1904, with the exception of one year when I was forced to be absent, owing to an accident, supervised the making and distributing of the Altar Wine made at the Beaulieu Vineyard cellar in Napa County, California. The Vineyards in which the grapes used for the making of these Altar Wines belong to Mr. Georges de Latour and to St. Joseph's Agricultural Institute. From my personal supervision of the making of these Altar Wines, extending over this long period of time, I hereby testify to the purity of all of the Altar Wines manufactured at the Beaulieu Vineyard Cellar.

> (Signed) Father D.O. Crowley[20]

Not only had Archbishop Riordan of San Francisco dispatched the official ecclesiastical winemaker to Latour's winery many years ago, his successor, Archbishop Edward Hanna, continued Crowley's arrangements with the vineyard during Prohibition. He also endorsed Latour's products. His letters of support were strewn liberally throughout Latour's sales literature:

> March 25th, 1920
> My dear Mr. Latour:

> With great pleasure, I have heard through the Reverend D. O. Crowley that you have enlarged your Beaulieu Vineyard winery at Rutherford, California, and I am pleased that your business has necessitated such development.
> I have had many favorable comments on your wine and, personally, consider it to be of the very best produced in California. Therefore, I again authorize Father Crowley to renew the contract which we now hold with you for crushing all the grapes grown on the property of St. Joseph's Agricultural Institute, situated at Rutherford, California, and which you make into Sacramental wine. I also authorize Father Crowley to continue his supervision of the manufacture and distribution of your Altar wines.
> Please accept this as a mark of my high esteem for you, and of my appreciation of your success in producing wine so fitting for the Holy Sacrifice.

> Very sincerely yours,
> Edward J. Hanna
> Archbishop of San Francisco[21]

When the owners of the successful and award-winning (Paris, 1889 and 1900; Dublin, 1892; Chicago 1893, among others) Beringer Vineyard in St. Helena, only a few miles farther north of Beaulieu, asked for a similar vote of confidence for a single sacramental sale and promised not to use the endorsement for any further solicitations of business, the response from the office of the archbishop was not nearly as generous as that afforded Latour. "The fact that His Grace has not endorsed you or your altar wine is not meant in any way as a personal reflection. His Grace understands from your Pastor that you are a reliable and honorable firm, and feels sure that the altar wine produced by you will be valid for the Holy Sacrifice of the Mass." Notwithstanding the lack of ecclesiastical endorsement, the Beringer Brother letterhead announced it produced "Pure Altar Wines."

Archbishop Hanna's relationship with Latour and the rest of his flock in Napa and Sonoma was warm. Hanna spoke beautiful Italian that impressed even the most cultured Italians; and it was said that Dr. Hanna, who had been educated at the Vatican where Pole Leo XIII had singled out his scholarship and natural oratory skills, was "the best Latinist among American Catholic clergy."[22] That warmed winemakers, many of whom had Italian roots. He personally contributed $1,000 to the University of California at Berkeley "to create an endowed chair in Italian culture," reported Richard Gribble in his book, *An Archbishop for the People: The Life of Edward J. Hanna.*[23] In 1922 as Prohibition began, the King of Italy made him a Commander of the Crown of Italy. In Hanna's acceptance speech, he "spoke of Italy and Italians as "a land and people I have always loved and admired."[24]

His warm relationship with his winemaking parishioners in Napa and Sonoma proved an advantage when it came to applying for sacramental wine licenses. The archbishop knew well the troubles visited on his flock by Prohibition legislation.

It is not clear when or how the archbishop and Latour first became acquainted. Whatever the tie, when Latour formed the Beaulieu Vineyard company in 1904, among his first directors were two men named Hanna and Crowley.[25]

One can only wonder why Latour was granted the singular honor. There was talk that the heftiest donations to the church often resulted in the most favorable outcomes for permit applications, but there is no evidence of Latour making such donations.

Like Catholics across the country, the wine-producing Reverend Crowley had made it clear long before Prohibition began that he thought the whole idea misguided:

"I believe that every sane and honest citizen of the State of California thinks, as we do, that prohibition is a measure of extremists and extremes are always dangerous. Prohibition aims not only to deprive people of their personal liberty, but in a hidden manner, it also strikes at the very foundation of that religious liberty which is guaranteed by the Constitution of our country."[26]

His words echoed a more pragmatic comment from the very top of the Catholic Church in the United States, Cardinal Gibbons, the most eminent Catholic prelate in the country: "I am intuitively persuaded that prohibition can never be enforced. It is calculated to make hypocrites and to lead to a manufacture of illicit whiskey, replacing the good material with bad, while at the same time robbing the government of a legitimate tax. Prohibition will never be enforced in any Christian country."[27]

The daily business of producing sacramental wine fell to Crowley to manage, but the relationship between Archbishop Hanna and Latour also grew over the years, and by the time Prohibition began, it prophesied terrific advantages for Latour. Beyond the wine sales themselves, the relationship with the church was also beneficial to the Latours when it came to amassing the valuable land of Rutherford. During Prohibition Latour later bought 110.5 acres of St. Joseph's land.[28]

Beyond making wine for religious customers, Prohibition authorities approved other possible moneymaking ventures for those in the wine industry. Wineries already had crushing equipment, and vineyards did, too, if they had the wherewithal to purchase crushing and bottling equipment; both could prepare and sell bottled grape juice or syrups. In the later years of Prohibition, when freezing technology had improved, some of the better-heeled operations also began producing frozen grape juice.

Again the vineyards and wineries owed the continued usefulness of their crop and the possibility of selling wine-grape juice to Justus Wardell of the Internal Revenue. Before Prohibition began, he declared that even California grape growers without sacramental or medicinal licenses could proceed with the crushing of the grapes for beverage purposes just so long as they did not allow the juice to ferment—a somewhat challenging proposition. Wardell's only real caution, which winemakers were urged to keep in mind each harvest, was that he did not want them to be hopeful about Prohibition's downfall when they made wine. Although he warned they should not hold it ready "for any expected lifting of the prohibition ban," that was hard to do.[29]

Wardell was right to suspect that an end to Prohibition was always on grow-ers' minds. Most wineries had retained stocks of wine, in spite of the tax liability, as insurance against a time when wine could be sold legally. Whenever that fi-nally happened, they figured, wine prices would rise dramatically, as pent-up de-mand pushed prices into the stratosphere. Another reason to retain wine was more practical: Wine tanks that held thousands of gallons of wine after crush were made of redwood. If they were drained and the wood was allowed to dry out, the tanks would be ruined for all future winemaking. The tanks had to be kept topped off with liquid. As a rule, though, the wine stored as a legacy vintage would be left undisturbed.

It soon became clear there was no single way to attempt to survive Prohibition. Contacts in San Francisco and across the nation, capital, risk, and winery loca-tion—all of these were factors in surviving the ordeal. Not all wineries and grape growers were large enough to benefit from the markets for grapes or for wine. Buyers first looked for large deliveries, which made it easier for them to work with the bigger grape growers and wineries in Napa and Sonoma. And not all grape growers were enthralled by the new business.

Many were country folk used to dealing in handshakes and cash. The idea of sending their grapes off across the country to a market they had never seen, in the hands of a company they did not know well, then waiting for payment was not something they were prepared to chance. They had their own reliable contacts in San Francisco. If they wanted to sell fresh wine grapes, they preferred to put them on their own truck and drive the load to a buyer they had known for years.

For those who chose to try out the new wine-grape markets, planning for harvest became more critical than ever, especially in good years. If the vines pro-duced a bounty, boxes had to be found for the grapes, railcars organized, and buy-ers one could trust signed on with. Crushing grapes for wine juice was as risky an option too, as the market for that produce was not well established: "Should we plan for a crush or not?" was a question that must have been asked countless times in every vineyard during the years of Prohibition.

In the past, consumers had not perceived wine-grape juice with much en-thusiasm—the processing necessary to keep the juice from fermenting gave it an unpalatable, cooked taste; but new technology was beginning to overcome that problem, it was said. In Napa, grape grower Bismarck Bruck was preparing to make grape juice as an alternative to wine. Bruck was going to crush about 1,000 tons of grapes. The superintendent of the magnificent cellars at Greystone, just north of St. Helena, had installed all the necessary apparatus for making grape juice too.[30] Another operation in Napa was producing another wine-based product, wine syrup, in a process that reduced every four gallons of grape juice into one of syrup. One of the advantages of this production, the owner explained, was that the ratio of four to one saved three barrels and the freight charge to eastern markets. It was reported in the *St. Helena Star* that the "dry vacuum" did eradicate the cooked taste, "which up to the present has so often been the enemy of grape juice.[31]

In Healdsburg, Edoardo Seghesio, his son-in-law Enrico Prati, and two brothers connected to the original Italian Swiss Colony, had formed a partnership to manufacture grape juice and syrups. Making the syrup was part of a program to reclaim some of the hillsides at Asti that the Italian Swiss Colony had abandoned when Prohibition threatened to wipe out the wine-grape industry. The company gave its new product the fanciful name Moonmist.

Advertisements declared it was "a drink that delights and satisfies. Only the fine wine-grapes, grown on the uplands of the Valley of the Moon, are used in making Moonmist and none of their enchanting flavor and bouquet is lost in the process. Notice its ruby redness—its clearness. Its taste is a revelation."[32] Golden State Products of San Francisco had also launched a nationally advertised wine-grape syrup and given it an even more imaginative name whose wry meaning probably was not missed: Forbidden Fruit Grape Syrup. It made, the company claimed, "a wonderful drink [made] by diluting with water, seltzer, ginger ale; delicious when poured on hot cakes or waffles. Forbidden Fruit Grape Syrup is the concentrated goodness of California wine grapes."[33] Wine grapes products had become anything but rare. Soon even more companies invested in the infrastructure to produce wine-grape syrup and industry promoters added medicinal properties to the growing list of grape syrup's supposed benefits. According to the *California Grape Grower:* "The form of sugar which is found in grape syrup is so delicate and harmless and so instantaneous in its effect that a person fatigued from heavy work or strenuous exercise or feeble from any cause may feel himself regaining his vitality and energy within a short time after it is consumed."[34]

The relatively high price of wine syrup made it decidedly less popular than other syrups marketed to home cooks. The industry hoped that housewives would so love grape syrup they would serve it as they served any other table syrup: at breakfast, for fruit punches, for making drinks with ice cream or soda, or for cooking. Touted as a product with almost unlimited uses, it supposedly tasted more like blackberries or loganberries than grapes.

Clarence Grange, who had invented the Grange Dehydrator, was drying grapes rather than shipping them unprocessed or turning them into syrup, and he soon reported that it was uneconomical for individual vineyards to operate small plants profitably and economically. He had hopes of eventually setting up community driers that would make the process even more affordable.[35] His large grape drier at Stag's Leap, near Yountville, had cost $14,000 and was powered by 840 gallons of distillate daily.[36]

Napa's Beringer vineyard was also drying grapes.[37] The Beringer operation had been started by two brothers from Germany, Jacob and Frederick, who knew about quality winemaking before they arrived in St. Helena in Napa County. By 1878, Jacob was producing 100,000 gallons of wine a year. When Frederick joined him in 1884, Jacob began work on his impressive Rhine House, which contained 17 rooms and thousands of dollars worth of stained glass.[38] Although both men had died long before Prohibition began, the winery was still in the family. On its premises was now an impressive Banks Fruit Evaporator, which used an electric fan to drive hot air into the drier. It took 24 hours to process each load of fruit, operated by four men during the day, one at night. Jacob Beringer thought early on that it might be profitable to construct two additional units the following season to handle all the grapes grown in the Beringer vineyard.[39]

But if wine grapes made an impressive syrup, they were decidedly unsuited to making raisins. However positively grape growers touted their new dried product, they realized that white wine grapes made particularly unpalatable dried fruit, and the red grapes, though slightly better than the white, were still far from delicious. Consumers shied away from raisins loaded with seeds. The cost of removing them made wine-grape raisins uncompetitive with those from the state's Central Valley—but only until consumers nationwide realized that dried wine grapes made good wine long after fresh grapes were out of season. Wine grape raisins stored throughout the long winter months allowed people to top off wine stocks throughout the year. In addition, California raisins became the basis of another popular homemade liquor across the nation: distilled raisin jack.

Perhaps because home winemakers had reacted so quickly due to the 200-gallon per household wine allowance, a dealcoholized version of the real thing never took a firm hold on the industry. The *St. Helena Star* reported early in

Prohibition that several Napa Valley winemakers had "shipped 1,200 gallons of claret by express" to a New York company, Virginia Products, Ltd., for experiments in de-alcoholization. But despite the Prohibition authorities' agreement that wine could be produced if it were later dealcoholized, the company's own California representative rendered a disappointing verdict on the perfectly legal product that resulted: He was "not fully satisfied with the result myself." His lack of enthusiasm dissuaded winemakers from pursuing the project with any vigor.[40]

The investment and time—new packaging, new marketing, and new machinery—that these products took made the fresh grape market look like a gift from the gods. Consumers could absorb only so much grape juice, syrup, and jam; what they really wanted more of was wine, and making it at home turned out to be much easier than anyone had expected. California growers planted their grapes accordingly—not just the instantly popular Alicante Bouschet, but also Carignane, a black grape with white juice and a thick skin; Mission, a black grape with white juice that had the benefit of growing in large bunches; and Zinfandel, California's most widely planted grape prior to Prohibition and still an enduring symbol of the state's wine industry. Other reds in demand included Grenache, Mataro, and Lenoir, even though its juice was often described as "slightly foxy." Popular white grapes included Burger, with its medium berry and neutral flavor; Chasselas, whose crisp taste became softer with maturity; and Sauvignon Vert, a large-berried grape that grew in medium-size bunches.

If growing grapes in the wine counties' ideal climate was no problem, getting them to market was more of a challenge. A critical shortage of railcars dogged grape growers from one harvest to the next, cutting into sales and profits. Grapes needed refrigerator cars for the long, hot journeys in August, September, and October. Professor Richard J. Orsi, in his book *Sunset Limited: The Southern Pacific Railroad and the Development of the American West 1850–1930*, explains that a shortage of refrigerated cars, "reefers" was, first, a legacy of World War I, when the government temporarily assumed control of the railroads as a wartime emergency measure and secondly and more important, the result of the growth in irrigation in the West that had created a huge demand for refrigerated transportation.

Pacific Fruit Express, a refrigerator-car subsidiary, was created by the Southern Pacific and the Union Pacific just after the turn of the twentieth century. To cool its first reefers, a massive ice-making facility was built in Roseville, a town northeast of Sacramento. It would be the first of many such plants designed to get California's fresh fruit to market in the best possible condition. Orsi recounts that by 1921, "the company manufactured 1.4 million tons of ice; by 1924, the annual production of just the Roseville ice plant, the largest in the world, had soared to 200,000 tons." Roseville could ice "hundreds of refrigerator cars simultaneously and thousands per day."

"Each car required 10,500 pounds of ice for initial cooling and 7,000 pounds for re-icing," explains Orsi. Huge blocks of ice were placed at each end of a reefer: They could be replaced many times on a car's journey across the country.[41]

The *Grower* had already warned early in 1920 that "California faces the greatest refrigerator car shortage ever known," declaring the state's supply of reefers short by 20,000 cars even though construction was underway on 8,000 to 10,000 more. Some of the cars were scattered "from Maine to Texas. Some have been 'lost' for months—another inspiring feature of Federal operations," the journal noted wryly, while others were being held by small railroads who can't afford their own, others were just stalled at small stations and being used for storage.[42]

Some grape growers eventually but reluctantly concluded it would be safer to tear out vines and plant other crops than to wait for more refrigerated railroad cars to show up. A number of cautious grape growers had decided to diversify even earlier. In Napa, apple, pear, and apricot plantings were all increasing. Sonoma planted many prune trees. Some grape growers interplanted the fruit trees in their vineyards so they could take advantage of a broader market while maintaining some wine production. But more wine-grape growers than ever believed there was a future for the wine-grape industry and intended to cultivate their vineyards as carefully as in the past. And a network of brokers sprang up to support them.

Advertisements in California newspapers proselytized the services of grape buyers across the country. From New York, John Pirung & Company asked for Alicante and Zinfandel grapes and offered a tempting inducement: "We will advance money."[43] Another wine-grape buyer, this one in the Fruit Exchange Building in Pittsburgh, declared that 60 million people could be reached within 12 hours from his city[44]—a market that could absorb huge amounts of fruit. Chicago dealer Jay H. Twitchell declared: "We have an outlet for six to eight hundred cars of juice grapes. If you have one or a hundred cars that you wish to market, get in touch with us before you make other arrangements. Reasonable advances made at time of shipment."[45]

Contrary to expectations, Prohibition had created such a grape boom that soon some vineyard owners went looking for more land on which to plant more vines, in some cases taking over land vacated by shuttered wineries. In November 1920, Sam Sebastiani, already owner of a great winery in Sonoma, purchased another 12 acres, which he planned to rig with his own system of irrigation before he planted it with new vines.[46] By January 1921, the *Grower* was asking "Have Prohibition Laws made Growers Prosperous?"

If some growers could answer with a resounding yes, the trade journal opined, one cause was now obvious: the fact that 700 wineries in California had been supplanted by millions of in-home manufacturers of wine.[47]

The phenomenon of a country making millions of gallons of wine in kitchens and cellars seemed not to have registered on the leader of the country's Prohibition Department. When Prohibition commissioner John Kramer reported on the first anniversary of the Dry laws implementation in the *New York Times,* he declared himself hugely satisfied with his department's activities throughout the country in the previous 12 months. It was clear to him now, he said, that the appetites of the steady drinkers in the nation were soon to disappear. Drinking, he explained, was simply a "hang-over" appetite from pre-Prohibition days. And he assured the public that social drinking had since passed into oblivion. He credited his agents across the country with making life difficult for bootleggers, vowed he could absolutely "see changes for the better," and believed that public sentiment against bootleggers would soon compel many of them to "give up."[48]

No one working in the major grape markets of the country was going to change his habits due to those comments, it was clear. And in March 1921, one New York broker, Kenneth Day of the firm Sgobel & Day, said in the *California Grape Grower* that he was off on a one-month's tour of the vineyards in California to book purchases for even more grapes that year than his company had bought the year before.

Day also described a typical day's grape-buying activities at the big-city markets that supplied home winemakers. When grapes were in season, he said, 75 to 100 carloads of grapes were sold each morning to buyers who flocked to the great

Erie Docks. The fruit was not sold from the cars, but buyers could inspect it at three large auction houses, Connolly Auction Co., Fruit Auction Co., and Brown & Seccomb.

The sales started at about nine in the morning, and if they did not get off to a bright start, auctioneers tried to move the goods fast and close the auction before prices dropped too far. But if there was a lot of interest on the part of the buyers, auctioneers drew out the morning so as to build up prices as much as they could.

Day stated that the jobbers on the East Side handled a great percentage of the fruit, although buyers came not only from New York City but from Brooklyn and from cities up the Hudson, and from New Jersey too. "You must remember that some 10,000,000 people live within a radius of 50 miles of New York," he explained.

Most of the wine grapes were sold to Italians and to people in "the Ghetto, no matter how many grapes have been bought by the jobbers." According to Day, the record number of railcars of grapes handled in a single day in New York was 150.

The most coveted wine grapes in the New York area continued to be the Alicante Bouschets, related Day. "The Italians are simply crazy for them and the brand most in demand is the Native Son brand, which the Italians have dubbed the 'Baby' brand because the label features a tiny native son." Oftentimes, Day recollected, he had seen boxes marked with the word "baby" written in the red fruit juice from the Alicante grape itself, and Day declared that he believed buyers would have paid from 50 cents to $1 more for a box of those color grapes over any other sort.[49]

Not all the news was as heartening: There had been damaging frosts again in the spring of 1921. But by June, the vines were recovering somewhat, and a reporter for the *Grower* wrote that a "stranger traveling in a machine from Napa [City] to Calistoga, would hardly realize that only a short time ago the vineyards, now covered with verdure, were black and looked as if a raging fire had swept over the land."

And in a nod to the felicitous landscape now before him, the reporter continued:

Even this year, after the disastrous frost, a motor trip through this pretty valley along the new cement highway will be found a treat, for just now the trees and flowers are beautiful indeed. Here and there your attention is attracted by the wild grape vines that festoon the trees along the roadway. The fuzzy blossoms appear a bit later on these vines than those that are cultivated, and have a sweet odor all their own. In fact, as you drive along, the drowsy morning air is heavy with the perfume of new-mown hay, multi-colored sweet peas that clamber over fences, thickets of wild roses, immense bouquets of buckeye blossoms, and catalpa trees thick with lavender blooms that are very fragrant.[50]

It appeared the killing frost would not dampen tourists' enjoyment of the valleys that summer. And it also appeared that the shortage of grapes might yet be an advantage. By September 1, 1921, the *California Grape Grower* was reporting that though the Alicante Bouschet crop was short that year, since frosts affected this varietal more than others, "and the bunches were loose and straggly, yet . . . buyers by the hundreds are wiring for Alicantes," hoping not to be cut out of the market.

Napa and Sonoma were so excited about the possibilities of the wine-grape market: Sonoma had planted 200 new acres to vines, Napa had planted 250.[51]

At San Francisco's public grape market, held on the tracks at Drumm Street near the downtown Ferry Building, railcars full of grapes sat with their doors wide open with salesmen inviting customers to climb up and try the fruit. The first of the grapes had arrived at the end of August from Asti in Sonoma County and from Modesto in the Central Valley. Even though they were in excellent condition, at first sales were sluggish; the buyers thought that prices might get lower once more grapes arrived. Instead, prices continued to rise.

Depending on the distance, trucks would take consumers' purchases to their homes from the market for $2.50 to $5 a ton.

All the salesmen at Drumm Street had different styles. Reported the *Grower* with yet another dash of broad-brush stereotyping directed at Italians: Most of the men doing the selling were well-known Italians who had a regular following of customers, and while some had the reputation of being absolutely square, others were looked on as "slippery eels": All "are hustlers and while you cannot believe what they say about the quality or the place from which the grapes were shipped, you have to give them credit for getting rid of a large quantity each season."[52]

But despite the high prices and the welcome revenue they were getting from their wine grapes, grape growers were becoming anxious about some nasty cracks in the wine-juice market that they were beginning to see.

Some growers had shipped grapes that had spoiled during the long waits for trains and days spent embargoed outside eastern unloading depots. They had shipped off thousands of tons of perfect fruit only to hear back from the shippers that the fruit was not acceptable at its destination, that it had been destroyed, and that there would be no payments coming for it.

The hardworking Domenichelli family of Geyserville had been one such victim.

Felicina and Remigio Domenichelli were toughing it out day by day. They had been blessed, and they knew it: They had seven sons, the greatest fortune any farm parents could ever have. Three had been born in Italy and the rest in Sonoma County, not far from Geyserville. The Domenichelli family story of life during Prohibition was related to Louise Davis in 1989 in a Sonoma Wine Library oral history by George Domenichelli and Alice Senteney Stockham Domenichelli.

Every member of the Domenichelli family of nine was used to hard work. When Remigio first came to the United States from Italy, he earned 97 cents a day at the Italian Swiss Colony at Asti. Work was tough, vigorous, physical. If he did not work for some reason for a day, he was charged 15 cents room and board. It was better to work.

Said his son George later: "There was no watch [time clock], it was from daylight to dark." They worked from one end of the vast vineyard to another. "At noon, they'd bring a big pot of soup down, they'd eat." And at night they would walk back to their quarters, exhausted, over acres of land.

Life was not any easier for Remigio's wife, Felicina, waiting back in Italy. She faced daunting working conditions herself. While she waited for Remigio to save enough money so that she and the three boys could take the boat to New York and then the train to San Francisco, she labored on the land in Tuscany, and not with oxen—that was for the lucky ones. The land she worked was hilly, and only hand tools were possible—she had a wooden shovel. After a day out on the hills, she would work on through the night to haul sand up from a creek to sell to masons. Her strength impressed even her tough, hardworking sons. One of them, George, later said: "She worked as hard as any man. Up till she was 85, she'd carry all the brush out of all of our ranches, and we had a lot of them, and burn it. Now you couldn't get ten men to do it, but she used to do it all by herself."

If Felicina was ever asked if she would like to return to Italy, she would swear, "No way, I've had enough of hard times," as if life in California on a ranch in the 1920s was Easy Street itself.

In 1908, after 10 years of sweat and toil, Remigio had saved enough to buy a 52-acre ranch for $5,500 that included not only the perfect fertile growing land of Alexander Valley but a winery, a barn, and a charming house with gingerbread trim and stained glass windows and doors.

Remigio grew grapes and prunes at first, later adding a pear orchard.

By 1918, the family was prospering even more. He and his wife and the boys had continued to sweat blood in the fields, and the family was able to make a down payment of $17,000 on a $50,000 purchase of an additional 580 acres; 130 acres were cultivated in prunes and grapes, the rest were hills.

That land was sold to them by a local lawyer, a man George Domenichelli despised, believing he had sold his land to the family in the hopes that they would default on their mortgage. "That's what he did—he bought up mortgages of people that could not pay, so he took them over." Then he would keep the down payment, said Domenichelli, all the while pocketing the mortgage payments, and own the land, as well, when it reverted back to him at foreclosure.

The Domenichelli family had once heard gossip that the lawyer had publicly boasted that even though Remigio had seven hardworking sons, he would find it impossible to pay back what he owed. And before long, they would have to give the land back. The family was doing everything they could to make that a hollow boast.

Remigio had set up a winery in the barn on the larger piece of property and produced a blended wine that consisted mostly of Zinfandel. And he made what seemed like a fortuitous deal with a "fella from New York" who wanted them to make wine for which he offered to pay $1.25 a gallon.

Said George: "We had just under 50,000 gallons of wine. The fella come and said, 'I'll take it.' And then Prohibition come and there it was, we couldn't sell it. So we lost everything then of that year's crop."

Early during Prohibition, the family had decided to sell their wine-juice grapes to the big eastern markets. "This fella who was with Pacific Fruit Exchange, he said the timing was great:" He said to the Domenichellis: "Those are the first grapes to leave . . . you'll make big money." And so the family picked the grapes, boxed and lidded them, and shipped them east.

The result was heartbreaking. Said George: "Out of 12-ton, we got a 17-cent check."[53]

Some grape growers who had cut deals with shippers had not read or completely understood the fine print of their contracts carefully. Some could not read English, and all were stunned to receive railcar bills for ruined fruit—their contracts insisted that if the fruit was found to be in substandard condition at destination, the originator of the fruit was liable for transportation. If many railcars arrived at a large market at one time, there were embargoes on new arrivals being unloaded: They could be shunted onto a siding to wait their turn. Grapes left sitting in a railcar for a few days in blistering end-of-summer or early-fall heat could rot completely by the time their turn came to be unloaded. One invoice for a situation like that, and a small grape grower could be out of business permanently. Other growers became disgusted with a process they had little control over and pulled out before they too lost shipments.

Railroad officials had not warned the grape industry that there could be problems getting the fruit to market in a timely manner. Poor traffic management had made for both embargoes and for a lack of railcars. The grape growers' were frustrated. Would the beautiful grapes, packed so carefully at the vineyard so that grapes would not split and bleed red grape juice out all over the pristine packaging, get to market while they were still in prime condition and could garner premium prices?

There were also other costs that grape growers had not considered: Successful harvests started to push up wages for field workers. Grape growers had to get the grapes out of the vineyards, packed into lugs (boxes), and then into railcars in a hurry once picking started. If one or two shipments went awry, profits vanished fast.

The demand for wine grapes throughout 1922 was extraordinary, though the year's harvest fared no better when it came time to transport it. There were railroad strikes; a coal strike (deadly in those day of steam engines); labor troubles; another shortage of refrigerator cars; days of embargoes of perishable crops; slow delivery of wooden box components to the growers themselves; and on top of all that, increased competition by eastern states, which also grew grapes and were trying to cash in on the bonanza.[54]

Chapter Six

If We Hadn't Bootlegged, We Wouldn't Have Survived

Although there is no formal date for the first bootlegging in Sonoma and Napa, by the time Prohibition was a few months old, it was most likely a new and very promising business that was well and truly thriving in Wine Country. From the beginning of Prohibition in 1920, the Prohibition Department was not quick to fully comprehend the incredible bonanza to grape growers that was the new wine-grape market and the threat it posed to Dry plans for the country, but it had definitely become rapidly aware of the import of another of the wine counties' entrepreneurial enterprises. Padlocked in the cellars of numerous wineries were hundreds and hundreds of thousands of gallons of wine made prior to Prohibition. And, of course, as Prohibition got going, winemakers wondered what they could do with it besides watching it, with their hearts breaking, turn sour. Some small part of it, the highest quality of those wines, would last for 10 to 30 years and could be considered a long-term investment if the winery had enough money to keep paying for the federal permits required each year to maintain it in storage. But much of the other wine made then was not suitable for long-term cellaring. It could last three to eight years; after that it would turn sour and would be worthless. And for those who had no other income to pay for wine permits, the problem was immediate.

It was the future of their cellars of wine that the winemakers contemplated long and hard.

For many of them, selling the wine while they could appeared to be the only sensible answer.

And so they did.

Virtually en masse, they turned to bootlegging. Some winemakers did hold out from this illegal business, but very few. Bootlegging became an overnight success story in the Wine counties. And it drove the Prohibition authorities into a ceaseless state of war with them. This explains why, not long after Prohibition began, along the roads mostly at night, heavily laden trucks or cars weighed almost to the pavement, would set off down the two main highways of Sonoma and Napa to San Francisco and other points south. A great deal of wine began to be moved secretly—illicitly—from wineries to bootlegging wholesalers, bars, hotels, speakeasies. In the battle to sell off their family's major financial asset before it was ruined, the two wine counties were blessed by geography. Both were situated near a big city with a well-deserved reputation for alcohol-fueled festivity. And the fact that San Francisco was full of immigrants from countries where wine was an integral part of a normal day's nourishment created a demand that continued unabated no matter what nasty edicts blasted out from the nation's distant capital. Napa and Sonoma had a lot of wine to sell, and San Francisco wanted to buy a lot of it.

It was a truly satisfying symbiosis.

Bootlegging soon became big business for some of the counties' winemakers. "A lot of people here made a lot of money during Prohibition," Sonoma County winery owner Lou Foppiano recalled in his ninety-seventh year. "There was no tax to pay on the money they got, and customers paid good money for wine and grappa."[1]

But bootlegging was risky, and most families, however worthy they thought the activity, bootlegged in terror, many driven by necessity. "If we hadn't bootlegged, we wouldn't have survived," said the Dry Creek grapegrower and winemaker Gene Cuneo, just before his death in 2007 at the age of 94. "We had to pay taxes on our land. If we hadn't bootlegged, we'd have lost our land."[2]

Making the decision to bootleg must have been very difficult for many of these winemakers in Napa and Sonoma, especially those who were relatively recent immigrants who had arrived in the United States with nothing and were still establishing themselves in the one way they knew how: by making wine. They were all aware of the tremendous advantages that life in the United States offered. They knew the value of living in this still-young country; land and the resources needed to create new vineyards and wineries were amazingly accessible, especially compared to their countries of origin, where real estate was so often reserved for the wealthy, influential, or aristocratic. As new residents proud of their hard-earned assets and their small bustling businesses, they were people who, given a fair and honorable chance, wanted dearly to obey the laws of their adoptive home. To choose to be a bootlegger was, for them, a cruel blow to their self-respect and a huge risk: of being arrested or paying an onerous fine, having their wine-making facilities knocked apart by the axes of federal agents, trucks confiscated, children and wives terrified. Many new immigrants who had not yet acquired their naturalization papers must have worried that their futures in this great country of opportunity would be in jeopardy. What helped them make the decision to bootleg, recounted longtime Sonoma county grape buyer Bob Meyer, who had lived through Prohibition, was that "No one in Napa or Sonoma looked at bootlegging as anything very bad."[3] Wine had been sold for decades in the wine counties. Only months earlier it been a dignified business; doing it well had brought winemakers respect and stature in Napa and Sonoma. Could one stroke of a pen in Washington change that? Bootlegging seemed merely to be a reasonable variation on the same business of selling wine. The work was the same; it was just more covert. Northern California voters had never given a plurality to Prohibition. The laws were made by people far away who did not offer a cent in compensation for the loss of income suffered. So as they had done in the past, winemakers and winery owners sold wine. Wine, after all, was an honest natural product of the earth and the sun and their talents and, most important, the result of a decent and honest day's work. No wonder, many winemakers of Napa and Sonoma felt they had a moral prerogative—to sell their wines to customers in San Francisco or wherever else they could find them.

Some of the wine was extracted from their padlocked wineries by skullduggery. Many of them constantly made wine throughout Prohibition and kept it in barns, in big tanks dug under ranch outbuildings, in tunnels hollowed out of hills. Gene Cuneo's father, John, had excavated under a garage to make the space to keep his secret tanks of brandy and wine. Winemakers would remove some of the older wine from their cellars and replace it with new wine made illegally. That way when government agents came to check out whether any wine was missing from the padlocked cellars, all looked well.[4] Some removed a great deal of wine from their secret stashes and replaced it with water, though this was very risky as federal agents did, from time to time, test that it was wine not water in tanks and barrels. There was a trick, perhaps apocryphal, that some winemakers used if they had removed the wine from a barrel and filled it with water: hanging a small container of wine below the spigot of a barrel, so that when the barrel was opened and the tiny amount of wine for the test was removed it came out of the smaller container. But this was a nerve-wracking experience not often worth the stress involved. It was easier to hide wine under the barn.

Getting the goods to market was the trickiest part of the bootlegging process. If a winemaker could not sell it to a dealer who would send a truck to the winery during the dead of night, he would have to get it down to the city himself. To be out on the highway with a truck packed with illegal wine or brandy took bravado, but wine families did it often. And it wasn't only federal agents they feared. It was said that some families had their goods highjacked by thieves lying in wait around dark corners of the roads to San Francisco late at night, but there are, not surprisingly, no official police reports of complaints by wine families about tragedies like that. If the wine was taken from them, they kept their mouths shut, sucked up the losses, and tried a delivery run another night.

On a good night with no interceptions from legal or illegal forces and after the wine was transported down the highway south to the city, it had to be taken across the San Francisco Bay. In the 1920s and early 1930s, that still meant crossing the bay by car ferry. Ferries were, for a long time, the lifelines of the wine business. The iconic Golden Gate Bridge opened as the first road connection to San Francisco's northern hinterlands in 1937. Until then, freight and passengers from Napa and Sonoma reached the city by boat. Lou Colombano, still fit, jolly, gregarious, and socially active at age 93 in 2008, grew up on a grape ranch in Geyserville; later he ran a bar in downtown San Francisco that served the nearby predawn vegetable and fish markets and the city's federal customs house. He recalled that so much wine arrived in San Francisco by ferry during Prohibition that the boats' fire security officers got rich.

"Cars back in those days had lots of fires and there were guys who walked around the cars on the ferries watching for smoke or flames," he said. "They knew what was going on and they made sure they got paid for keeping their mouths shut."[5] Bob Meyer, who attended elementary school with Colombano in Geyserville, confirmed his good friend's story with one of his own. His uncle had been a ferryboat engineer. "One night he took me up on deck to show me two or three cars," Meyer recalled. "He said they were bootleggers' cars full of five-gallon containers of high-proof grappa."[6]

A regular flotilla of cars and trucks left the wine counties each night, and the ferries were constantly filled. County roads were rough. It took nearly a day to make the return trip from San Francisco to Geyserville—a four-hour journey today—and cars and their tires were not as durable as they are now. "You'd see cars with two, three spares tied on the back coming up from San Francisco," Colombano said. "It was a rare trip when you could get all the way home from the city without changing a tire at least once."[7]

Gene Cuneo's parents used the ferry whenever they wanted to take the illegal brandy that they had distilled from their own wine to San Francisco to sell. They liked to take 8 to 12 gallons of brandy to the city at a time, sell it, and then buy some staples for their family; often a 100-pound sack of flour for $6, or 6 gallons of Spanish olive oil for $6. "They would come home with the car loaded. We always had more than enough to eat," recollected Gene.

It took hours to drive from the Cuneo farm on Dry Creek Road along the two-lane road that wound through Santa Rosa, Petaluma, and San Rafael to the ferry at Sausalito. Cuneo's father always polished and cleaned the family Dodge for the long brandy run. Then his mother and father would dress in their best clothes, hide the brandy under a picnic basket in the backseat, and head south. They always tried to catch the 3 P.M. ferry, making it appear that they were heading to the opera or a night out in the city.

"My mother would drive and my father sat there looking henpecked," said Cuneo, who remembers that seemingly no one ever suspected the real purpose of the trip. At least, they were never stopped. They would transact the necessary business with the brandy and then would stay in San Francisco for a day or two, visiting relatives and buying groceries.[8]

Nearly everyone who had wine bootlegged, even if it was just a little. And sometimes it was a great deal.

The Colombano family's experience with bootlegging was one that was played out many times. At first it was a small enterprise; later it grew in size until the family feared for their lives and their freedom, explained Lou Colombano who was born in 1915, five years before Prohibition became law.

"My parents, Eligio and Angela, were married in 1913," said Colombano. "They had come here together from Piedmont in Italy. Eligio had been in the United States on an earlier trip and then he'd returned to Italy to marry. His brother Camillo had arrived in San Francisco after the big earthquake"—the 1906 quake and fire that leveled much of that great city. At first, Eligio worked for a marble company, where there was so much opportunity thanks to the work of rebuilding a city with pretensions to even greater grandeur than it had known before the catastrophe. At the same time, Camillo ran a wine and brandy emporium in North Beach. A photo of Camillo taken at that time shows a strikingly handsome young man perched on an immaculately kept wagon, freshly painted with lavish decorative script. The photo shows the wagon full of five-gallon wine demijohns and drawn by two dark horses—one of them named Blackie—standing poised to deliver wine. The demijohns are wrapped in raffia in the style in which Chianti bottles once were.

But a business founded in such promise in the years after the earthquake did not have long to prosper before Prohibition stopped it in its tracks. "When the country went dry," Colombano explained in 2008, "my uncle said, 'I'm out of business. I can't make a living.'

"My father had been a farmer in Italy. He understood grapes. And he knew how to make wine. So my uncle suggested to my father that they should go north and find some land—hopefully somewhere near Asti, which was where the biggest winery was then," said Colombano. The brothers believed the owners of the Italian Swiss Colony operation would have bought fine land and that they would do well to be close to it.

The two Colombano brothers did find a suitable ranch near Asti, about 80 miles north of San Francisco, and promptly planted a vineyard of about 30 acres. Before long, Eligio was making good red wine and Camillo was trucking it down to San Francisco in the middle of the night. And the two black delivery horses that used to trot through the hilly city streets of San Francisco had been trucked to the ranch and were now pulling plows.

"Camillo drove a green Chandler touring car," remembered Colombano. "The car was full of tanks made to carry wine and brandy—but the tanks had been constructed, then upholstered to look exactly like the bottoms and backs of seats.

"Dad and my uncle made a pretty good living. Yes, they were doing pretty well. My father said his share of the business was $55 a month."

Like most farm families, Colombano said, "we also had cows, pigs, chickens, vegetable gardens. We made our own cheese and butter and once a week, made bread in the outdoor oven. But we didn't yet have electricity on the farm."

The business was such a success that the car's secret holding tanks were soon inadequate for the demand, so the brothers "bought a truck to carry their wine and grappa and they'd set off from the winery with the barrels covered with oat sacks," Colombano said.

Their first run-in with trouble both surprised and infuriated them. Said Colombano, "Two guys came in the middle of the night to the ranch and told us they were Prohibition officers and that our truck was confiscated." One of the supposed government agents drove off with the truck full of wine and grappa; the other hung around the Colombano home all day before he finally left. The men were never seen again—and had nothing to do with the government. "Eventually the truck was found abandoned in San Rafael, a few miles from the Sausalito-San Francisco ferry with nothing on it," Colombano said.

The armed men had been hijackers, not Prohibition agents.

Given the night work and the worry of an official raid at any time, Colombano's parents eventually grew tired of bootlegging and closed their business. Camillo bought a ranch at Morgan Hill, about 200 miles south of Geyserville, where he established a vineyard of Carignane. Eligio resettled a few miles away in Geyserville, establishing a new farm and raising grapes and prunes. Everyone contributed to the family's well being.

"I even had a little milk route. We had extra milk from our cows. When I got back from school every evening I used to get on my bike and deliver to six or seven customers. I used to sell it for 10 cents a quart."

But the lure of the wine business, so much a part of the Colombano family's heritage, was too powerful to ignore. Eligio Colombano decided again to make and sell wine illegally, and soon he decided to add to his inventory. He was going to make grappa as well. Eligio bought a still and took advantage of his new property's fortunate geography to defy the government. "In winter, the river used to come up around the farm," Lou recalled of his teenage years. "We couldn't get to school and nobody could get to our ranch." It was a perfect situation for a bootlegger.

"My dad would work the still all day and I would work it at night." His father's wine and grappa "sold locally or to folk who would come up in the good months of year from San Francisco to buy a gallon of grappa for $1.50, or to get a gallon or two of wine. If you bought your own jug, wine was 25 cents a gallon."

Business flourished yet again.

Soon "my dad bought us a truck, too. It cost $75. It was a Ford Model T. You bought just a chassis, the frame, and the wheels in those days. There was no platform. There were no closed-in cabs in those days. You'd buy the basic car. Find something for a platform. Then you'd get a seat from another old car and bolt it down. And if you could find a windscreen somehow you felt very lucky."

Even though Eligio's still was contributing healthy sums to the family coffers, one day he got a bigger and better offer that made the idea of running his own small still pale in comparison.

Eligio's brother Camillo had a friend named Palosi, "a big-time bootlegger, big-time. And he came to see my dad at the ranch." Palosi had heard the Colombanos lived on a dead-end road with no through traffic. "So he came to my dad with a deal. He said, 'If you let me put a still in your big barn, I'll give you $50 a day for every day we run it.'

"My mother was terrified. She thought we'd be found out by Prohibition agents and lose everything we had. But we'd had a terrible frost that spring, which took all our grapes. Everything got burnt by the frost—there was just no crop that year. My father had said he would not be able to pay his property tax. So when Palosi made the offer, well, my father felt he had to accept for the good of his family."

Palosi required a large barn well out of the way of prying eyes. He had recently acquired—he did not explain how—a huge supply of port, which was sitting padlocked in a winery about a mile from the Colombano farm; he needed not only a still to convert the port into grappa but a place to store it; then, when the times were right, he would get it moved down to San Francisco.

"Well, we knew where the winery was that he was talking about," said Colombano. It was the winery of a family they knew in Geyserville, located near the Hoffman House. (The Hoffman House, built in 1903, was a substantial home back then; the well-preserved building has been transformed into a popular restaurant that now serves breakfast and lunch to wine tourists and the winemaking community around it.)

Money was no object to Palosi, it appeared. The project required running a two-inch galvanized tin pipeline underground from the winery to the large new still under construction in the Colombano barn, a distance of over a mile.

"He had men dig all night and they even dug right under the railway track, which had a fair amount of traffic on it. My mother would feed the hordes of workers it took to do this, and they slept at our house on cots."

Then came a serious, possibly deal-ending glitch in the plan.

"Palosi found out that we didn't have electricity to the farm yet. And he needed it desperately for the turbines that were going to cook the port." The solution took time to engineer, because the Colombano farm's geography—so convenient for hiding a still—also placed it some distance from the nearest power lines. Once again Palosi revealed considerable business acumen. He spliced into the nearest power line of the electric company that serviced Geyserville, running power all the way to the still via a line burrowed into the ground next to the already constructed galvanized wine pipeline.

That electric company and its shareholders was unknowingly but effectively subsidizing one of the largest stills in the county.

Palosi's still was huge: At a time when many stills were about the size of a baby's bath and held five gallons of liquid, this one stretched 10 or 12 feet in diameter—about the volume of a medium-size room.

Now that the pipeline was dug and camouflaged and the power was in, it was time to start up the still.

The Colombanos were by turns stunned then terrified at the noise.

"It made a terrible roar," remembers Colombano. "Terrible."

"You could hear it everywhere, we thought. We had one neighbor to the side of us, who must have heard it but never said a thing."

"My mother was hardly sleeping by then, she was so scared."

But the gambit had worked. Grappa poured out of the still in an endless stream day and night. Palosi's crew could fill a five-gallon can, kept camouflaged by hay in the barn, in just a few minutes.

"There were three shifts each day and four people were needed on each shift. Twelve people in all, each day, were working on it, and my mother struggled so hard feeding them, but they did purchase all the food for her to cook."

The liquor was taken away to San Francisco at night. Some was transported down to the city in a big car driven by a hefty woman from Hawaii who would stop and eat a meal prepared by Angela before she set off on her journey through the night. "This woman used to eat her dinner, have a glass of wine with it, maybe even a grappa and then light up a cigar," recollected Colombano. "We couldn't believe our eyes. Back then, we'd never seen anyone smoke in our house ever. My mother was dumbstruck."

Colombano's dad was making his $50 a day for the use of the barn, and the still had been operating 24 hours a day for 10 days, when Palosi suddenly announced that operations would cease immediately.

"I'm going to send a crew in," he said. "We have to get this thing out of here in 24 hours."

Palosi had received a tip from one of his paid informants that the barn was to be raided. They had only a day to erase all traces of the giant still. It seemed impossible. First, the vast copper pot, with its chimney and all the cooking and evaporating paraphernalia, had to be completely taken apart, piece by piece; and then there were the cans, some empty, many filled and hidden under straw. The staff, their cots—everything had to vanish by the next day.

"But, by God, they did it," said Colombano. "They worked and worked and in 24 hours every single thing was gone from the barn. The only things left from the operation were the pipeline and the electrical connections. But the Prohibition agents missed those completely when they visited."

Eligio and Angela decided that their family ranch would not be involved in bootlegging again.[9]

Like other bootleggers, they had heard tell of the mighty force of the Bureau of Internal Revenue's Prohibition Unit (it would be renamed the Bureau of Prohibition in 1927) had arrayed against them. Breaking Prohibition law was hazardous.

Far away from the precarious life of the Colombanos and their neighbors across the wine counties of Napa and Sonoma was an army of employees of the Prohibition Unit. Thousands stood at the ready to do battle against those small-holding grape growers and winery owners. There were commissioners, agents, assistant chiefs, shipment posting clerks, senior typists, stenographer-typists, clerk-typists, administrators, deputy administrators, telephone operators, legal advisors, attorneys (plus associate and assistant attorneys), assessment clerks, chemists (plus assistant and junior chemists), law clerks, file clerks, permit clerks, disbursing clerks, audit and payroll clerks, stock clerks, suboffice agents, telephone operators, machine operators, investigators in charge, auto mechanics, chauffeurs, field supervisors, secretaries, withdrawal chiefs, and chiefs of all sorts: of bonded accounts, returns, withdrawals, enforcement, padlock departments, automobile and freight departments, case reports, mail, and files, and even chiefs of major conspiracies—and on and on.

The nation had been divided into 27 Prohibition districts, each consisting of one or more U.S. judicial districts. New York and Pennsylvania had two district offices, as did California, with one in Los Angeles and the other close to the wine counties, in San Francisco.

The staff of the Twenty-first District Headquarters in San Francisco, responsible for both Napa and Sonoma counties, consisted of another entire militia of new employees: an administrator with his own secretary; a chief clerk with another secretary; a disbursing clerk aided by a payroll and audit clerk, a voucher clerk, and a travel audit clerk; a chief of mail and files, with two clerks; an information clerk with a staff consisting of a supply clerk, a telephone operator, and messenger; a legal advisor aided by an associate attorney, assistant attorney, assessment clerk, abatement clerk, reporting stenographer-clerk, and a secretary; a chemist in charge of a field laboratory who had an assistant chemist and stenographer on his staff; a chief of withdrawals whose department included a prescription book clerk, specially denatured alcohol and tax-free withdrawal clerk, a signing and registration clerk, and a senior typist; and 12 inspectors, and 21 storekeeper-gaugers. At the San Francisco suboffice, 40 agents worked under an agent in charge.

A branch office in Sacramento also took its orders from San Francisco; it consisted of one agent in charge, six agents, and a clerk. The lowest salary in San Francisco was $1,200 per year for a clerk while the highest-paid employee was the administrator at $5,600. Agents received from $1,800 to $2,300. In Washington, the national commissioner of Prohibition made $9,000.[10] By comparison, the mayor of New York would earn $15,000 in 1920[11] and a railway policeman or watchman would have made about $1,150 a year in 1918.[12]

Employment tests for some of these positions had been held in 16 cities across California on January 7, 1920. Given that Prohibition was going to start 10 days later, the competition seemed late—a lack of timeliness that eventually would seem to be just the tip of an iceberg of disorganization that revealed itself more and more as the years of Prohibition went by.[13]

The agents were the public face of Prohibition enforcement assigned to search for miscreants. What exactly did an agent do in a typical workday?

Official reports took up the first part of the day, usually followed by court attendance to help prosecute those who had been charged the day before—the process could work this quickly; then it was out into the field, which could last till evening or through the night. Without civil service protection, agents' workdays were as flexible as their employer, Uncle Sam, required. A few years later, when the battle against bootlegging and other liquor crimes looked like it was being lost, there was a discussion at Washington headquarters to decide whether agents should work on Sundays. Nothing formal came of that. A typical daily report of federal Prohibition agents and inspectors, filed in the San Francisco office on September 13, 1922, reveals a fairly busy day of operations in Sonoma County:

9 A.M.
Office, reports, etc.

10 A.M.
U.S. Com Court on cases of: Tollini, Bruce, Ferrero, Brocio, Ligi, & Biagiotti

1.30 P.M.
Hired Auto and left for Boyes Springs with Agents Krumhansl, Bernhard, Curtis, Bennett, Myers and self. And made following arrests:

- George Darling, Darling's Resort, Boyes Spring
- Gene Cazes, Mason Dorce, Fetter Spring
- James Moore, Shamrock Inn, Fetter Spring
- Ed Peters, Cabonettes Resort, Boyes Springs

Searched several other places but found nothing.

Finished 9.30 P.M.
Expenses: Ferry for Auto and self S.F. to Sausilito [sic] and return $2.30[14]

Although some of the immense Prohibition staff were industrious, honest individuals, it became clear very soon that not enough of the ranks had these sterling qualities. From the very earliest days of the Prohibition bureaucracy, agents and officers regularly were arrested across the country for embezzlement, extortion, intoxication, disorderly conduct and assault, trespassing, theft from hotels, and behaving in an unnecessarily destructive manner during raids. Agents were accused of roughing up customers and bootleggers; their bosses were charged with stealing seized alcohol and even giving away books of official prescription forms for "medicinal" alcohol as Christmas gifts. Theoretically, medicinal alcohol was available in small but regular amounts from a drug store by prescription from a doctor, but drug stores in some towns across the country were considered good places to find a drink with or without official permission.

That the criminality on the inside of the Prohibition Unit often matched that on the outside was evidenced by a shocking event that became first the subject of a grand jury indictment, then a case before a district court judge in Sacramento. It stunned friends and relatives of a Wine Country family and became a cautionary tale to every other immigrant winemaker in Sonoma and Napa.

The event happened among some of Sonoma's most ravishing hills and gullies.

When travelers on their way north from San Francisco rode over the final crest of land into Alexander Valley, they may well have gasped with delight at the sight before them. Ahead, as if dropping out from under their feet, lay a spectacular valley as rich and fecund for grape growing as could be found anywhere.

Stretched out before them was a vast, deep bowl surrounded by high hills. In the far distance the hills would have been dusky blue; the nearer ones glowed emerald green all winter, then turned to a bleached-out soft gold when spring warmed up and the soil dried. In the early months of the year, the valley was aglow with fruit tree blossoms flowering on every farm, blue and purple spikes of larkspur and lupines decorated the roads and byways, and everywhere was the delicate dance of bobbing white milkmaid blossom. Soon the color would be intensified by wild grasses and drying wild herbs, their spectacular golden hues a perfect contrast to the azure blue skies that the valley's grape growers could count on through so many summer days. Then as the vines leafed out, the valley would have been gently transformed into an ocean of glossy green from one end to the other.

Today this is the home of many microclimates that allow a spectrum of varietals to flourish, but the valley's greatest wine is Cabernet Sauvignon, though it is renowned too for its Zinfandels, Chardonnays, and Sauvignon Blancs. The valley's two sleepy municipalities, Cloverdale and Geyserville, have been important even from the early days of settlement with their agricultural services, hotels, and gas stations.

At night, as the sun goes down behind the coastal hills, peace settles on the valley. This is a landscape in which people work all year at tough physical chores both indoors and out. Unless it is grape harvest time, the workers pack up their pruning shears, put aside their hoes and plows and lock their winery doors well before evening comes, and a great quiet comes over this land. On many nights in summer, the fog slides in before the moon comes out, but by September, the fog has receded back from the hills well out over the Pacific, and Alexander Valley skies are clear and the stars are bright and sparkling in the pure air.

It was on such a September night in 1922 that three agents, George H. Crawford, Henry W. Meyer, and Waldo E. Curtis, headed out from the San Francisco office of the Prohibition Unit with trouble on their minds. That trouble would reverberate for years. It would bring those agents and the Seghesio family to court, faced off against one another both with their differing recollections of a horrifying incident, documented in files of the U.S. court.

Nearly three decades earlier, Edoardo and Angela Seghesio, a young couple who had been married only two years, purchased their first vineyard and planted Zinfandel on a ranch backing onto the pretty hills between Geyserville and Cloverdale.

Long before the agents arrived at the Seghesio home, Angela was not only a hard-working mother and housewife; she had established herself among her family as an astute businesswoman. The Seghesio household was a vineyard away from the country railroad station named for Italy's Chianti region. From her front window, Angela could see the train that carried passengers back and forth across the Wine Country to the ferry for San Francisco. Family legend has it that before Prohibition whenever the big steam train stopped at Chianti and Angela could see across the fields that a man in a suit had disembarked, she knew he was a wine dealer from San Francisco. She would call to her farmhand to kill and clean a chicken and she would get out the wine. And by the time the buyer had walked through the vineyards to the house, Angela had a good meal bubbling on the stove and a jug of wine readied to make business run as smoothly as possible and to show the dealer how fine the wine was.

Prohibition had not stopped the trains, but from January 1920 on, whenever men in suits appeared in Sonoma County, they were more likely to be feared—or merely tolerated—than welcomed with a hot dinner. Angela and Edoardo had believed to the last that Prohibition would never pass in a nation so wedded to new business endeavors; they optimistically had invested in another vineyard only months before Prohibition began.[15]

If the couple had been one of the last to see the nightmare coming, however, they were among the first of the wine families to experience its full fury.

It was about 3 A.M. on a warm September night when a loud knock at the farmhouse door interrupted the wonderful life they had known for decades. The Prohibition agents had arrived, and their guns were pointed squarely at Edoardo Seghesio. Angela soon came running

Crawford dictated an official report to a stenographer two weeks later under the questioning of Alfred Oftedal, Special Agent in Charge, Bureau of Internal Revenue, who would have been a boss to Crawford. Crawford told his version of events, with its dark allegations, of that remote country night:

Some time ago I received information that quantities of wine were being transported nightly from the vicinity of Santa Rosa, and Healdsburg, and Geyserville, and especially the Asti wine company. We agents figured that if we could devise some ways and means whereby we could get a truckload of wine coming directly from the Asti Winery Company we could pull over one of the largest transactions since prohibition went into effect.

Accordingly, "we went and stationed ourselves some distance above Geyserville."

The roads would have been completely silent and devoid of traffic most of the night, and Crawford said he had "quite a little snooze" before he was awakened by one of the other agents (Henry Meyer or Waldo Curtis) on the job with him saying "here it comes, here it comes." Then "on the road, about 3, or shortly after, we seen a truck coming down the road. When it passed us we seen that it was loaded with wine, heavily loaded."

The agents took off after the truck, they said, and stopped the driver for questioning. The driver was not talking, but Crawford figured he could trace the truck's journey by its distinctive tire tracks.

Eventually, alleged Crawford, "We found a roadway where this truck had turned into a private house, the tracks showing in the soft dirt." The driver of the truck denied picking up wine at the house, claiming he had only stopped by for a social visit. But the agents checked up on it anyway.

> Arriving there, we found two men on the premises, awake, a light in the house, they were sitting eating some bread—I think it was bread and wine, but I don't know for sure . . . Immediately upon entering this young fellow (from the wine truck) said something to those two men in Italian which I didn't understand. They pretended they did not talk much English, and denied they had ever seen him before, and said that they had not sold him any wine.[16]

Documents later revealed that the two men were Edoardo and his son, Arthur.[17]

Crawford's allegations continued as he explained:

> Immediately a woman came out, whom we afterwards found to be the wife of the man that lived there, and saw that I had handcuffed this boy that had the truck to the old man.

She started to cry and exclaimed, "What is the trouble, what is the trouble?"

Crawford said he questioned the couple about the truck and its contents of wine and demanded reports from the family's winery. The older man said he'd call his son-in-law there to have him bring the reports.[18] The patriarch's relationship with the Swiss Colony winery well-predated this event. It had helped him rise from poverty to being a respected landowner in Sonoma. When he first arrived in the United States, he had labored in its vineyards 10 hours a day, six days a week, until he was able to buy his first 56-acre vineyard some years later,[19] a splendid parcel of land where, on the night of the agents' raid, he was living. A few months before total Prohibition came into effect, Edoardo had bought the Swiss Colony winery for $127,000. Although he made a down payment of $75,000, there was a hefty loan to be paid back[20] just as the wine market underwent a terrific upheaval. Edoardo owned the winery alone for only one year. In 1920, two men who had been involved with the Colony earlier joined with Edoardo and his son-in-law Enrico Prati, to form a four-way partnership under the name Asti Grape Products. Later, Seghesio sold even more of his holdings.[21]

When Enrico Prati arrived at his father-in-law's house with the winery records, Crawford claimed Prati offered the agents a $5,000 bribe to release the truck driver. He would increase the offer to $10,000, Crawford claimed, if the agents would also guarantee safe passage for future bootleg shipments from Asti to San Francisco. Crawford alleged he ran this idea past the other two agents and they agreed, since they were really after the Asti operation, much bigger game than the Seghesios. They would allow Prati to continue assembling the wine convoys, Crawford alleged he masterminded, and spring the trap later. Asti, Crawford told his superiors in the official report, was he believed:

> the biggest wine concern there is, practically, in the United States. That is my understanding. It is a big bunch of people that is worth several millions of dollars. It is composed of the richest Italians in the State. We thought that was the only way they could be caught. . . . If they were caught, it would be the biggest catch that ever has been known. That is what I understood.

Crawford alleged Prati made arrangements with George Warfield, the Healdsburg National Bank's president, to have the $10,000 ready at nine the next morning. Crawford stashed the money in a safety deposit box at the Humboldt Bank, checking on it every few days to make sure it was still there.

But the law was already alerted to Crawford and his fellow agents. That next morning, after Prati had handed the $10,000 to Crawford, he drove down to Santa Rosa where he informed Attorney Wallace Ware about what happened to him and his family. Ware then informed U.S. intelligence officers in San Francisco. Henry Meyer and Waldo Curtis fled, leaving Crawford alone to face his superiors.

When asked which of the agents was in charge of this official expedition to the Seghesios, Crawford responded, "Well, I'll be darned if I know. We hardly have anybody in charge. I don't know if there was anybody in charge." Agents, Crawford continued, had standing instructions to use common sense when intercepting wine shipments; few credible leads came from their superiors, anyway.

Agent Oftedal also asked Crawford—who had suspiciously failed to file an official report of the $10,000 payment—whether it had occurred to him to tell his superiors about accepting a vast sum of money that might place him in "rather a questionable position." "Absolutely," the agent replied; he had simply failed to do so, he explained, while he waited for the deal to develop.

"Did either of these agents suggest to you, or was the suggestion made by anyone that this $10,000 should be divided up?" Oftedal asked.

Not in so many words, Crawford answered, but he did allow that he thought it was Curtis who said, "Jesus Christ, Crawford, that's a lot of money, what's the matter with splitting it up?"

But Crawford said he shot back with "Not by a damn sight, you won't split it up. I am not taking any chances of that kind . . . I am not monkeying with that kind of stuff."[22]

George Crawford had been a government agent for nearly three years at the time of this statement, one of a dozen agents hired in April 1920 and paid $1,800 a year to police the Wine Country.[23] By March 1923, he and his colleagues— who were still missing—were facing a federal grand jury investigation for bribery. The Seghesios, the *Healdsburg Tribune* reported, had been mentioned in connection with the case.[24]

Crawford's story didn't pass muster with the courts. Instead of the Seghesios or Prati offering a bribe to the agents, it was decided that it was the *agents* who had demanded money from the Seghesios, in return for not arresting them and promising not to report any violations of the Volstead Act. Nor were the Seghesios and their associates fabulously wealthy as Crawford had intimated, able to call their banker in the middle of the night to arrange a $10,000 payment first thing in the morning. Instead the Seghesios and Prati had been forced to sign a $10,000 loan— the signed promissory note was introduced as evidence. Apparently, there was no pot of gold to which the hardworking family could resort to in times of emergency.

On June 21, 1924, nearly two years after the cruel incident in the lonely farmhouse, the *Sonoma Index-Tribune* reported on the surprising resolution of the case: "George H. Crawford, former prohibition agent, was found guilty by a federal jury in San Francisco a few days ago, the courts said he had accepted, " a $10,000 bribe from Eduardo Sighesio [*sic*], a Sonoma County vineyardist, for prohibition protection."

Then Crawford's original tale changed on the witness stand.

Now, reported the paper, "the final session of this dramatic trial . . . was marked by Crawford's contention that he accepted the money to tempt the owners of the Sighesio [sic] winery into a huge plot to flood San Francisco with Sonoma county wine."[25]

Crawford was found guilty and sentenced to 18 months in Leavenworth penitentiary. Nothing more was heard from Meyers and Curtis, who were thought to have fled to Mexico. But even though the court laid the blame for the bribe directly on the shoulders of George Crawford, the Seghesios and Prati still faced litigation over the ownership of the $10,000 payment, which Prati still claimed had been extorted and which the government still said had been offered freely.

Not until December 27, 1924, more than two years after the incident, were the winemakers finally exonerated. That day's *Tribune* reported that the $10,000 had been returned to Enrico Prati.[26] Finally, the family had won its good name back. Though further details of this case are not extant, Prati was right: The agents had extorted the money. The shame that had pursued the Seghesios for two years was now wiped away. Instead of being a party to an expensive bribe, the Seghesios had been the victims of a vicious extortion.

Some years after federal agent Crawford had blundered into their lives, the Seghesio family had to deal with the Prohibition Bureau again. This time the final resolution was much sadder. The family had long been storing about 46,000 gallons of once eminently drinkable wine that could be taxed but not sold. By 1929, officials reckoned it had passed its prime while padlocked as the law decreed and was not permitted to be sold. Now, it was no longer fit for "any thing other than distilling material or vinegar stock." Now, many harvests after it had taken Edoardo and Angela Seghesio so much hard work to prepare, it would be destroyed. The law moved slowly and it was not until June 1931, that two Prohibition inspectors from San Francisco showed up at the Cloverdale ranch to supervise the wine's destruction. "This wine was destroyed by allowing it to run upon and be absorbed by the surrounding soil," the inspectors reported to their superiors.[27] If they had stayed around longer, they would have seen that eventually some of those 50,000 gallons made their way through gullies and ditches down to the

Russian River. In 2007, legendary grape grower and winemaker Gene Cuneo still recalled the scene—the Russian River running red for a day, shocking passersby downriver in the little town of Healdsburg and killing fish.[28] The event is still part of the lore of Healdsburg.

Those thousands of dumped gallons was all the wine the family had owned, said the Prohibition inspectors in their report. And thus the industrious and frugal Seghesio family, like other families in Napa and Sonoma, was cruelly deprived of its major movable asset.

Far away from the lush Alexander Valley, officials were becoming more and more concerned that the tentacles of the business of illegal wine with its massive profits, had reached too far and too wide. Officials were worried not only about bootlegging but because a great deal of wine made and originally sold for sacramental purposes did not end up being used in religious services as it should have been. The regulations and oversight of that market made it ripe for crime of all sorts: bribes, thefts, embezzlements, holdups. Sacramental wine sales increased exponentially, but religious services and congregations did not increase accordingly.

Even as early as September 1922, just two years after the Dry laws were put in place, Prohibition zone chief John D. Appleby, in charge of New York State and New Jersey, planned a "crusade" with his agents to investigate the hundreds of wineries and wine stores that were supposedly selling sacramental wine illegally throughout New York City's Lower East Side. Appleby's officers, reported the *New York Times*, suspected that bar and restaurant owners might have been paying $200 to $500 to rabbis, or people pretending to be rabbis, for the use of their names to buy sacramental wine.[29] Some of the wine involved could have been prepared by wineries who followed Jewish dietary laws, but some of it was most likely the illicit product of California grapes sold in New York and illegally labeled.

Three of Appleby's agents seized a variety of wines from Kalmer Rosenbluth's Zion Casino at 96 Attorney Street in New York City in September 1922. Included in the seizure were "9 barrels, each containing 50 gallons (of alcohol); 20 bottles of Tokay, 80 half-gallon jugs of wine, 76 gallons of kosher wine, 61 one-half-gallon jugs of wine, 7 one-gallon jugs of wine, 28 one-half pints of wine, . . . quarts of wine, and 70 bottles of wine," valued between $5,000 and $10,000.

A rabbi owned the wine, said Rosenbluth. And a certificate was on the door leading to the cellar, it was said, showing that the wines belong to that rabbi.[30] Whether the rabbi was an imposter or not was not reported.

The very next month, the infamous New York Prohibition agents Izzy Einstein and Moe Smith, masters of disguise, got involved in a complex case involving sacramental wine. Einstein and Smith were both rotund and did not fit the general expectation of what a Prohibition agent would look like. This was a decided advantage in their business. In order to infiltrate every kind of operation when illegal liquors and wines might be sold, they polished their innate talents for dressing up: as football players, coal men, longshoremen, streetcar conductors, even musicians if it would help bring liquor dealers and wine sellers to justice.[31] The duo was believed to have arrested thousands of bootleggers and confiscated 5 million bottles of bootleg liquor. As reported in the *New York Times*, this time the men posed as cigar salesmen, one of their favorite and most successful ruses. According to the agents, the case was initiated by an informant who let them know that they could buy wine from someone who worked at the Hammondsport company on Fourth Avenue, by using a password. They telephoned the secretary of a rabbinical bureau on East 28th Street, who was also, it was alleged, a salesman for Hammondsport Products, and arranged to purchase 10 cases of assorted wines from him. The agents said the wine needed to be delivered to them under a fictitious name, Mike Lopeano, at a saloon, but the seller asked that the name be changed to Joseph Levine and that he would leave the goods at a cigar store on a different street to the saloon. The seller said the change of name would make the deal look more legitimate.

The wine arrived. Einstein and Smith had paid for it with marked notes and revealed their true identities. They then seized not only their 10 cases of wine but 20 more that had been loaded on the same truck. The 30 cases of wine were described as sacramental wines for religious use at home.[32]

Other sacramental wineries were soon under investigation and some of the sacramental wine agents that did business with the Napa County winery of George de Latour were also involved in questionable practices.

William McKinley Sodenberg, who ran a garage in Minneapolis, declared in an affidavit that during 1920, he occasionally had been invited to have a drink with acquaintances in a company situated upstairs from Mid-West Church Goods Company, agents for Latour. The company had had a sales permit to sell wine for sacramental purposes. Mid-West sold all sorts of religious articles. The wine for those happy hours enjoyed by Mr. Sodenberg appeared to have come directly from

Mid-West downstairs. When Sodenberg's host ran out of wine, he alleged "more wine was procured by going to the elevator shaft and waiting a few minutes. The wine always came up in bottles." At Christmas time, said Sodenberg, Mid-West also gave him wine as gifts.[33]

On December 18, 1922, Mid-West had also come to the notice of Minneapolis Prohibition officers, when two general Prohibition agents wrote a letter to their divisional chief explaining that they had recently been assigned to investigate the company's records, files, papers, and premises. They reported that its sacramental wine supply was kept in a locked cellar to which only two people had keys: the owner and the employee who filled the orders. The two agents had allegedly discovered that nearly a fifth of the wine stored in the cellars was missing. The owners laid the blame elsewhere: they said George de Latour's winery operation had not sent the ordered amount; that they had had a railroad loss, and that they generously filled bottles for customers up to the limit. But they did admit they had been offering "lots of samples" of the wine to potential customers. The agents dismissed those excuses and declared the company to have what they described as "haphazard" business practices. And, their report said, that the company was just "too lax to enjoy the trust of the government." As for giving samples, it was "a direct violation of the National Prohibition Act." The agents recommended that Mid-West's permit be revoked.[34]

Latour himself had been outraged at an investigation of his shipping practices when a number of barrels and kegs of wine were found to be full of water when they arrived at their destinations in Milwaukee and New Mexico. "I need not tell you that the water was not put in the barrels and kegs at my winery—we do not do that kind of business as you know well," he declared in an August 1922 letter to Edward Yellowley, the federal Prohibition commissioner. Latour explained that he had had a great deal of wine pilfered in the past but had put a stop to that by shipping small packages of wine in double casks. "If the package is very small," he explained, "it is stolen altogether, but if the package is large they cannot take out wine so easily; that is why I advise priests to buy a larger quantity at a time, for instance, a half barrel or a barrel, as it is easier to take kegs of 5 and 10 gallons."[35]

Two agents headed to Beaulieu to investigate but found there was no internal tampering with barrels or kegs. They reported back that the wine had been shipped to the customers through another of Latour's agencies, run by two salesmen called Baker and Hunt. "As you will remember," reminded the agents, "Baker and Hunt are reported to be bootlegging down on the border." Whether Latour knew about the alleged bootlegging of his agents is not reported. In Washington, Prohibition Commissioner Haynes eventually put an end to the issue with, "Beaulieu Vineyard appears to have committed no violation of the law . . . the case is hereby closed."[36]

The Latour wine headed to Milwaukee had been traveling on a Chicago, Milwaukee, and St. Paul railroad car when it went missing, the enforcement officers discovered. When the train was detained at Atkins, Iowa, the seal on the car necessary for the carrying of alcohol was broken, allowing workers to enter, supposedly for the purpose of repairing the car. Instead they stole the wine in an act probably repeated thousands of times during Prohibition. How they would have known which car contained sacramental wine was not revealed. According to Wine Country lore, many losses of sacramental wine in transit were inside jobs involving trainmen or wine clerks: Crime syndicates paid well for information about the contents of railcars.

The Davini Brothers—The vineyards tucked throughout the hills and mountains of Sonoma and Napa were established by brave, tough, hard-working settlers and immigrants who wrestled year after year with the lonely landscape throughout intense summer heat and lashing winter rains. Here the Davini brothers— Carlo and Vince—work to establish a vineyard on Lytton Springs Road in Sonoma County. Photo courtesy of Aileen Lencioni Steadman.

Tree Stump—Removing vast oaks and towering redwood trees was backbreaking work. Chains and horses were used to prepare the land for planting vines, and building wineries and homes. In 1890, Luther Bell stood proudly by a stump removed from land near Windsor, Sonoma County. Photo courtesy of the Windsor Historical Society

Passalacqua Wagon—Many immigrant families in Sonoma County who later grew into dynasties in the wine industry began their lives in America as market gardeners growing vegetables and fruit for sale. This is Ed Passalacqua's vegetable wagon. Photo courtesy of the Healdsburg Museum and is part of its permanent collection.

Foppiano Family—The beautiful and hardworking Mathilda Foppiano, center, shown here in a 1910 photograph, with her husband, Louis A. (left), their two daughters, and an unnamed man, had to watch in horror as as much as 140,000 gallons of her family's wine was disposed of in a ditch during Prohibition. In this photo, Mathilda is pregnant with her son, Louis J. Foppiano, who went on to create one of the most important wineries in Sonoma County and was instrumental in introducing the Petite Sirah grape into northern California. Photo courtesy of the Foppiano family, Foppiano Vineyards.

Greystone—The California Grape Grower *reported the unbelievable and heartbreaking news in 1921 that the "beautiful Greystone" plant of the California Wine Association in St. Helena in Napa County where some of northern California's best wines were cellared, would crush no grapes that year thanks to Prohibition. Photo courtesy of* Wines & Vines, California Grape Grower.

Nichelini Family—Proud and loyal parents Antone and Caterina Nichelini—photographed with their twelve children in 1920 just as Prohibition was beginning—would eventually have to resort to bootlegging from their Chiles Valley homestead in Napa County in order to survive. Front row left to right: Josephine Delaphine, 26; Antoinette Louise, 7; Mother Caterina, Father Antone, Inez Leona, 4; Emma Virginia, 24; Middle row, left to right: Fred Walter, 13; Allen James, 11. Back Row, left to right: William, 29; Edith Dora, 23; Rose Elva, 21; Catherine Angelina, 16; Mary Carolina, 18; Joseph Frances, 27. Photo credit: Toni Nichelini-Irwin (daughter of William Nichelini) for the Nichelini Winery.

Russian River—The Russian River wine appellation is now known all over the world for its Pinot Noir, but during Prohibition this pristine, winding waterway was widely recognized as a bootlegger's dream come true as the area surrounding it ran through remote grape ranches and the lonely countryside where liquor stills and illicitly stored wine could be easily hidden from federal agents. From time to time its waters ran red when wine, dumped by the government for winemakers' infractions against Prohibition legislation, poured into it down streams and gullies. Photo courtesy of the Healdsburg Museum and is part of its permanent collection.

Federal Agents—Federal Agent Harry Dengler, right, stands with Sonoma County Detective John Pemberton (left), and another unnamed agent while raiding a still. Photo courtesy of the LeBaron Collection.

Colombano Couple—Eligio and Angela Colombano would not have known on their San Francisco wedding day in 1913 that during Prohibition they would be forced to bootleg wine. During those tough, frightening days, they lived at the end of a quiet country road, which made their property attractive to even bigger bootleggers. Photo courtesy of Lou Colombano for the Colombano family.

Uncle Camillo—The strikingly handsome Camillo Colombano sold wine and brandy throughout North Beach and other parts of San Francisco before Prohibition. The contacts he made then served him well when his business was declared illegal by federal law and he decided to buy a 30-acre vineyard with his brother Eligio and turn to bootlegging. Photo courtesy of Lou Colombano for the Colombano family.

Grapes Being Sold—Grapes were sold for home winemaking throughout Prohibition at San Francisco's Drumm Street tracks. Here, in this California Grape Grower *photo of 1921, salesmen are working as they always did—directly from railcars. Grapes came from all over the state of California but the preferred grapes for home winemakers, especially in San Francisco's discriminating North Beach Italian community, came from Napa and Sonoma. Photo courtesy of* Wines & Vines, California Grape Grower.

Grapes Crushed—After San Francisco customers had bought wine-juice grapes they could avoid the messy "crush" in their kitchens and cellars by paying Golden Gate Grape and Juice Company to do it for them. Then a grape buyer would merely have the juice delivered and let it start to turn into good, hearty homemade red wine. A strange loophole in Prohibition legislation allowed wine to be made in homes across the nation throughout Prohibition. Photo courtesy of Wines & Vines, California Grape Grower.

Resorts Thrived During Prohibition—This photo, taken circa 1920, shows the Agua Caliente Hotel, one of the many resorts that dotted Napa and Sonoma counties both before and during Prohibition, many of which were located close to train depots. Resorts provided a full range of accommodations from luxury rooms to family tents and they attracted fun-loving tourists from the Bay Area and beyond along with good orchestras, dancing, and a myriad of outdoor activities which were made even more delightful by the weather of the wine counties. Their meals of good fresh food, or evening dance parties, were often accompanied during Prohibition by the fine but illicit wines of the region. Photo credit: The Sonoma Valley Historical Society.

Cuneo Family—The Cuneo family members are pictured together circa 1927, some five years before its hard-working, thrifty patriarch, John, was jailed for illegally making brandy on his grape ranch from his own wine and then selling it. Front row, left to right—Virginia Cuneo; Emilia "Babe." Back row, left to right: Maria; parents John and Emilia; and Eugene, who passed away in his nineties after a long life as a kind and generous man and a hugely respected grape rancher. Photo courtesy of the Healdsburg Museum and is part of its permanent collection.

Healdsburg Depot—This 1915 photograph shows the tiny rural train depot where during Prohibition hundreds of car loads of fresh wine grapes would be sent off to markets across the United States; many thousands of sacks of sugar would arrive to service the many stills that thrived so profitably in the surrounding farms, hills, and valleys. Photo courtesy of the Healdsburg Museum and is part of its permanent collection.

Edoardo Seghesio and Angela Dionisia Seghesio—seen here on their wedding day in the summer of 1893, worked hard and had a rare wine business acumen that helped parlay simple beginnings into a dynasty that today produces award-winning wines from a family winery, even though during Prohibition they were the victims of one of the cruelest of extortion schemes by government agents. Photo Credit: The Seghesio Family, Seghesio Family Vineyards.

Chapter Seven

Almost as Ubiquitous as the Radiance of the Moon Itself

By the end of 1922, grape prices had risen again. The news of continuing troubles with the trains ferrying the grapes from California to major markets in the East had pushed prices skyward, as consumers panicked that the grape supply could slow down, perhaps even stop, at any moment. All this brightened the finances of California's wine-grape growers.

But the beginning of 1923 brought infuriating news that there was another serious competitor in their best market: Italy was sending wine grapes to New York. Packed in long wine barrels, the kind used in the south of Italy and each containing about 500 pounds of grapes treated, it was suspected, with sulfuric acid to prevent decay and fermentation, these grapes were said to have been eagerly bought up by New York's Italian population, and there were contracts out to deliver more at harvest time.[1]

But as the year progressed, the sales of Italian grapes appeared to make no dent in the sales of wine grapes from northern California. The number of railcar loads of wine grapes shipped east from Napa grew satisfyingly through 1923. The scenic little town of Calistoga had shipped 101 carloads in 1921; 337 in 1923. Rutherford in the heartland of Napa Valley had shipped 112 carloads in 1921; in 1923 it sent 340 carloads east.

About 20,000 tons of fresh wine grapes left Napa County in 1923. Not included in that number were the many loads of grapes that had been hauled by road to the bay cities. Although it was impossible to get an accurate estimate of the tonnage of those grapes, industry watchers believed it to have been large.[2]

That year the weather had been cool during the early summer months, and early September rains caused heavy losses in Sonoma, ruining thousands of tons of Zinfandel and Petite Sirah. Again trains of grapes were halted, fully loaded, before they could be unloaded in major markets as too many cars filled with other perishables from around the nation created "congested terminals" at markets in the East.[3] A great deal of California fruit would rot as it waited to be unloaded.

Curiously, the real impact of the boom in wine grapes seemed to have escaped the very forces that had willed Prohibition into being. Wayne Wheeler, the very visible and influential head of the Anti-Saloon League, insisted with his usual air of authority that home winemaking had run its course.

"Like home brewing, it was taken up as a fad, but quickly abandoned," Wheeler declared confidently, either oblivious to the evidence or deciding to ignore it the hopes that it might go away.

Outraged by the dissembling, a story in the *California Grape Grower* asked the Dry leader what had become of the 30,000 cars of wine grapes that were shipped out of California in September, October, and November 1923.[4]

Grape growers slapped each other on the back in amusement. If government and its cronies were this dull-witted or this duplicitous, they told each other, they were almost beholden to flout the law.

By 1924, there were more than 670,000 acres of grapes in California, 127,000 of them wine grapes.[5] Business was bustling, and grape growers in Napa and Sonoma were shouting impatiently for more railcars to get grapes to major markets. The demand had become so acute that grape prices were booming, and the industry expected the season to establish new price records. Grape dealers were desperate to ensure their fruit left California before it spoiled. Noting this, central California vineyards in Kern, Fresno, Madera, and Tulare counties, where a glut of Thompson Seedless table grapes was ripening, were planning to graft new grape varietals to their vines in order to further cash in on the wine-grape market. This angered the grape growers of Napa and Sonoma, who worried that those valley grapes would eventually flood the markets and depress the prices of the entire California wine grape supply.

Central Valley counties were planting Alicante Bouschet vines too—still the most demanded grape in the markets—further antagonizing northern Californians. They had not forgotten that most of those counties had pushed hard for Prohibition.

The *Grower* sarcastically warned growers in the Central Valley that if they grafted their vines over to wine-grape varieties and if juice-grape prices slumped, there would be only one course open to them: "to dig up their vines and plant cotton, alfalfa or some of the other wonderful crops" that the Drys had earlier advocated for the unirrigated hillside vineyards of Napa and Sonoma in 1914, 1916, and 1918 when the state was voting over and over again on Prohibition.[6]

The year 1924 was notable not only for its record grape harvest but for a general election that, sadly for Napa and Sonoma, seemed to solidify and strengthen Prohibition forces.

The election came after Commissioner Haynes claimed in August that during the previous fiscal year, Prohibition law violators had paid more than $7 million in fines across the country, up $2 million from the previous year. Dry law violators had received, he claimed, sentences totaling 3,148 years, 3 months and 11 days. The year previous they'd totaled more than 2,000 years.[7]

None of the candidates for president that fall had faced the Prohibition issue head on. Calvin Coolidge, running for reelection, was concise, as usual, in one of his few pronouncements on the subject: "Our country has adopted prohibition and provided by legislation for its enforcement. It is the duty of the citizen to observe the law and the duty of the Executive to enforce. I propose to do my duty as best I can."

His Democratic opponent, West Virginia lawyer John W. Davis, was, if anything, even more prickly about the matter:

> For no reason apparent to me this question has been asked, as perhaps it will continue to be asked until it has been definitely answered, what views I hold concerning the enforcement of the Eighteenth Amendment . . . ?
>   Why is the question:
>   Is it not the law?[8]

The third candidate for president was Progressive Robert LaFollette, lawyer and ex-governor of Wisconsin, who had voted against U.S. participation not only in World War I but in the League of Nations and the World Court too—a world-view that was perceived as ominously exclusive by the multinational voters of California.

Whatever his view of Prohibition, Coolidge won Sonoma County by nearly 2 to 1 over his nearest opponent, LaFollette, with Davis running a poor third. Nationally, Coolidge won by a landslide, with the electoral votes of 35 states and 54 percent of the popular vote; Davis got 29 percent and LaFollette, 17 percent.

Amid the cheering about grape sales, Sonoma and Napa watched helplessly as Prohibition kept its iron grip on their lives.

As 1924 ended, worries about wine-grape overproduction grew more and more pronounced, inciting the grape growers to become more and more strategic about their product. They were beginning to apply a rule of thumb about regional demand: The larger the foreign-born European population, said the *California Grape Grower,*—Italians, Germans, French, Spanish, Austrian, Hungarians, and others for whom wine was a part of their culture—the better the market. It was a primitive calculation, but one they felt they could depend on. Philadelphia, for instance, whose population was 20 percent foreign born, was a booming destination for wine grapes. Its 1920 population included 63,000 immigrants from Italy and 40,000 from Germany, who bought Muscats, Tokays, Zinfandel, Mataro (a black grape now more commonly called Mourvedre), Carignane, Mission, Alicante, and Grenache.[9]

Detroit, its population nearly a quarter foreign born, took more than 1,000 cars of California table and wine grapes in 1924.[10] New Orleans, however—a once-great wine market whose wholesalers and restaurateurs had had close relationships with California winemakers before Prohibition—was proving a surprising challenge. In 1919, the city's hotels, cafés, and French and Italian restaurants had purchased four million gallons of wine, but now the city was a disappointing market for wine grapes.

With no basements or cellars in the often waterlogged city, consumers had little space to store boxes of grapes, let alone the 200 gallons of wine they were allowed to maintain each year. New Orleans' wine lovers were forced to produce wine a few gallons at a time, and they did that mostly from easier-to-store raisins, purchased in 25-pound boxes.[11]

Boston was third largest market in the nation for California wine and table grapes, partly because it was the dominant trade center in its area—grapes that arrived there were sent out to Maine, New Hampshire, Vermont, Massachusetts,

Rhode Island, and half of Connecticut—but also because it had a healthy immigrant population.[12]

Chicago, California's second most important grape market, took 7,000 cars of California wine and table grapes in 1924. Nearly one-third of Chicago's inhabitants were foreign born, including 138,000 from Poland, 112,000 from Germany, 59,000 from Italy, 30,000 from Austria, and 5,000 from France. On one day alone—October 20—289 cars of California grapes arrived in the city, most of them destined for wholesalers on South Water Street. In those days the street was full of noise and shouting, with an endless stream of horse-drawn wagons jostling for space to pick up goods from sidewalks piled high with supplies.[13]

The finest of all markets for California wine and table grapes was New York, continued the *Grower*. Thousands of cars arrived all through the first years of Prohibition, and more than 12,500 railcars of grapes arrived in New York in 1924. A few were shunted into New York terminals, but the bulk arrived first in New Jersey, which usually sent them into New York within hours. The city's four great auction houses, located on Franklin, West and Harrison streets, handled more than 95 percent of all California deciduous fruit. A quarter of all the grapes that left California were headed for the New York market. It was estimated that more than 50 nations were at that time represented in the cosmopolitan population of New York City, and it was thought that most of the demand for wine grapes came from the 390,000 Italians, 193,500 Germans, 126,000 Austrians, the 22,500 French, and the 64,000 Hungarians who lived there. The top-selling grapes in New York were Alicante, Zinfandel, Mission, Petite Sirah, Carignane, Grenache, and Mataro. New York was rated an especially auspicious place to sell grapes as, " . . . the income of the average New Yorker is exceptionally high and they are liberal spenders."[14]

While the wine industry was unsettled and constantly worried by the fresh juice grape market, everyone knew that the market for wine in barrels or bottled could not be dampened. The *Sotoyome Scimitar* newspaper complained in January 1925 about the broken glass of wine jugs left behind in city streets by partygoers who had attended a dance in Healdsburg, saying "it is a remarkable thing that some wineries will continue to sell their product apparently to whomsoever will come to buy."

That very same month, the federal government decided to take on the issue of the embarrassing performance by its agents that was permitting the sale and consumption of wine to be carried on so publicly in Sonoma County. A special convoy of Prohibition enforcement authorities arrived in the area, reported the

Sotoyome Scimitar newspaper, some of them members of the "secret service" working undercover to pick up what intelligence they could about illegal goings-on. Other officials openly advertised their presence, holding public hearings on the illegal sale of wine.

Q. J. Bone, assistant federal Prohibition director, Don C. Reid, assistant legal adviser of the state prohibition forces, and A. Housel, a general prohibition agent, were looking into whether more bonded winery permits in Sonoma County should be revoked as the river of wine leaving the county continued to amaze and dismay authorities. They were particularly worried by the flow of wine, it was said, from vineyards to big city bootleggers run by "a well-organized ring of state and city employees who permit cargoes of wine to traverse the highways and cross the bay to San Francisco unchallenged."

An investigation in the San Francisco Bay area had led to the discovery that over $1 million worth of wine had been removed from bonded warehouses where the wine was supposedly guarded 24 hours a day. Because of the mysterious removal of this wine, and because of countless and continuing failures to comply with internal revenue regulations, 81 wineries in the state had already been seized and locked down by the government. But the mysterious losses of wine continued. Embarrassingly for the Prohibition authorities, wine valued at more than $1 million, more than $10,000,000 in 2008 dollars, had disappeared from government control *after* being placed under seal.

Federal authorities claimed it had somehow been sold wholesale to bootleggers, but everyone knew what really must have happened: The missing wine could not have been sold from under the government's nose unless the bootleggers had official assistance from conspiring Prohibition employees themselves.[15]

By now the wine counties were rife with the activity of the illegal wine trade and the force of the Prohibition Unit was hustling to keep up. At the start of the year, Officer William Navas had staged a raid on the dining room at Healdsburg's Hotel Sotoyome and discovered "jackass" brandy, the possession of which had cost proprietor, A. Barsotti, $350 when he appeared the next morning before Judge Royle. Barsotti paid the fine immediately. One Sunday morning a month later, Healdsburg's chief of police, James Mason, "pulled his coat collar up about his ears," said the *Sotoyome Scimitar,* and "his hat down to meet it," and knocked on the Hotel Sotoyome's kitchen door. "He was readily admitted and almost immediately recognized," but he had already placed his hand on a bottle of the same sort of jackass as had previously gotten Barsotti in trouble.

Barsotti was arrested yet again and issued a further $400 fine, which he also paid immediately. The speed with which Barsotti paid his fines made it clear both to his customers and the law that bootlegging was more profitable than running a legal saloon ever had been.[16]

The extent of a Napa County bootlegging ring both amazed and amused locals when, late on a Monday night in March, a squad of 15 officers, under the command of Sheriff J. R. Harris, swept down through damp and dark roads to a number of upper valley resorts tucked away in the wooded hills but blazing with lights and loud with dance music, and arrested seven men and seized several thousands of gallons of wine and jackass brandy along with three stills. Deputy sheriffs, constables, and town marshals at Yountville, Calistoga, and St. Helena had all been convened to assist in the lightning raids, which were made shortly before midnight—a time when the resorts were crowded, even though it was a Monday in midwinter. Those arrested were placed under heavy guard and rushed to the courthouse in Napa, while other officers loaded four trucks with the liquor and other evidence seized in the raid. Justice of the Peace Charles H. Snow roused himself from his bed and held a special midnight session of his court to handle the raid, fining the defendants a total of $5,250 when they pleaded guilty, though he offered to substitute jail terms if they preferred.[17]

The raids were a constant irritation in Napa and Sonoma. But perhaps no one in the two counties had better reason to be vexed with the relentless pressure of the law than Nate Ghisolfo, the proprietor of a bonded winery in Calistoga. In April 1925, a Prohibition agent had marched uninvited onto his premises to check the state of his cellars and discovered that 25 percent of Ghisolfo's previously cataloged and padlocked wine had gone missing, reported the *Sotoyome Scimitar.*

Ghisolfo claimed the shrinkage was entirely explainable: It was from natural causes like evaporation. But when the matter came to the desk of U.S. Attorney Alma Weyers, she pooh-pooed the excuse immediately, and set in motion the volumes of paperwork required to secure a federal court order to destroy the remaining 31,000 gallons of wine that Ghisolfo had on hand. It had a value of more than $60,000—a great deal of money at a time when a new car cost $1,500.[18] While the documents were making their way through the courts and bureaucracy, Deputy Marshals John O. Hanlon and William Foster were sent to guard the wine to prevent any further "leakage" or "evaporation." But despite the insult of the imminent threat of destruction of the asset he had worked years to accumulate, and into which he had invested the cost of not only his own labor but of field workers too, the warm-hearted and gracious Ghisolfo treated the two agents like welcome visitors.

The agents spent the days relaxing in the green heaven that is Napa in the summer, dining with the family on fine homemade food, including fresh chickens and good fruit and vegetables from the family's own land.

By July, the days are long and hot in Napa Valley. In the kitchen early in the morning before the heat becomes too oppressive to work, salamis to be dried or juicy sausages ready to be browned to a crunchy crisp over the family's wood-fired stove are prepared, along with long-simmered sauces and meat stews. Outdoor ovens are readied for loaves of breads, rubbed with olive oil, that have risen in their pans under spotless dishcloths. Cantaloupe, though small, are ready to eat, juicy and almost erotically perfumed. Tomato plants as tall as your shoulder are bearing their first sweet, ripe fruit. Sunflowers bend their heavy heads. The first corn arrives. And long, sweet Italian peppers are getting ready to turn from green to red. Roses are on their third bloom of the year. By noon, nothing moves in the still and heavy heat of a vineyard. The low vines that stand alone (un-trellised) and are dubbed "head-trained" as the leaves fall from the top-knot of the vines, now have elegant trains of leaves reaching to the ground, the leaves arranged around the fruit to protect it from burning in the relentless sun. But when evening comes, the gardens in the valley are cool and refreshing.

Surrounded by all this beauty, the agents spent happy days guarding the wine. But after three months of feeding the agents and treating them to a virtual vacation on his property, Ghisolfo grew weary and began providing them with an increasingly less elaborate menu while they were on their watch. After all, they *were* there as enforcement officers. Eventually Ghisolfo enlisted the help of an attorney in San Francisco to help him find a way to get rid of the two men. His lawyer informed the authorities that Ghisolfo wanted the two deputies to leave and that, if necessary—and even though it would mean a sickening financial loss to him—they could take the remaining wine with them. Ghisolfo, said the lawyer, was even prepared to put up an $18,000 bond if they would leave him alone. The U.S. Attorney refused to recall the deputies or accept the bond, saying that Ghisolfo might be using this as some sort of cunning ruse to get rid of even more wine in some illegal manner. A judge refused to make a ruling without the U.S. Attorney's consent. "Mr. Ghisolfo," reported the *Sotoyome Scimitar* newspaper, "does not know what to do. And the deputy marshals face a life of stale sandwiches."[19]

The numbers of arrests, in these and many similar apprehensions, was becoming mind-boggling. That summer, federal officers destroyed 9,000 gallons of choice Sonoma County wine held in two bonded warehouses, when the wine's owners were found guilty of violating Prohibition. An inability to explain "shrinkage" in their stocks was the reason for the punishment. The wine, 6,000 gallons at the De Mercantonio winery at Cloverdale and the remainder at Pieta, some miles farther north, was destroyed by dumping. As usual, the agents knocked the bungs out of the huge tanks, allowing the contents to empty out onto the ground and into surrounding ditches and creeks.

More wine flowed again into ditches and creeks the very next day, when Marshal Fred Esola and a corps of agents poured out 21,160 gallons at a winery owned by G. Gondola near Santa Rosa's Monroe schoolhouse.[20]

As winemakers felt more and more pressure on their home turf, they were by turns more angered, then more dispirited when Dry forces in Washington continued to agitate for tougher penalties for illegal activities involving alcohol. Lobbying for even worse poisons than kerosene to be placed in alcohol held in bond, so it could never be sold or bootlegged or drunk, heated up after it became clear that few laws were effective in slowing down the supply and manufacture of alcohol.

Drys were having some effect. Earlier that year, Congressman Gale H. Stalker of New York had introduced a bill to increase penalties for Prohibition violations. The existing fines, proponents claimed, were so low as to amount to nothing more than a license fee for law violation. House Judiciary Committee Chairman Earl C. Michener, a Michigan Republican, observed that existing laws also precluded arresting those possessing liquor on their first offense, a serious weakness.[21] Debate at the highest levels occurred about whether those responsible for selling poisoned liquor should be indicted for murder. However, since the government itself was condoning adding "denaturants" to liquor, it was a tortuous argument.

The Coolidge administration declared in May 1925, that it would make a "tremendous effort" to *finally* enforce Prohibition laws. Senator James E. Watson, an Indiana Republican, admitted in a story that appeared in the *New York Times* that across the country: "Everybody knows that prohibition is not being enforced and that everybody knows that the law is being wantonly violated." However, Watson had words of what he hoped were reassurance for Americans, "I can say this, that from the President down, they have determined to make a tremendous effort to enforce Prohibition in the United States and they are going

to use all the agencies at their command to enforce it." These disappointing plat-
itudes insulted many Americans and were not mitigated by the additional intelligence that Major Haynes, prohibition commissioner, had prepared guidelines on
Prohibition for children in schools preparing to apply for citizenship. The first
question: What brought about the need for the Eighteenth Amendment (which
banned alcoholic beverages)? The answer: "Power of the liquor interests in politics. Welfare of children." And this answer drummed up from where? Folks believed "powerful inventions of today demand steady nerves, sound bodies, sober
judgment." The reasoning behind Prohibition now seemingly was as changeable
as the weather in fall vineyards.[22]

Inefficient or corrupt though so much of the enforcement had been, and no
matter how hollow the harangues in Washington turned out to be, there was no
question among the winemaking community that the pressure against them was
already painful. Grape growers and winemakers who had seen friends and family
go to jail, pay fines, or have their property smashed and wines destroyed realized
that they were fighting an onslaught of battles that required wit and will, and became even more determined and resolute to win as each day of the war went on.

They were heartened by a growing sense that small cracks had begun under-
mining the very foundations of Prohibition, and they poised themselves to take
every advantage of that. They saw these weaknesses in the desperation of the enforcement forces; in the use of glib euphemisms and plain fabrications about the
success of Prohibition from Congress and by special interest groups in Washington; in the creation of special committees on the Hill to look into what was going
wrong with the grand plan; and in the growing public outrage at rising crime rates.
Time, they began to think, might be on their side. A few more harvests and things
might be really begin to fall apart.

But that same defiance was becoming more and more aggravating to enforcement officials in San Francisco and Washington, who were repeatedly embarrassed at the winemakers' cunning and their own inability to control the
situation.

Soon Congress, unable to explain the growing liquor-related crimes and the
obviously constant supply of liquor in every corner of the nation, called for a
shakeup of Prohibition authorities. Commander Roy Haynes, the nation's first
commissioner of Prohibition, whose official pronouncements were once derided
by *TIME* magazine as "optimistic ballyhoo,"[23] was stripped of his authority on
September 1, 1925, his rank reduced to inspector. General Lincoln C. Andrews

had been Haynes's boss since April, 1925. He had maintained his head spot as assistant secretary of the treasury but had also been given the additional responsibility for Prohibition.

Besides wanting to deal with Haynes's inability to deliver successes to the government in managing Prohibition, Andrews faced a crisis that was the sacramental wine problem in the United States. Wine, ostensibly being shipped from wineries for religious use was being sold in such large quantities across the nation that it was obvious that religious organizations could not be absorbing such a torrent. By 1926, after a year on the job, Andrews said he had conquered some of the most egregious issues facing Prohibition enforcement and vowed that he had been especially successful in curtailing the tidal wave of sacramental wine. In a statement to Congress, he reminded politicians that not only Catholics had been involved in the illegal trade of sacramental wine; those of many other faiths or pretenders to those faiths were implicated. Indeed, he said, there were thousands of Americans pretending to be rabbis to take advantage of the sacramental wine regulations.

Andrews had found that under the law, no basic permit was required for a minister or other religious representative to buy sacramental wine, although the dealer had to have a permit. And while religious purchasers were supposed to have an application approved by a local administrator, this had appeared to be no roadblock at all to massive fraud. Dealers and bootleggers had been able to take wild advantage of the loopholes.

Andrews explained that he had spent some months working with senior rabbis in New York "trying to work up a regulation, and they were very helpful. They did not want this thing to go on, and we got that matter worked out very satisfactorily."

Andrews also related one astounding fact about the veritable flood of sacramental wine. He explained that one lone Prohibition department employee in its New York office might have single-handedly enabled much of the vast business of sacramental wine in that city to flourish. "Unfortunately the man who was charged with the granting of these permits," explained Andrews, "either through failure to understand or through sympathy with the bootleggers, did not cooperate." He had been relieved of his job. Since that time, said Andrews, sacramental wine supplies in New York City had dropped until the flow was a "negligible quantity, and it will remain so. I think I am justified in saying that there will be no more diversion of sacramental wine to beverage purposes."[24] Andrews's weak excuse for the rogue New York bureaucrat behind the flood of sacramental wine was not convincing: most people wondered how fabulously wealthy such a person had become—the approval of so many illegal sacramental wine permits must have resulted in massive and lavish payoffs from bootleggers and their syndicates.

Still Andrews got the credit for the dramatic decrease in illegal sacramental wine sales after 1925, although it is still hard to comprehend how he cut the country's sales down as much as he did. From nearly 3 million gallons being sold in 1924, his efforts would eventually reduce that number to 642,000 gallons of wine for religious use across the nation,[25] which seemed more in line with demand for bone fide religious ceremonies. Before Andrews, the wine that was flooding into New York and Chicago and other large cities must have poured back out into the suburbs and states around them like a Niagara Falls of booze. And it certainly made some impressive fortunes for bootleggers along the way. Back in California in 1925, the same subject had engaged lawmakers. The state senate passed a public morals bill that was intended "primarily to stop the illicit sales of wine by fake rabbis" and would compel every priest or minister of any religious congregation to secure a permit from the district attorney of his county before being able to buy wine for religious rituals.[26] This legislation was the result of two rabbis, Rabbi Robinson, and his son Paul of San Francisco, and Rabbi Garfinkle of Oakland, being charged by Prohibition officers after a quantity of liquor had allegedly been discovered in each man's home by undercover officers who were said to have purchased wine from them.[27]

Even Archbishop Hanna in San Francisco took legal advice about the public morals bill. It was opposed by Orthodox Jews, by the California Circuit of Lutheran Churches, and Bishop Moreland on behalf of five Californian Episcopal dioceses. The archbishop's adviser explained that, although the bill specifically exempted the Catholic Church from its provisions, it asserted that the distribution of sacramental wines was a proper subject for the police. "If the state can require the Jews to go to the District Attorney for a permit to practice their religion, it can whenever it so desires, require that the Catholic Church conform to the same procedure."[28]

To the winemakers of Napa and Sonoma, the real crime regarding sacramental wine had nothing to do with bureaucrats or bootleggers or wine stores. An editorial in the *Sonoma Index-Tribune* in August 1925 explained that the real crime in Wine Country was the cheap prices received by legitimate winemakers who were forced by Prohibition law to sell their padlocked and aging wines at a heartbreaking discount to sacramental wine producers. Under the headline "Here is a Crime—Wine, Fourteen Cents," the paper noted that while leaks of sacramental wine had led to the arrest of senior Prohibition officers and their agents in Chicago and elsewhere, the more deplorable events were closer to home: A recent shipment of 7,411 gallons of wine sent from a Sonoma Valley cellar to Lodi, in the state's Central Valley, where it was to be converted into sacramental or medicinal wine sold at a shockingly low price. "The wine, made in good faith by an expert wine maker, represents a big investment and has been tied up ever since Prohibition," said the paper, noting that the real value of the wine had been 75 cents per gallon, yet the owner had been compelled to accept 14 cents per gallon for it.

"Those fortunate enough to have the special government permit to manufacture legal wine (sacramental or medicinal) will make lot of money out of it, while the Sonoma Valley property owner who toiled early and late to cultivate his vineyard, bring it into bearing, harvest its crop and make his wine must either suffer a complete loss or take what he can get."[29]

As predicted, the weakness in the process of getting Napa and Sonoma juice grapes to dealers and consumers in the largest marketplaces—troubles with transportation, the vagaries of nature, increased competition from other parts of the state—soon caused a perfect storm that cut sales and increased red ink.

First, the weather played havoc with the growers. A heatwave "raisined" grapes before the fruit reached harvest. Then early fall rains, particularly feared by grape growers, tumbled onto Napa and Sonoma before harvest. September rains that last for more than a few minutes can encourage mold and split fruit, both nightmares for a grape grower.

Prices were disappointing owing to the poor quality of much of the shipments. The average price for a box of Alicantes was $1.97 compared with $2.59 the year before. Petite Sirah grapes, in particular, which had sold at record prices the year before, had arrived at the markets in poor condition and had brought more red ink to some growers.[30]

The season had petered out early not only in the eastern markets, but even close to home in San Francisco. By the end of October, the city's Drumm Street railcar market was dead, though still packed with white wine grapes that could not find buyers at any price. The point of saturation seemed to have been reached by the middle of October all over the country.

While the grapes had found ready customers in September, by October too much fruit had arrived. By the middle of the month, prices had dropped drastically and before the month was done they had struck bottom.

The markets never recovered, and dealers suffered some frightening losses—the heaviest ever experienced for grapes. Industry watchers estimated that New York dealers and shippers lost at least $200,000 the first week in November. New York traders would long remember the grape season of 1925 as one in more than 16,000 railcars had arrived from California—more than ever before—but too many were filled with fruit in the poorest of conditions.[31]

It had been a bumper harvest for all California's field and fruit crops with grapes, cotton, walnuts, raisins, peaches, prunes, and lemons all showing increases. But that bounty had made for a dangerous excess of grapes. And the growers realized that sending too many grapes to market had helped create the disaster.

George de Latour's sacramental business, however, was continuing with great success. The volume of wine and brandy Latour was handling was consistent with the large volumes of sacramental wine sold annually throughout the United States. By December 1925, Prohibition officials said they were discussing a request from Latour for permission to increase the amount of wine it produced in the third or fourth quarter of the year from 600,000 to 1 million gallons—this when most other wineries were unable to sell even small amounts of wine legally.[32]

Archbishop Hanna's backing was not Latour's only support in the sacramental wine business. Earlier, in 1923, when the vineyard had made more wine than allowed according to its bond, Latour appeared to receive genial treatment from Prohibition authorities and he was not required to destroy that wine. Instead, Latour's company informed the Prohibition Department that a "strengthening" bond of $25,000 had been paid up to cover the excess production and it seemed to offer up the mildest sort of apology by explaining "climactic conditions at Rutherford had compelled them to crush more grapes than had been anticipated."[33] In fact, while the manufacture of wine was illegal unless for sacramental or medicinal purposes, there appeared no procedure or power to stop what was seemingly antithetical to the Dry philosophy of the nation.

Earlier excuses made by others in Napa and Sonoma, and other places in California, to explain ongoing wine production had been eventually questioned by testy Prohibition authorities, said a *San Francisco Examiner* piece that had run in that paper in the fall of 1924 and reprinted in the *Sonoma Index-Tribune* a week later. "Why are most of California's wineries running full blast in these supposed days of dryness and what do they expect to do with their surplus stores of liquor,'" was the question being asked of Samuel F. Rutter, the local Prohibition director. He quickly declared he needed to launch an investigation into "into the peculiar situation," saying that Wine Country winemakers continued to offer him irrational reasons for increasing their production. One year, he explained, they declared that because of a shortage of railcars, grapes could not be shipped east, so they had to make wine with them; another year, the winemakers had blamed the weather, which had forced them, they said, to gather their grapes quickly and press them immediately. "This year, with both good weather and plenty of cars," a frustrated Rutter reported that winemakers were "storing up supplies [expecting] the return of the 'good old days.'" In the previous year, 1923, Rutter said California's wineries made 17,000,000 gallons of wine; now they had 40,000,000 gallons on hand.[34] The growers were squeezing every advantage they could from authorities in California—and some of them no doubt were making sure they had enough wine to pass onto bootleggers. And as for the bribes and presents to officials that might have smoothed the road for some of that wine to be made and held, well, no-one was talking. But Rutter, who had to explain the continual wine making to higher-ups in Washington, was annoyed and embarrassed. And the ease in which Latour had his "overage" approved, proved that nothing had been resolved a year later.

And while things were well at Latour's winery, over at St. Joseph's Agricultural Institute, both reports extant for that operation in the previous decade had criticized the state of its vineyard, including the 1926 report citing the deplorable state of its farm, with its "old" vineyard missing many thousands of vines and its "new" vineyard poorly laid out with an unfortunate mix of varieties.

While so much was different between the Latour and St. Joseph vineyards, what they did have in common it appears, beyond having shared the services of Reverend Crowley in charge of sacramental wine production at both places, was the labor of the boys of the institute. One of Latour's marketing pamphlets made that detail clear: Printed alongside a photo of a dozen or so young boys picking fruit in the middle of a spectacular vineyard with the "foothills of the Coastal Range Mountains" behind them was the text: "Panorama of a section of the Beaulieu Vineyard . . . The grape pickers in the vineyard are boys from St. Joseph's Agricultural Institute."[35]

Not visible in some of the files of the institute are notations for Latour's payment for the boys' work. Perhaps it is elsewhere or was credited directly to the archbishop's office, or to some other long lost account. But church authorities may have felt discouraged at the inequities in the wealth Latour's vineyards were creating while the vineyards of the orphanage were in deplorable state and obviously in great need of improvement. The church still hungered, it was clear, for more re-sources for its many charitable ventures.

As the Christmas season arrived, those in the wine counties tried to turn their thoughts to family celebrations, as they always had. The large, extended families always celebrated the season with gusto. Waves of family members would arrive from San Francisco and elsewhere for the festivities via the ferries across the bay, their cars packed full of gifts and boxes of aged sausages, olive oil, and pastries and sweet breads, lots of it from North Beach, San Francisco's vibrant Italian neighborhood. Visiting friends and neighbors was one of the things that you did in those days. You did not wait for an invitation, said Gene Cuneo. "You just headed on over and knew there'd be a fine welcome along with a bottle of wine or brandy, maybe both, on the table as soon as you arrived, and soon something good to eat."[36]

Early in the New Year, fog froze on trees, windshields, window screens, tree limbs, as the temperature dropped to 29 degrees. Locals were dumbfounded when they checked the calendar and realized that 22 days of the New Year had been consecutive days of fog.[37]

The coast road between Fort Ross and Mendocino was closed for an expected two months, blocked in several places by slides.[38]

During the foggy and rainy weather, many field workers stayed at home, en-thralled and later outraged over tales of a gun battle that occurred between two po-licemen on busy Kearny Street in downtown San Francisco that had shoppers diving for cover and mothers dragging children behind parked cars in an effort to avoid bullets whizzing past their heads.

"It was a duel to the death," declared the *San Francisco Chronicle,* as two offi-cers fought a Prohibition feud of more than three years' standing. Fred Grant, the special policeman, was killed by a bullet through the heart. Samuel Shipman, his patrolman opponent, was in Harbor Emergency Hospital in critical condition with a bullet wound to his right chest and another to his thigh.

"Both men were in uniform. The ferocious battle was witnessed by scores of pedestrians." Cars stopped at the scene, terrified to move as bullets ricocheted from building to building.

It was a bootlegging wrangle. On his cot in the hospital Shipman said: "He [Grant] accused me of being a bootlegger. For more than three and a half years he has been threatening me." Grant, who believed Shipman was bootlegging on his beat, which was next to his own, received his fatal wound as the two men shot at each other at close quarters. Grant had crumpled to the sidewalk but kept up the fight until his revolver was empty. Shipman, who used five shots in the duel, kept firing his revolver as he ran away from the scene. One bullet went through a cigar stand and continued through into the Nicholson barbershop, where eight men were waiting for haircuts.[39]

Turf wars and vengeance over liquor were everywhere.

Far from the city streets in Napa's Chiles Valley, bootlegging was also very much on the minds of the Nichelini family, which had now settled into a life of bootlegging as if they had been trained for it. Hoping that their remote location would keep them out of the ears and eyes of officialdom, yet still anxious about the fines and imprisonment they risked, the Nichelinis kept on selling their wines. Like so many others, they asked themselves what else they could do to ensure they had a cash flow for taxes and food they did not grow, including such staples as flour, lard, and sugar. They had no other substantive income. Perhaps in a few years they might pull out their vines and replant with some other legal crop. But that would take time they did not have now: bills needed to be paid. So the Nichelinis continued doing what they had done for years—they made wine and they sold it.

The eldest son, William, made the most of his friendship with James Rolph, Jr., San Francisco's longest-serving mayor, and became, William's daughter Toni Nichelini-Irwin related in a 2008 interview, "pretty much Rolph's personal bootlegger." The mayor owned a grand Lincoln limousine in the early years of Prohibition, Toni explained. Her father bought that Lincoln from the mayor. With no explanations offered as to why or how, the car had arrived with a vast space built in under false floorboards in which William could pack jugs of wine for his trips into San Francisco or wherever else he had wine business. "He'd fill up jugs with wine, carry them out to the car, tuck them into the bottom of the limo and then head to the city," explained Toni. "A substantial part of my father's income came from successful bootlegging on into the Depression," she added, recounting that her father did well enough in that line of business to wear silk suits and smoke 50-cent cigars.

Antone, William's father, always had a talent for construction, and he used it well during Prohibition. He dug a pipeline from wine tanks hidden in a barn, tucked deep back into the hills above his house. That pipe led directly to the family's water supply in the kitchen sink. As needed, the kids in the family would be sent up the hill: If they turned a hidden spigot one way, water came out of the kitchen faucet; if they turned it another way, wine appeared. It was an easy, convenient way to fill the many jugs needed for the bootleg trade, Toni explained.

But even with their strong entrepreneurial talents, the Nichelini family found that things did not always go so smoothly for them during Prohibition.

One day early in Prohibition, Joseph Harris, the sheriff of Napa County, had received a letter about the family's clandestine business operations. The author of the letter lived in the tiny town of Monticello in the Berryessa Valley, just a few miles beyond the Nichelini homestead on a twisty, unpaved road. Monticello was a sleepy farming community. At least one resident was outraged by his neighbors' activities.

> Friend Joe:
>
> Virgil Anderson has rented the hotel here and it is reported that several good times, drinking wine, have gone on about the place. I am told that a jug of wine is placed or hidden, and the fellows put wise as to where it is, so they just help themselves. Whether Anderson buys the wine and sells it I do not know. It is possible someone donates the wine and uses the Hotel for a meeting place to drink and have a good time.
>
> There is no question but that the wine comes from Nicolines [*sic*]. If the revenue men would get busy, and put the lid on him, I am satisfied drinking would end here.
>
> Yours respectfully,
> Clifford Clark

Some time later, Prohibition agents arrived at the Nichelini home and, pretending to be casual passersby, they bought lunch from Antone's wife, Caterina. They also purchased at 50-cent jug of wine. Immediately after the sale they arrested the mother of twelve. Says Toni Nichelini-Irwin, the granddaughter of Antone and Caterina, luckily when the case later came to court Antone was able to convince the judge to sentence him rather than his wife, on the grounds that the household would suffer greatly if a mother of so many children was incarcerated. Now that they had been alerted to the family's hidden wines, federal agents drove up the lonely scenic road to the family's homestead. They would dump the offending wine stores that they believed Caterina had drawn from to give them a drink. Soon the bungs were knocked out of wine tanks in the family's beautiful stone cellar and 15,000 gallons of fine wine poured down the family's scenic acres and raced over steep rocks into the pristine creek below.

Yet another watershed in Wine Country ran red for many ugly hours. How many fish and other critters who lived in the creek might have died will never be known.

It was cold comfort to the Nichelinis to know that the agents' laziness had precluded them from finding another store of wine hidden up a hill not too many steps away from the front of the house.[40]

Raids continued everywhere. And however many people were stopped from selling or making or drinking wine, just as soon as they had been fined, others would be found conducting similar operations. Northern Californians came to consider the fines as merely a tax on the way they lived and worked.

In January 1926, in Dry Creek Valley, J. Rudolph was found to have 756 gallons of illegal wine and a small amount of "jack" on his ranch, and the entire liquor consignment was seized.[41]

One wet night not long after that, seven arrests were made in Healdsburg and Santa Rosa. Federal Prohibition officers, under the leadership of W. R. Paget, had descended suddenly on a Wednesday evening in a lashing rainstorm: Emilio Buffi, proprietor of the Oak Lawn Hotel, and Mrs. Susie Moretti, proprietor of the Italian-American hotel, were both arrested. Simultaneously, federal officers led by Agent David Pinckel raided six places in Santa Rosa and arrested seven people. From the Fior d'Italia Hotel, they took Frank Cassani, proprietor; at the Hotel United, they took John Merlo, proprietor, and Ben Deprizzi, bartender. Chester McKay, proprietor, was arrested at the Central Rooming House. Mrs. Onorea Rossini, proprietor, was arrested at the Italian Hotel, and at the Cigar Store, John Faccini was taken into custody. C. Arrighi was arrested at the Pool Hall. At each place, the officers had found small quantities of liquor, which they seized as evidence.[42]

A week later, county Dry officers set out at night and raided the Mile House operated by G. Nardi on the highway north of Healdsburg at the junction of the Dry Creek Valley road; 620 gallons of jackass was seized.

Four other places in that end of the county, all near Cloverdale, were raided on the same night. They included two hotels, a residence near that city renowned for its citrus industry, and a resort on the highway north of Cloverdale at the base of the grade leading over the mountain to Hopland. Eight men were in the raiding squad, headed by E. F. Westphall. At the Toscana Hotel, operated by E. Mazza, one and a half gallons of red wine, a quart of white wine, and a pint of jackass were seized. The Dante Hotel, owned by John Gianecchini, yielded a pint of jack and a pint of wine. A two-quart jug of red wine was taken at the home of A. Bellotti. The Alder Glen resort, of which A. Pardini was proprietor, gave up a quart of jack to the raiders. The raiding party split up and worked simultaneously, so one raided establishment could not warn others that trouble was on its way.[43]

The news got worse.

Suddenly at the end of November 1925, the 200-gallon tax-free wine permits that allowed wine to be made at home appeared to have been canceled. The announcement from the U.S. Treasury Department made thousands of families in northern California that were legally making wine juice for home use tremble for their personal prospects and for the future of the wine-grape market in the East. Hundreds of thousands of Americans across the nation now used to making their own wine from California's wine grapes greeted the news with grim dismay. The *Sotoyome Scimitar* reported that Assistant Secretary of the Treasury Lincoln C. Andrews had been moved to act in the hopes of plugging up, "a source of supply for the bootleggers," although "other government officials" stated the new ruling could have no effect as the right to "manufacture wine in the home was granted originally by an act of Congress and [can] only be changed by congressional action."[44]

No one appeared to know quite what the announcement meant. "Whether this new move means that the government hereafter will wink at the householder's press, or whether the day of home made juice in home cellars is past was a subject of anxious speculation," reported the *Healdsburg Tribune*. Some government officials believed that, given all the other chaos in policing Prohibition, Washington had ceased wanting to enforce the making of wine to be consumed in the home. Other officials believed the calling in of the permits marked the end of crushing California grapes in the home.[45]

But while grape growers held their breath, many people continued to make wine at home. There was no destruction of home wine, and the *California Grape Grower* considered the decision merely a tax grab.

Although Prohibition legislation did not permit an individual to make wine, an old Treasury regulation apparently had not been nullified, explained the *California Grape Grower*. The new head of Prohibition, General Lincoln C. Andrews, appeared to have promptly closed that loophole.

Eventually the situation cleared up, and it was established that citizens were being asked to pay the taxes on the 200 gallons of wine allowance, not give up their 200 gallons of wine. This whole new federal initiative exercise might have arisen to offset the huge revenue losses from the lack of liquor taxes and business taxes from saloons and hotel bars, along with the spiraling costs of the Prohibition bureaucracy.

When agents called on winemakers in Sonoma County to levy the new tax, some people promptly destroyed their 100 to 200 gallons in front of the agents so they were exempt from paying the tax.[46] This was not such a terrific hardship or sacrifice; probably hundreds or thousands more gallons of illegal wine lay hidden beneath their barns and garden sheds. The just-emptied barrels would be refilled as soon as the agents drove away.

Early in 1926, Wayne Wheeler, the still-powerful head of the Anti-Saloon League, had issued another statement to the nation reviewing the glowing progress in Prohibition enforcement. He declared:

> The *popular* approval of this [Prohibition] policy of government has been increased by the improved health of the Nation, the drop in drunkenness, crime and alcoholic insanity; the economic gains registered in steady employment, stimulated retail trade and home building, multiplied savings and insurance, and more wholesome recreation.[47]

While some of those benefits were true, the policies were receiving anything but popular approval, according to the results of a number of public polls that soon riveted the nation.

In March 1926, more than 700 newspapers, with a circulation of more than 40 million across the country, participated with the Newspaper Enterprise Association (NEA), a national news service associated with Scripps newspapers, in a nationwide poll asking readers to complete a ballot on which there were three choices. Readers had to mark a cross beside the statement that best represented their view: marking the first box would indicate that the reader favored the Prohibition amendment, strictly enforced. A mark by box number two would indicate that the reader favored repeal of the Prohibition amendment. Marking box three would indicate that the reader favored a modification of the Prohibition law to allow the sale of light wine and beer but not liquor of any other kind.[48]

By March 13, the first tallies came from California cities: in the north of the state, San Francisco had voted 2,700 to maintain enforcement, 10,000 for outright repeal, and 26,000 for legalizing beer and wine. In San Diego in the south of the state, enforcement was beating repeal by three to one with surprisingly the largest vote for the beer and wine choice. [49] Three days later, some national numbers were tabulated. More than a million votes had been counted from 44 states and the District of Columbia, and of those more than half were in favor of modifying the law to allow beer and wine. Of the other half million votes, "Repeal" votes were beating "Keep Prohibition" votes by three to two.[50]

Other newspapers picked up the idea of investigating a possible change of heart in the country. The *San Francisco Chronicle* launched a nationwide poll in conjunction with 20 other newspapers, and on March 22, it announced that 33,535 voters opposed any change to the Prohibition law while 313,966, favored change or repeal.

Hearst newspapers, including its San Francisco paper, the *Examiner,* also launched a poll across 45 states, which resulted in a vote of 196,049 in favor of the existing Prohibition law and 921,367 against. For changes that would allow light wines and beer to be made and sold, more than a million voters voted yes, while only 182,000 voted against.

The Hearst poll showed some intriguing county differences. It was no surprise that Sonoma County voted 35 to 1 against the law. Voters in Fresno County in the state's Central Valley, which had always voted for Prohibition, now tallied 172 votes to 6 votes against the continuation of Prohibition. The income from the wine-grape market in that county may have changed many minds.[51]

Though pro-repeal and pro-modification voters had hoped to nudge Washington with the national vote project, it appeared to do little when it reached the overwhelmingly Dry Senate. A new AP poll found 68 Dry senators, 15 Wets, and 13 "Doubtfuls."[52] And while public polling on any subject is never scientific, the Prohibition poll certainly hinted at some deep dissatisfaction across the nation.

Perhaps it was the shocking experiences of many Americans at the hands of Prohibition Department employees that explained why public agitation appeared to be increasing. Mabel Walker Willebrandt, the Assistant U.S. Attorney General in charge of the legal affairs of the Prohibition Department, wrote: "The prohibition force, largely as the result of political influence, was for several years filled with unfit men is proved by official records."[53] During its first six years, more than 750 Prohibition agents were dismissed for delinquency or misconduct, 61 were dismissed for acts of collusion or conspiracy to violate the very law they had sworn to enforce.[54] This was no way to increase the public's confidence in the men at the helm in Washington.

One reason the force was so ineffectual said Wayne Wheeler, counsel for the Anti-Saloon League, was that, "agents are chosen in most places because of their political qualifications . . .

"Many agents . . . hesitate to enforce the law aggressively . . . they know that if they reach certain violators with large political influence it may work against them."[55]

A Prohibition administrator of New York, Major Chest P. Mills, agreed and when he testified at the hearings by the Judiciary Committee of the U.S. Senate in 1926 he concluded: "Prohibition . . . is a party-spoils system. Three-quarters of the twenty-five hundred dry agents are ward-heelers and sycophants named by the politicians. . . . (Prohibition is) a reservoir of jobs for henchmen and of favors for friends."[56]

Some unsavory characters got unsuitable jobs in the force and it showed.

Said Harvey Rose, a man of many talents, who, among other things, worked on and around the vineyards of Geyserville in Sonoma County in his 97-and-a-half years: "I never did have any time for those agents, they thought they were big shots and shoved their way around here with no respect for anyone."[57]

Mabel Willebrandt would have agreed with him.

A teacher before becoming a lawyer, Willebrandt had built a fine reputation in Los Angeles, where she eventually opened her own legal practice and was active in influential women's clubs. After her experience as an assistant police court defender who had seen more than 2,000 cases through police courts, she knew she did not want a career in criminal law. At 32, after a phenomenal run of good luck not only with lawsuits she was involved in but in making important connections in Los Angeles, she had been appointed assistant attorney general of the United States and prosecuted Prohibition cases with great success on behalf of the government.[58] She quickly became one of the most famous women in the United States. She had gentle features, was often photographed in a dark suit with her hair pulled back sharply, and was one of the first high-profile single mothers. After her marriage broke up, she very much wanted a child and eventually adopted a little girl called Dorothy.

Her first experience with Prohibition was discouraging: "I had not been in charge of prosecutions under the Prohibition law more than a few months before I realized what many people since have acknowledged: that hundreds of Prohibition agents had been appointed through political pull and were as devoid of honesty and integrity as the bootlegging fraternity."

Her exasperation was palpable when she declared: "I refuse to believe that out of our one hundred and twenty million population, thirty-five million eligible adults of whom can be reasonably counted as favoring Prohibition, it is impossible to find four thousand men in the United States who cannot be bought."[59]

Willebrandt was faced with a long laundry list of offenses. Official reports cited the infractions committed by some of the 752 employees fired from the department in the first years of Prohibition: 20 had been let go for making false statements on their applications; 121 fired for extortion or bribery; 80 for falsification of expense accounts; 187 for intoxication and misconduct; 119 for unsatisfactory service and insubordination; 6 for theft; 2 for robbery of a warehouse; 8 for assault; and 1 for issuing a worthless check.[60]

The Senate had its own sense that trouble was brewing across the country. In April 1926, with much hoopla, the country heard that the senators had launched their own investigation into Prohibition, reported the United Press. Senator James A. Reed, Democrat of Missouri, a nationally known lawyer, had been selected by the Senate Wet block to conduct the prosecution, and some 25 Wet witnesses had been asked to appear. Senator Thomas J. Walsh, Democrat of Montana, who had conducted the Teapot Dome scandal inquiry into oil reserves, had been chosen chief counsel for the defense.[61]

Some weeks later, when the dozens of witnesses had finished testifying, *TIME* magazine moaned, "A great talk fest came to an end. So much of a propaganda matter was it for both sides.

"In the closing weeks, any number of bishops and leaders of prohibition-supporting societies declared their faith in prohibition. Mayor Dever rushed down from Chicago to deny testimony given by a Federal attorney that Chicago was full of bootlegging."[62]

One high-profile witness of the many who spoke in front of the committee was Senator William Cabell Bruce of Maryland:

> From the extent to which Prohibition monopolizes private conversation everywhere in the United States without or within doors; from the amount of space that is given to its merits and demerits in the editorial, reportorial and news columns of our newspapers; and from the innumerable polls that are now being taken for the purpose of testing public opinion with respect of it, one might well imagine, at the present time, that the Eighteenth Amendment and the Volstead

Act, instead of having been technically in force for more than six years, had never passed beyond the ordinary stages of popular agitation.[63]

Arrests for violations of Prohibition law made by federal officers had increased from 34,175 in 1921, to 62,747 in 1925. Convictions had increased from 4,315 in 1920, to 38,498 in 1925. These were federal convictions only; state offenses are not included in these figures. Seizures of illicit distilleries, stills, fermenters, etc., had climbed from 95,933 in 1921 to 172,537 in 1925.[64]

Bruce continued:

> Moonshine (and jackass), instead of being made before [Prohibition] in a few crude, sequestered localities, is now made, as the daily discoveries of the Federal and State prohibition forces evince, in swamps, in mountain fastnesses, in dense thickets, on rivers, in attics, in basements, in garages, in warehouses, in office buildings, even in caves and other underground retreats. In other words, moonshine is almost as ubiquitous as the radiance of the moon itself.[65]

The situation in the courtrooms of the nation was dire; the Volstead Act was clogging the courts. Arrests for drunkenness under Prohibition in some of the biggest cities of the United States told the same story of irrepressible law violation: There were 6,000 arrests in New York in 1920, 13,000 in 1925; in Philadelphia, there were 14,000 arrests in 1920, 59,000 in 1925; New Orleans: 2,400 in 1920, 14,000 in 1925; Chicago: 32,300 in 1920, 93,000 in 1925; Los Angeles: 3,300 in 1920, 11,000 in 1925; and close to the wine counties of northern California in the city of San Francisco: there were 1,800 arrests in 1920, 8,000 in 1925.[66]

It was no surprise really to anyone in northern California's Wine Country that sales for the 1926 wine grape harvest were disappointing. They'd already seen their receipts and heard the prognostications as the harvest progressed. Though the market was more buoyant during October and prices were better than in August and September when extremely low prices prevailed, they never were as good as growers had hoped—many cars of grapes from California arrived too early, many said, for consumers to be interested in making wine.[67] Uneven prices had dashed hopes yet again. And while the perennially popular Alicante Bouschet grape was still in demand, it was selling at lower prices than the last year. It had once enjoyed some spectacular rises in the past, but it was selling at 60 or 75 percent of those prices now and not expected to ever again reach the great heights it ascended to in, say, 1924.[68]

That grapes from the coastal counties were still most in demand on San Francisco's Drumm Street helped out the growers in Napa and Sonoma immeasurably. Dealers often marked "Cloverdale" or "Healdsburg" or "Geyserville" on the boxes even if their contents had never been within 100 miles of those places. Before the going got tough in the grape markets, the Golden Gate Fruit and Juice Company had been contemplating enlarging its grape-crushing plant next to the railroad tracks in San Francisco; local wine lovers could have grapes they'd just bought from the railcar market crushed there, avoiding the messy business of making juice in their kitchens and cellars.[69]

In California, the discouraging news about the national markets of 1926 crystallized around the time of the November vote to determine whether the Wright Act, the state enforcement legislation for Prohibition, should stay in force. It was a more decisive victory than ever for the Drys, who were mostly in the south of the state; much of the northern half of California voted against it, as ever. Wets were convinced that the question on the ballot was poorly framed and that the increase in yeas was not indicative of citizens' true state of mind. The vote to repeal the Wright Act would have been merely symbolic at this point, but it would have put wind in the sails of California's Wets and encouraged them to continue to beat the drum for repeal.[70]

The year ended with another spirited discussion at the highest levels over the best ways of rendering liquors undrinkable. The federal government intended to make seized alcohol, already treated with "denaturants" (poisons) and dangerous to drink, and planned to double the use of poisonous wood alcohol as one of its many new plans to deter drinkers. By April of 1927, denaturants would consist of ethyl alcohol, methanol, aldehol, and benzine. Many believed the mixture to be lethal and that the government had no right to employ poison use against its citizens. In support of the addition of more poison, Wayne Wheeler of the Anti-Saloon League declared, "The Government is under no obligation to furnish the people with alcohol that is drinkable . . ." Democratic Senator Edwards of New Jersey declared that the move would be "legalized murder." Was it right, detractors asked, that the government would kill its citizens in order to enforce a law originally construed to improve the health of the nation?[71]

While discussions were held on Capitol Hill in 1927 about the never-ending problems with the enforcement of Prohibition, both houses of Congress had majorities of Drys. Although the public grumbled ever more loudly, the Volstead Act was in no danger of modification, let alone reversal. However, continuing and deep dissatisfaction with Prohibition officials and their enforcement failures initiated some changes to their organization.

In March 1927, the Bureau of Prohibition, virtually the same organization as before when it was called the Prohibition Unit, but now under a new name and reporting to the secretary of the treasury, was officially re-created. Its track record was horrendous and not made any easier by the constant reinventions and reorganizations it had gone through since inception. The government could not come to any good conclusions about how it might do its work. And the revolving door of Prohibition management continued spinning, as it had done since 1920, guaranteeing confusion, misdirection, and a serious lack of focused enforcement on the ground.

The 1927 harvest in Napa and Sonoma was no better than the disappointing one of 1926. The problem was a simple one: There were far too many grapes for sale, and although Napa and Sonoma did not suffer as much as the Central Valley, the juice grape bubble had burst in the two wine counties and growers debated their next moves. Few people in the wine industry had made any long-term plans—most hung on from harvest to harvest in the hope that the nation would come to its senses. Now nearly eight years after Prohibition's inception they began to feel dispirited. Perhaps their hopes of an end to Prohibition had been entirely misplaced. Grapes increasingly sat unpicked on vines, and growers again spoke of planting more profitable fruit crops. An atmosphere of unease and futility settled over much of Napa and Sonoma: The mood of the two wine counties was low and dark, like one of the heavy grey fogs from the Pacific that drifted on a damp and chilly November evening across the mountains and around the vineyards.

Chapter Eight

A Million Dollars to Go away to France

One winery that had had its heart cut out of it by the end of the 1920s was that of Domenico Pelanconi. Domenico, a native of Gordona, a small Italian municipality tucked just below Switzerland north of Milan, had arrived in the United States with his brother Giuseppe. They had left their home together and traveled to the southern French port of Marseille, where they had signed onto a merchant marine ship headed to Halifax. Then they took a train cross country to Vancouver and hopped on another boat for San Francisco, where they disembarked and started to look for somewhere to settle where they could find work.

When the duo arrived in the Dry Creek area, there were many "Anglos," as immigrants called them, who wanted to homestead land but could not qualify, as they already owned other land in the district which disqualified them immediately. One of the requirements of homesteading was that the applicant live on the land, or else ownership could not be granted. In order for a landowner who wanted more land to sidestep that significant stipulation, immigrants were sometimes paid to "sit" on the land as ersatz homesteaders; then, as payment when the homestead was granted, they would pass it onto the new but essentially unlawful owners. The immigrant "land-sitters" would be paid off for their troubles with a lesser—but to them just as highly valued—piece of land somewhere else in the same district.

It was rumored that the Pelanconi brothers had to resort to this sort of employment to survive when they first arrived in Dry Creek. To earn some additional income, they gathered the bark from tanoak trees and took it into town by wagon, either selling it directly to leather tanning businesses or sending by train to purchasers elsewhere. It was tough work.[1]

When Prohibition agents were assigned to Domenico Pelanconi's farm to scrutinize his winemaking facilities and business practices, it was to determine whether the appraisal would result in the renewal, or not, of his all-important bonded winery permit which allowed him to store what little wine he had already made. If the permit was renewed, Domenico would have to furnish the government a $1,000 bond, but he could keep the wine and perhaps even sell it to a winemaker with a sacramental or medicinal wine permit.

To get to their assignment at the Pelanconi ranch, the agents had driven through the hills up to a small plateau in Dry Creek Valley. The clouds and rain in late winter along this finger-thin sliver of rich wine-growing land, 16 miles long by about 2 miles at its widest, can be so thick that it is difficult to see where the sky starts and the horizon ends. Huge gnarled oak trees appear and reappear through the mists like giants with beckoning arms. The tall, dark hills vanish into the distance behind a shifting wall of fog, making the landscape look more intimate than it ever does on a sunny spring day, when the vineyards and fields stretch into soft green waves as far as the eye can see. When the clouds are thick and the rain is an endless downpour, daylight time is short. No doubt, the agents would have wanted to get through the rough, muddy roads early enough in the day so that, if they did get stuck anywhere on the wet and lonely roads, they would have time to extricate themselves and get home before night settled in completely.

Wine folk say that Dry Creek Valley, about 70 miles north of San Francisco, has a similar climate to another great winemaking terroir: Bordeaux in France. Today it is the home of wineries respected across the world: Yoakim Bridge, Passalacqua, Ferrari-Carano, Nalle, Preston, Rafanelli, and Lambert Bridge.

When the agents set off to see Mr. Pelanconi that time, wine from the vineyards surrounding them was already well known in markets across the country, with thousands of barrels leaving each year for Chicago, New York, Newark, and

Boston. The agents Huffman and Adams drove their official car past orchards of peaches, pears, apples, and prunes nestled among the innumerable rows of mani-cured vines, farmed by large and small vineyards of varying reputation. The pic-turesque creek after which the valley was named often dried outright in summer, its diamond-clear waters getting slower and slower on the peaceful journey to the Russian River until they finally ceased almost altogether in the heat; yet, after the spring rains, the creek was like an angry child trying to break its bonds as it ebbed and flooded the valley floor along its muddy, furious way.

Thanks to Prohibition, Dry Creek had become a valley of fear. No one knew then that so many of its wineries would eventually be defeated by Prohibition, though some, to be sure, would make a lot of money from bootlegging wine, jack-ass brandy, and grappa. Still, the future looked eerily uncertain and the wine fam-ilies were always in a state of anxiety as they wondered whether their ranches, and the families themselves, would be able to pull through the year's harvest.

The agents knew that Domenico had been a vineyardist and winemaker since 1911. They inspected the building; they officially tested his simple security—just "a padlocked door"; they then inspected the machinery, the wine tanks. After they finished, they headed back to San Francisco to file their report. The agents rec-ommended that Domenico again be licensed, noting in their report that he "de-sires privilege of manufacturing wine only as a safeguard against financial loss in case he cannot dispose of his grapes which are his sole source of income. . . . Inas-much as he appears to have conducted his winery business in good [order], rec-ommendation for approval is made."[2]

But while that appeared a definitive assent to Domenico's request, only two months later, in correspondence contained in the Pelanconi tax files now held at the Shields Library at University of California at Davis, more senior officials rec-ommended that Domenico's permit be canceled, not renewed. The matter of the rancher's small stock of wine in a remote location suddenly became, it appeared, a matter of national proportions for the Prohibition Bureau—or perhaps it was just a make-work project aimed at giving headquarters in Washington a sense that the San Francisco office was a bustling hive of activity.

In any case, James Robb, the Prohibition division chief in San Francisco, dis-patched a letter to his superior in the nation's capital, Edward Yellowley, then chief of the general Prohibition agents, recommending that Domenico lose his license. "Mr. Pelanconi," Robb wrote, "does not have the proper facilities for the operation of a bonded winery in that there is no press or cooperage for [the] manufacture and storage," although "nothing could be learned against the applicant's character."[3]

In April 1924, the same issue went further up the Prohibition ladder of command, right to the top, in fact. Yellowley sent a letter with the same details to the head of all Dry operations in the nation, Major Roy A. Haynes, the country's Prohibition commissioner. This letter added a cavalier note to the saga: It suggested that Domenico should "be advised to file for an application for a special permit to dispose of the wine."[4]

What Haynes, or Yellowley, or the San Francisco agents might have known at that time about how long certain wines can be stored would never be clear—the complex debate about aging wine is one for experts. Although Domenico might have known how long his wine might last, the officials likely had no idea whether it needed to be drunk that year or be aged for a decade or more. It was this kind of high-handed but uneducated decision that infuriated winemakers whenever they heard about them.

Even then, the Prohibition Department was not yet finished with Domenico. The future would bring more, and regular visits from agents, more forms, more letters. Domenico once again applied for a permit, perhaps unaware that the bureaucratic staff in San Francisco had had problems with his previous requests. In 1926 new agents visited Domenico and reported back to headquarters: "There is no equipment adequate for the manufacture and storage of wines, being but one storage tank, capacity about 925 gallons which is in a cheap farm building, shaded by mature trees."[5] Since this was Prohibition and the manufacture of wines was now forbidden, at least in the legislation, it's not clear why the state of the winemaking equipment of this rancher was relevant to whether or not he would be able to keep his wine in storage. Would he be able to continue to keep his wine from the vines he had tended? Could he store that under lock and key as insurance against Prohibition's end? Or did it need to be destroyed? The information he needed apparently was in documents traveling slowly between the halls of power in Washington and the western Prohibition offices in San Francisco. Domenico hung on.

That same year, Domenico's family suffered an even greater tragedy than Prohibition: His brother, with whom he had traveled from the old country to California, died. The *Healdsburg Tribune* of October 19, 1926, related that Giuseppe "Joe" Pelanconi had been cleaning a wine tank when the poisonous fumes from the pumice he had been using had overcome him.

Pelanconi's lifeless body was found in the tank, which is six feet high, by his wife who went in search of him when he did not return for breakfast. There are two ranch houses on the place and Pelanconi stayed all night at the upper house, to do work at that portion of the farm, expecting to return in the morning to the residence below where the family resides.[6]

More harvests passed: Domenico would have been anxious about the prospects for his wine that was, due to the inexorable march of time, slowly becoming less and less valuable. Domenico was becoming poorer and poorer: His permit applications show that while he was worth $5,000 in 1923 when he was 44, three years later, he was worth just $4,000.

On May 19, 1927, the newly renamed Prohibition Bureau still had Domenico in its sights: More inspectors were deployed to the valley and headed up its dusty roads to reexamine the tiny winery and its insignificant cache of wine. Once again, the inspection report noted no violations of law or regulations, but did report that Domenico had 834 gallons of wine made in 1922 on hand.[7] The quantity of official manpower, reports, and files expended on this small amount of wine must have amazed Domenico. But not long after the inspectors' visit of 1927, a despairing Domenico must have tasted his wine and perhaps even raised his fists in fury about the glacial pace of getting his economic life in order with the Prohibition authorities. Finally, the wine did, in fact, become undrinkable, but many years after the first official correspondence. And so Domenico penned what must have been a hard letter to write to the western Prohibition director in San Francisco.

January 3, 1928
Dear Sir:

I am the proprietor of bonded Winery #3188 located about 8 miles Northwest of Healdsburg, Sonoma Country, California, and I have on hand at the present time 812–1/2 gallons of wine, which is unfit for human consumption. I ask that a representative of your office be sent to destroy this wine with the understanding that I am relieved of the payment of all taxes thereon.

Yours respectfully,
Domenico Pelanconi[8]

A little more than a month later, the wine, that might have represented a half year of living expenses to the humble Pelanconi family, was officially spilled out over the land surrounding Domenico's modest winery and the wine tanks drained by the chief inspector from San Francisco himself aided by a fellow Prohibition Bureau inspector. What a wretched moment for the farmer and winemaker, his wife, Caterina, and their two teenage sons: all that labor and fruit gone to waste in a few hours. The follow-up incident report stated: "On the 7th instant, accompanied by Inspector W. J. Walker, I visited the premises of bonded winery #3188 operated by Domenico Pelanconi, near Healdsburg, California, and witnessed the destruction of 809 gals of dry wine as per written request by the owner. Signed F. H. Driscoll, Chief Inspector."[9]

Thus the mighty, though sluggardly, weight of the nation's Prohibition forces came down hard on a humble, hardworking farmer.

The Pelanconis were not the only winemakers along Dry Creek who had their wine destroyed. Mike Teldeschi, a grape grower in the valley, remembered in an oral history for the organization Winegrowers of Dry Creek Valley that his grandfather and two friends had to dump their own wine into the creek during Prohibition when they could not afford to pay "the taxes and bond." He recollected: "I understand they put hoses out, and the creek was close by, and they just ran it right in there. Today you couldn't do a thing like that, but in those days they just did it . . . they just ran it out there and let her go."[10]

While winemakers and grape growers suffered, there was one sector of Napa and Sonoma's economy that continued to shuffle along. For decades, the two counties had been popular weekend destinations, drawing crowds of thousands from around the San Francisco Bay area who wanted to to relax in the sun and the heat and the dry weather. The ban on legal alcohol everywhere had helped keep that business buoyant as, unlike some other vacation destinations in California, it was always possible to get a glass of wine or brandy at Wine Country resorts, or visitors would be easily directed to where an alcoholic drink could be obtained. Upon arriving from San Francisco by train, vacationers were met at the tiny local stations by wagon or car sent out from the resorts. During Prohibition, more and more visitors began to travel to the counties by automobile as well. Hordes of fun lovers crowded the country resorts, and the many camps and hotels along the Russian River were filled to capacity on many weekends. Some of the resorts were designed for families, some were located on a river or high in the hills and offered fishing, boating, walking, even hunting, and many offered ballrooms or dance halls. The beaches were packed all afternoon, rental boats plied every navigable inch of the river although the river usually dropped lower and lower as the summer progressed and dance halls did roaring business.

There was a tremendous range of accommodations available, from tent camps where families shared one big room constructed of canvas around a wooden frame, to elegant buildings made of stone and surrounded by long verandas on which guests could nap or play board games in comfort. Napa County boasted some of the raciest resorts of northern California with secluded cottages where business-men and their mistresses would be left alone. Travelers seeking discreet accom-modations especially favored Stag's Leap Resort, in a Napa County district now known for its distinguished Cabernet Sauvignon wines. A number of the resorts were run by French immigrants, who served fine French food and good wines[11] which would have on occasions been served openly if arrangements had been made, as they so often were, with officials who would give tip-offs of imminent raids, recounts Healdsburg Museum's Holly Hoods.

Vacationers had headed to the counties' popular resorts ever since entre-preneur Sam Brannan's Calistoga Hot Springs had opened in the 1860s. Both Napa and Sonoma are dotted with hot springs whose waters are famed for their soothing, calming qualities. Brannan, one of California's most colorful pioneers, saw the possibilities and benefited from them. He had arrived in San Francisco in 1846 by boat around Cape Horn from New York bringing with him more than 200 Mormons whom he was leading at that time. Soon he owned a news-paper, a hotel, and other businesses including a general store at Sutters Fort in the Sierra Nevadas, when he realized that there was so much money in the area that men paid their bills with gold. He became fabulously rich and some years later built a resort with a mudbath, bathhouse, racetrack, and dancing pavilion at the north end of the Napa Valley. He named it Calistoga, combining the "Cali" in California with the "toga" from the New York's Saratoga resort. It is said after a tough divorce and an even tougher drinking habit, he died alone and impoverished.

Wealthy visitors, socialites, politicians, and well-known artists and writers signed in at wine counties' most exclusive resorts, including Napa's Soda Springs and White Sulphur Springs, where formality ruled and clothes would be changed a few times a day, from morning wear, to afternoon clothes, to a fancy get-up for dinner. For guests, the resorts offered the latest in newfangled entertainment.[12] In 1928, the Agua Caliente Springs Hotel and the French Cottage at El Verano, both in the Sonoma Valley, announced they had each installed a single "radio set" that would allow summer guests to hear up-to-date entertainment and dance music. One resort promised the radios would be tuned in to the Democratic convention at Houston, Texas, where Al Smith, thought to be soft on Prohibition, was expected to be nominated.[13]

Dry proponents in Washington were still declaring that Prohibition was a success that was wiping out the supposed national drunkenness epidemic, but their assertions would have been news to Sheriff Douglas Bills of Sonoma County. County authorities, beleaguered by the constant need to transport drunks (some of them violent) from Guerneville to the county seat 20 miles away for booking, opened a branch office in the Russian River resort town, reported the *Sonoma Index-Tribune*. A huge steel tank acquired from a local phenol plant was renovated to contain a number of cells, a sanitary convenience, and barred doors and windows. There were scores of arrests for drunkenness during summer months— most of them made at dance halls, where illicit cocktails were easy to come by.[14] Old-timers recall a great deal of drinking in parked cars; people would dance, then head out to their cars for a tipple or two from their private flasks, and then pop back into the dance hall for a few more rounds on the dance floor.

In June 1928, Sheriff Bills announced he was going to enforce Prohibition laws more strictly, in the hope of drying up some of the tidal waves of booze that washed through Sonoma each summer.

Bills's efforts began aggressively. At one Sonoma Valley resort, one evening agents suddenly and silently walked in, marched across a room, and boldly plucked a glass of whiskey directly from a guest's hands. The Prohibition agents told the guest the glasses would be used as evidence against him as well as against the resort's proprietor. A newspaper predicted that if Sheriff Bills and federal agents continued their program of enforcement, "the summer colonies, both here [surrounding Sonoma], and along the Russian river will be as dry as the Sahara desert before long."[15]

There was still fun to be had in Napa and Sonoma even though it had been a bleak few years because the juice-grape market—the one reliable source of income for so many grape growers—had imploded after a surfeit of grapes had devastated their best markets. In September 1928, the editor of the *California Grape Grower*, Horatio F. Stoll, reiterated his fierce argument that it was the raisin growers of California who had ruined the wine-juice market. In a front page story in the *Grower*, headlined "Raisin Growers Bring Disaster to Grape Industry," he stated his case. Raisin growers were sending their fresh grapes to market as juice grapes—Muscats, Thompson Seedless, and Malaga—instead of turning them into raisins, he said, and the oversupply was making prices for everyone crash and burn. The raisin-grape growers, Stoll thundered, had started their plotting as far back as 1918, when they began doing "all they could to help bring about Prohibition and wipe out the juice grape vineyardists."

The raisin grape growers' slogan was, said Stoll, "Down with the destructive juice grapes and three cheers for the good little raisin grapes." They wanted the wineries closed, and "they backed their campaign to wipe out the juice grape vineyards with their votes."

When a frantic public instead began buying up juice grapes, raisin growers climbed on the juice-grape bandwagon, added Stoll, and started to ship great quantities of grapes east to be turned into wine. Stoll asserted this amounted to a civil war among the vineyards, with the former raisin growers of the Central Valley pitted against the traditional wine interests of the coast.

Naturally, said Stoll, "the wine and table grape growers of California cannot be blamed for being peeved at these dry raisin grape growers for shipping their grapes in fresh form, instead of drying them." Carloads of those grapes flooded the market. To add further to the anger of northern California's wine juice grape growers, the raisin growers were even accused of monopolizing the refrigerator cars with their fresh grape shipments, so that wine juice growers were left with rotting products on their hands.

There was even resentment toward the raisin itself, which as everyone knew had been used in millions of homes in the manufacture of all kinds of alcoholic home-brew concoctions. New Orleans, which had been such a strong wine consumer before Prohibition, was now making wine from raisins, said Stoll, using about 125,000 25-pound boxes each year, all of which could make the equivalent of 750,000 gallons of wine, though to make it attractive to a wine drinker they had to color it red with aniline dye.[16]

With the markets in such dire straits, Napa and Sonoma worried about every indication that a winery or vineyard might be in trouble and jobs, even vineyards, lost.

Sam Sebastiani operated a large winery and canning operations in Sonoma. He was an extremely popular and considerate town booster and many jobs in the area were dependent on him. In March 1928, Sebastiani and Mike Gallo of Oakland had bought the Woodbridge Vineyard, putting down a deposit for the

$60,000 operation, said the *Sonoma Index-Tribune,* which included the plant and 650,000 gallons of wine.[17] Subsequently, Sebastiani bought out Gallo and had a trusted employee, E. Castagnasso, looking after the plant where wines were blended for the sacramental and medicinal trade. But while the partnership was still in effect, a quantity of wine was moved to Oakland, which naturally attracted the attention of Prohibition lawmen.

Ownership of the wine was traced to the two partners immediately. The *Sonoma Index-Tribune* pronounced Mike Gallo an "unsavory" character, identifying him as the "East Bay liquor king." He had also done time in San Quentin in 1913, the newspaper alleged, as a bunko artist. A warrant was sworn out, and Sebastiani surrendered immediately, to be released on bail.

Sebastiani did not appear unduly worried about the arrest, stating that the facts would clear him.[18] But his arrest unsettled the city of Sonoma. When Prohibition had arrived, the local newspaper reported, Sebastiani's reputation as a responsible businessman had helped him win permits to make sacramental and medicinal wines which had been a great stimulus for the local economy. The community rejoiced when the *Sonoma Index-Tribune* followed up on the story in November 1928, heralding the fact that federal officers had exonerated Mr. Sebastiani completely of all criminal activity.[19] The newspaper offered no further explanation of the officers actions; whatever they were, the town heaved a sigh of relief.

It was hard for the two wine counties to comprehend that things might get even worse than they were, but the harvest of 1928 was a catastrophe. "Nothing like the drop in prices this year has been witnessed since the advent of prohibition in 1920," lamented Stoll to the *California Grape Grower.* So many grapes, so little return. It had been a tough summer for growers: early heat, hot winds, mildew, mould, and straggly bunches. Wine grapes were sold at ruinous prices, and this time there were no fingers to point at raisin growers or fussy customers. Even poor quality was no longer to blame for falling prices; consumers just were not in the market for wine grapes. The nation's economy was limping along; the structural failures that would lead to the stock market crash a year later were beginning to make themselves felt. Demand had vanished: nobody wanted grapes.

When the season had opened, it appeared—worryingly—that eastern householders still had lots of wine on hand. Low prices at the end of last year, perhaps because of the raisin-growers who were now sending juice grapes to market, had encouraged sales and left people with more wine than usual. Unemployment had dampened the purchasing ability in the nation's cities where the "foreign" population, the most loyal wine-grape purchasers, lived. Grape shippers and grape growers were having difficulty collecting from dealers who could not collect from customers living in tough times. And because of the worrying state of the economy, that year no one wanted to extend credit.[20]

The result of grape overproduction was evident not only at urban grape markets but also in the vineyards. Vines hung heavy with grapes that would never be picked; the cost of picking them outweighed their sale price. Anyone who wanted to buy grapes could get them at bargain prices. A prominent winery in Sonoma with medicinal and sacramental wine licenses had bought hundreds of tons of grapes at only $4 a ton, thanks to the winery's ability to parlay its size and federal licenses into a lucrative deal.[21]

Under the circumstances, Napa and Sonoma residents watched the run-up to the 1928 presidential election avidly and weighed the two candidates carefully. Republican Herbert Hoover was a wealthy Californian with a long history of public service in the United States and abroad. He had been secretary of commerce in the Coolidge administration. Californians were enthusiastic about the idea of a homegrown president, and many admired the speech he gave accepting the Republican nomination. Hoover spoke at length about supporting agriculture and his plans for the creation of a Federal Farm Board. His proposals were near to the hearts of many voters in the state, as agriculture was of tremendous importance to all of California. However, northern Californians who knew that Hoover believed in the vigorous observance and enforcement of Prohibition hesitated to endorse the favorite son.

Hoover's Democratic opponent, New York governor Alfred E. Smith, appeared to be an ideal candidate for Wet Californians. He was the first Roman Catholic to be nominated for president by a major party, something that appealed to the many Italians in the wine industry. He was a governor of a state whose heart was Wet, a soul mate to California, which had never had a Wet majority in any election. But he played down Prohibition in his campaign and did not bring it up unless pressed; the Democratic platform allowed that the party believed in enforcing the law.

Rudolph Spreckels, owner of a fine estate in the Sonoma Valley, a banker and one of California's most prominent businessmen, endorsed Smith, explaining his position in a letter to the Democratic national chairman: "The only important conflict of opinion between Governor Smith and Herbert Hoover, so far developed, is in regard to prohibition. . . . A vote for Hoover would be a vote for murders, gang wars, the continued poisoning of alcohol, hypocrisy and debauching of youth."[22]

Despite these words in the *Sonoma Index-Tribune,* California voted 64 percent for Hoover, 34 percent for Smith. The rest of the country agreed with California, and Hoover won the presidency by a landslide.

The winemakers headed into the year of 1929 with dire foreboding. They worried that the wine industry and the criminal element associated with it might be forced into more reckless efforts to survive what they thought would be tough years to come as Prohibition continued—it was hard to keep hopes up that it would end.

Crime continued on at its roaring pace everywhere: scary when it was close to towns and still equally worrisome when farther out in the loneliest reaches of the wine counties. Though many understood why crime was rampant and could commiserate somewhat with locals who fell foul of the law, it was more difficult to sympathize with the many city criminals who were haunting Sonoma and Napa roads. They, too, loved to use the roads and byways of the two wine counties just as cunningly as those who lived by them, and locals hated them drawing official attention to their remote corner of the state where so many clandestine activities often went unnoticed.

Everyone knew that at night, the twisting narrow roads that zigzag through dense redwood forests on Sonoma County's western edge were perfect for transporting illicit liquor whoever you were. This area was considered a safe haven, tucked away in dark green timberland from the snooping eyes of Prohibition enforcement agents, and was much appreciated by locals headed to town with illegal barrels of wine or cans of brandy. These secluded roads, whose hidden turnoffs and secret detours could be used to elude the law were prized by San Francisco gangsters, who regularly used them when meeting boats that landed liquor on Sonoma's lonely Pacific beaches. Many millions of dollars' worth of liquor arrived in California from Mexico and Canada through that back door to the state. A fleet of liquor ships regularly plied the state's spectacular but dangerously fog-shrouded coastline with its endless rough surf and occasional but terrifying giant rogue waves that locals knew to watch out for. Ships could carry 40,000 to 70,000 cases of liquor, transferring their bounty to small boats that brought it ashore, 200 to 2,000 cases at a time.[23]

In March 1929, Sonoma County Sheriff Douglas Bills—the same industrious officer who was trying to keep the lid on his county's resorts—along with a deputy acting on a tip went in search of a convoy of gangsters they believed had arranged to pick up liquor worth $12,000 on a beach and transport it to San Francisco on the secluded county byways. The gang consisted of Joe "Deep Hole" Ferris, a one-time Alaska miner; Freddie "Bibleback" Marina, a San Francisco underworld character; and Frank Finney, a punch-happy ex-boxer, along with two other gangsters named Frank Willson and James Sanchez. They were reputed to be part of one the largest bootlegging syndicates on the West Coast. The cargo of liquor they were after was to be dropped in a few relays from a large ship onto a speedboat and ferried to a remote spot near Black Point Beach, located near today's up-market Sea Ranch Lodge. The smaller vessel was able to maneuver close enough to shore that a rope could be pulled out through the surf and the cases of liquor dragged onto the beach. The boys would then drive it to the city along the tiny, quiet roads that wound alongside the Russian River.

Anyone who has ever walked along the precarious cliffs of northern California knows well the raging surf and huge rollers that pound below on that rocky coast day and night; the bootlegging work must have been dangerous and very uncomfortable in the dark and the wind and the salty wet sea spray.

The gang, whose convoy consisted of both a truck and car, must have identified a rare spot where the waves would not have crushed the cargo against rocks. One of the two vehicles, a rope tied to its back end, dragged the cases of liquor up across a beach. Then they were stowed in the truck and the trip back to San Francisco was begun. However, soon after the gangsters passed over the little bridge at the tiny enclave of Monte Rio, the two police officers intercepted the truck, arresting and handcuffing the driver and his associate. Minutes later the car containing the other three gangsters raced around the corner and was stopped. This time the arrest was not so simple; the gangsters in the car brandished a submachine gun. Sheriff Bills had little alternative but to use his two captives as a human shield, marching them in front of him as he approached the heavily armed car.

"I'm pretty sure that submachine gun would have been turned on us if we had not taken the precaution to make [the gangsters] stand in front of us," Bills declared after the capture.[24]

When the case went to court, the defense mounted an impassioned argument that there was no evidence to tie the truck and the car together—which would have left the truck crew to face the music alone. However, the rope used on the beach had been found in the sedan, wet and covered in sand—and it had traces of the green paint from the truck on it. The judge sentenced the gangsters each to 15 months in jail and a $600 fine: a tough sentence.[25]

It was neither the first nor the last time the folk of Napa and Sonoma would hear about organized crime making use of their lonely roads to engage in the illegal liquor trade. The two counties' long tradition of "live and let live" made them attractive for business, both legal and illegal. Members of the illicit liquor trades in San Francisco were reassured by the fact that illegal wine made by the locals in the two counties was safely transported into the city day and night. They felt a strange comfort in a place where such operations were part of a regular day's work. They knew that if they kept their heads down when doing business, chances were that the locals—themselves often guilty of illegal dealings, too—would have little reason to turn them in. The motto in the two counties since Prohibition started had been "See no evil," a laissez-faire attitude that often extended to local law enforcement authorities as well.

Harry Bosworth today runs a Geyserville general store that looks, inside and out, much as it did in 1908, when his paternal grandfather opened it. Bosworth remembers that this carefree attitude allowed his maternal grandparents, German immigrants who arrived at the turn of the twentieth century and farmed in the Dry Creek Valley, to continue with their prosperous business that, thanks to Prohibition, was no longer respectable. The couple sold wine to German immigrants "who came up regularly from San Francisco in a motorcade complete with a policeman" to lead the procession. The customers would buy the couple's wine and brandy to take home. While they were in Geyserville, Bosworth's grandmother would fix a meal for them and also serve wine and brandy. It made for a festive day out for the visitors and a good source of income for the couple. During Prohibition, the couple had to keep their supply of wine and brandy under a false floor in the chicken house. "The sheriff let it happen with no problem," said Bosworth. As in most small towns in the wine valleys, the local authorities were as lax as they could be and still keep their jobs. And why not? Most of them were neighbors of winemakers and bootleggers; in many cases, they were related as well. And as for the police officer who led that procession to and from the city, he must have been paid off sufficiently in wine, brandy, or cash to have made it a worthwhile jaunt out of the city.[26]

Crime syndicates knew well that the wine counties were a good place to do business. Harvey Rose, of Geyserville, had an uncle who was in charge of a cooperative of local wine producers. "Everybody had put their wine together because they didn't think Prohibition would last," Rose explained. The uncle stored the wine in good condition for his neighbors; if the law ever changed, it would be ready for selling. Somehow, a bootleggers' syndicate found out about the huge cache of wine and offered Rose's uncle $1 million if he and his family would go away somewhere for a year or so. The syndicate would then make arrangements to get rid of the wine. Rose's uncle did not fancy getting involved with an illegal and dangerous offer like that, and eventually the wine grew old and soured; it was sold to a vinegar outfit in San Jose. "He didn't get anything for it, really, and eventually the bank took over the property where the wine had been stored," Rose recalled.[27]

Prohibition combined with the difficulties of the early years of the Depression made life more and more difficult, for adults as well as for children.

Mary Decia, née Perotti, was five years old when Prohibition began and in her teens when the Depression started to make its mark on Wine Country. Yet she does not remember desperate times. Her family worked hard, they had few, if any, luxuries, but neither did anyone else, she says, so there was no shame, for instance, in folks knowing you went down to the creek to wash.

For most of her younger years, Mary recounted in a 2008 interview, she lived with her aunt and uncle and five cousins on a grape and prune ranch in Dry Creek Valley, site of today's magnificent Ferrari-Carano winery with its colonnades and pillars and reflecting pools amid lavish gardens. Mary's mother had died in San Francisco "of flu or childbirth, I don't know which," when Mary was 40 days old. Her aunt and uncle, August and Theresa Perotti, took her in immediately. "My aunt already had a baby—he was nine months old and she took him off the breast to feed me. She was an angel." Later, when Mary's father remarried and lost his second wife to tuberculosis, Theresa welcomed Mary's stepsister into her family as well.

During Prohibition, the big Italian family lived on the land in humble surroundings. On Saturdays in the summer months, Perotti remembered with a smile, her aunt would gather towels and bars of soap and all would go down to Dry Creek for a weekly bath. "We'd have to find a 'hole' cause [the creek] ran low by midsummer," she explained, remembering the trickle that was sometimes all that remained by August. In the winter, a big tub was brought into the house and the kids took turns washing in the same hot water. "We preferred summer and the creek." It was easier to send the kids down to the creek in the long months of summer than heat water on the stove to fill a metal bath tub. With eight people in the house and a bath with no hook-up to a tap, bathing in the creek seemed like its own especial luxury in the long hot afternoons of a childhood in Wine Country.

"We never wore shoes all summer," Mary remembered. "We didn't know what a pair of shoes was in the summer." Like every other ranch family, Mary remembers, they grew all their own food and kept chickens, a rooster, rabbits, and two hogs. "It was my duty to milk the goat."

"We used to grow a lot of garlic and preserve it for the winter. When the chickens were laying heavily, we packed the eggs in water glass, a preservative, and put them in the cellar—they'd last all winter. At Christmas we'd hang our socks—my uncle's old wool socks, not some fancy Christmas stocking like today—behind the stove and if we got an orange and some walnuts, well! We couldn't wait till the morning to get that orange and those walnuts."

Theresa made all the kids' underclothes from flour sacks—underpants for the boys and slips for the girls. Were they comfortable? Mary Decia laughs. "We didn't know any better, they were just fine."

Her uncle had planted prunes on his land to help him survive Prohibition. "We all had to pick those prunes each year. We hated it. It was awful. You picked the prunes that fall to the ground. Trees were shaken with a big pole and then more prunes fell to the ground. Some of them were split and were sticky. Wasps were everywhere."

The family would dip the prunes in lye and hot water, then lay them out on huge trays in the sun to dry before they were sent to the packinghouse. "My uncle had an entire field set aside for that," she explained. "If it rained, we had to run out and gather up all the trays and stack them together. And I remember it always did rain once each summer."

August Perotti was not only a prune farmer, he was a bootlegger, too. And the fruit trays were useful not just for fruit drying. "Sometimes my uncle hid wine he had made under piles of old trays in his barn," Mary Decia recalls. She remembers many visits from the "Pro-his"—she still used the old name for Prohibition agents. "They used to come around real regularly and rip everything apart."

Her uncle also sold wine grapes; in her mind's eye, she can still see them leaving town on a railcar. And she remembers her aunt and uncle enjoying a glass of wine with every meal. "Wine was on the table all the time." The secret to survival through those days? "They didn't make much money but whatever they had, they retained."[28]

While many families like the Perottis clung to their land, others decided the struggle was not worth it. In Sonoma's Alexander Valley, vineyards changed hands as folk just plain gave up, says William F. Heintz in his book, *Grapes and Wine in California's Alexander Valley: A History.* When Tom Meek sold his ranch in 1921, he "was one of the first to throw up his hands," says Heintz. The "old Bud Cake ranch was sold in 1923," then the Cottle family ranch went, too; and the Clarence Hall family ranch was sold in 1924 after 70 years in the same family.[29]

Decades later, Luke Tedeschi remembered in a 2000 interview with Jim Myers for the *Russian River Recorder* what it was like in Wine Country during the Depression: "If you had a twenty-dollar bill you were rich! We were more self-sufficient. You didn't need to go to the store, because there wasn't any money. You tried to raise everything at home.

"Mother was a good cook," he remembered, "raviolis, lasagnes. She didn't have recipes. She knew how to make a meal with hardly nothin'. Go out in the garden, pick up a thing here, a thing there, make a big meal, and it was good. We didn't waste anything. If we killed a pig, we used everything but the squeal."[30]

Luckily the hills and rivers of Wine Country were still rich in those days: venison, ducks, rabbits, robins, quail, steelhead—so many critters that did not cost a cent could make a tasty stew or a sauce for pasta, and the fish were always a welcome treat.

But hunting and fishing held its own challenges. While wrestling abalone off the rocks at Bodega Bay, a popular pastime on California's Pacific coast, the pastor of a church in Santa Rosa was grabbed by four tentacles of an octopus. He could not break free, and one of his fishing party had to cut the octopus off him with a hunting knife. When it was dragged onshore, the octopus measured eight feet from tip to tip.[31] Remmel Griffith, a member of a hunting party in Napa, ran across a bear on Pine Mountain. It weighed 200 pounds and had badly hurt a dog before Griffith took it down. He was delighted he was going to be dining on bear steaks for a long time. Griffith's hunting party also bagged three ducks that same day.[32] Less traumatic was the fishing jaunt of a local fire chief, who hooked his limit of trout in a stream north of Cloverdale, including a 17-incher.[33]

Besides hunting and fishing to put food on the table, running a still was a financial comfort in these dark days. Stills were everywhere in the two wine counties. "If you had a barn," Lou Foppiano recalled, "you had a still."[34] But not everyone made brandy or grappa to sell. Some neighbors would share a small still between them, using it only from time to time to distill wine for their own use. Recipes were not needed; everyone knew how to turn wine into something stronger.

But others made thousands of gallons of distilled liquors for markets in San Francisco and beyond—and profited greatly. Some made grappa from wine; those who had no wine, or had run out of it during Prohibition, made jackass, a high-proof alcohol, with sugar.

As a teenager, Foppiano was acquainted with all the stills around his family's vineyard, delivering supplies to his neighbors each night. His typical routine was to pick up a truckload of sugar from a wholesaler in Santa Rosa in the afternoon. Then, after having dinner and sleeping till 3 A.M., he would deliver the sugar, earning $15 a night.

"They made alcohol just about any place in these hills. I knew of seven or eight stills. You needed water, a good supply of running water, of course. They'd make it and put it in five-gallon cans, and then they'd sell it to dealers who knew them or they'd take it into the city. They all made money. A lot of money," he added. They would "put" a little oak into it—by letting it rest in oak barrels—or add caramel to it to make it look a little more like whiskey.

It was hardly a dangerous business, said Foppiano, and most stills kept operating despite occasional arrests. "Oh, the Internal Revenue did capture stills. But if you paid the sheriff or somebody who knew when they were coming, he'd call the guys at the still, or have someone go round to tell them and they'd clean that place up in four or five hours and move out. The Revenue guys would go in, and there was nothing there. Every once in a while they'd get someone."[35]

If locals were going to bootleg, brandy made from wine and jackass made from sugar were eminently marketable. It was much easier and safer to hide a gallon of liquor in a truck or car on its way to San Francisco than to try to move a bigger number of five-gallon jugs full of wine.

Although winemakers had plenty of wine to turn into brandy in their hidden stills, making jackass involved buying lots of sugar. By 2008, Walter Murray, born the day before Christmas in 1912, had lived for 92 years in the comfortable Healdsburg house his parents built. His mother came to town in 1900 in a covered wagon from Wyoming. He remembers cowboys and their dogs driving cattle down the streets of Healdsburg on their way to the railroad depot. Cattle were still as important to Sonoma County's economy as grapes in those early years of the twentieth century.

Murray, who later owned a thriving local laundry business, began work when he was 14. During Prohibition, he helped to ship fruit from a packinghouse next to the railroad tracks. Carloads of wine grapes were sent out; sugar for the stills came in.

"We loaded grapes nine hours a day," said Murray in an interview in 2008, "and then we went home at 6 P.M. and had our dinner. Then at 7 P.M. we went back to work. The trains would be switched on the track and would bring in a carload of sugar. Sometimes three carloads." The sugar deliveries were perfectly legal. It was the still operations they were being sent to which were not.

"I think [the sugar] was made of beets," says Murray. "It was packed in 100-pound sacks, 600 sacks to a car. There was four of us working unloading anywhere from one to three carloads a night. There was a room in the back of the packing-house building: two of us would load sacks onto a two-wheeled cart, five or six sacks to a cart, and we would pile up the sugar in the storeroom."

Townspeople did not ask questions—not even Healdsburg's night watchman, who passed by on foot some nights. After loading the building with sugar sacks, the boys would lock up and go home. The next day, Murray said, "we'd come to work at 8 A.M. and there would not be a sack of sugar anywhere in that warehouse."[36]

They had all been spirited away during the night to the hills and vales around town.

The math is astounding. Each railroad car held 60,000 pounds of sugar, and local stills could consume all of it—or even three times that amount—in a single night. And Healdsburg was just one very small railroad station among many others. A little general store at Asti, a few miles north, is said to have sold more sugar than any other general store in the country during Prohibition—and that store was serviced by an entirely different railroad depot from the one at which Murray labored.

No wonder authorities and the Drys complained bitterly that there was a river of booze flooding into San Francisco from the wine counties.

As markets got tougher and tougher to San Francisco, the wine industry watched carefully to see if President Hoover would make good on his election promise of aid to agriculture.

In the summer of 1929, he did so when he signed into law a massive Farm Relief bill that had passed both houses of Congress. The Agricultural Marketing Act of June 1929 created a Federal Farm Board that would help establish farming cooperatives and have the power to sell or dispose of surplus crops. Grape growers recognized the need to stabilize prices and, most important, to manage surplus grapes. The new cooperative Grape Control Board would organize the production and dispensation of 85 percent of California's two million tons of annual grape production. Each fresh-grape grower would pay $1.50 to the industry's coffers for each ton of grapes he produced. This would provide an estimated $2,550,000 fund each year to take care of the industry's 300,000-ton annual surplus, which was to be disposed of as waste and by-products.[37] It was hoped that this would reduce the incentive each season to flood markets with grapes that would rot unsold and bring prices down for everyone.

By fall 1929, grape ranches were finally addressing the overplanting of grapes, which had caused the devastating glut of grapes on the market. As well, the grape growers pulled back at harvest time. This year's harvest would be the smallest since 1924. At the same time, Dr. James Maurice Doran, the latest commissioner of the Federal Prohibition Bureau based in Washington, decided it was time to pay a visit to the two wine counties.

Doran was already infamous for his comment that his department really deserved a $300-million annual budget if it was to make Prohibition work as smoothly as it should—that sum would have been more than 20 times its usual appropriation. His wife published the *Book of Juices* containing suggestions for nonalcoholic holiday beverages, noted *Time* magazine. The instructions for one recipe, served to a group of Women's Christian Temperence Union (WCTU) members, who rated it highly included: "Take a pound of seedless grapes chopped very fine and a quart of grape juice. Stir thoroughly and serve very cold."[38] Few winemakers would have traded an entire barrel of that for a glass of good Napa Cabernet.

Now Doran earned fresh ridicule in the wine counties by pronouncing his administration a success and stating proudly that his inspection of California showed that the state was effectively Dry. "That will be good news to bootleggers," said the *Sonoma Index-Tribune*.

"If California is dry, we are here to say that the Pacific Ocean must be dry and the Mojave Desert a lake," the paper scoffed in the middle of September 1929, asking why Uncle Sam continued to delude itself into believing that Prohibition had achieved its goals. Yes, the wine industry was by now beyond bitter humor. The only beneficiaries of Prohibition, the paper charged, were illicit liquor dealers who were "rolling in wealth," whereas the government had forsaken tax revenues it might otherwise have collected from a legal liquor industry.

"While the streets of America run with liquor and real crime is rampant," the newspaper continued, "mere boys continue to be shot down by dry agents who 'stumble' and accidentally kill suspected violators of this new, heinous crime of possessing a little liquor. An ignoble experiment, past the experimental stage and willfully indulged and continued by this country, is a blot on our national honor."[39]

October 1929 brought a perfect storm across the market, for grapes and everything else. A truck driver's strike halted New York markets for several days and hammered sales. The Jewish High Holy Days—on October 5 and October 14—always reduced sales in New York and coincided with the strike, further depressing sales.

Consumers were extremely slow to buy grapes and they been worried about rumor from Washington that the right to make 200 gallons of home brew had been canceled. The situation had not been officially clarified by the government enough to reassure consumers who were now hesitant to invest money into wine grapes. Why bother, they thought, if they would then find that the wine they would make could not be stored in their homes, or kept anywhere else as a matter of fact, because moving wine would require special permits—almost impossible for private citizens to obtain. In order to comfort consumers with the sure knowledge that grapes were still a good investment for the future, the managing director of the California Vineyardists' Association, Donald Conn, traveled to Chicago and New York and other markets to reassure consumers and sales people alike that the right to do this continued. He spoke to editors of both American and foreign newspapers to make sure the message was loud and clear. Somehow he was also able to inveigle a representative of the Federal Prohibition Bureau to speak at most of the large markets: a reassuring move in the marketplace.

The *California Grape Grower*, by now completely perplexed as to how to explain the worsening market conditions, wondered whether wine sales had been damaged when Italian construction workers, idled by a downturn in housing starts on the East Coast, stopped buying wine.[40] If Italian Americans were not buying grapes few others would be buying either.

Then came October 24, 1929, Black Thursday. The Depression was starting to take the heart out of the two counties.

November 1929 was a particularly cruel time for a proprietor of one famous Sonoma Valley resort to be duped by government agents. He had been approached by two sporting types, who had shown him some local references, including one from a well-known winemaker, and he served them a fine dinner including wine. The next day four men turned up with the same references and enjoyed yet another fine meal. Upon finishing the dinner, they abruptly revealed themselves as Prohibition agents and arrested the proprietor. One observer was amazed at the nerve of agents who would accept food and then bite the hand that gave it: "Such a business," the observer commented, "I'd rather wash bottles any day than do that kind of dirty work."[41]

The nation's unemployment rates continued to rise to unheard-of heights and farm prices were tumbling. But if you had to live anywhere during a depression, the countryside of Napa and Sonoma—which could provide foodstuffs for its inhabitants year round—was a healthier, safer choice than any city. If you wander today through the peaceful little Olive Hill graveyard tucked into a pretty hillside under huge oak trees near Geyserville, where so many winemakers rest in their final sleep, you will see few children buried during that period, a testament to the area's plentiful food and clean water.

But still the wineries continued to close.

In 1920, when Prohibition began, there were 700 wineries in California, 256 in Sonoma, and 120 in Napa. Two years after Prohibition started, 6 had closed down. But soon thereafter, the numbers started to tumble precipitously as many wineries stopped production, their owners completely bewildered about what to do about the wine in their tanks. It was often the greatest asset they had. By the beginning of the 1930s, it was gut-wrenching for winemakers to consider how so much of it had already spoiled or had been destroyed by Prohibition agents. By that time, probably fewer than 160 wineries were operating in the entire state.[42]

The cost of the loss of all that wine, in capital, in hard work, in financial security, was astronomical. Prohibition was a national shame. As of this writing, many decades later, winery people still speak of it with bitterness.

The loss was palpable each year at certain times in the wine cycle. Long gone was that heady moment of excitement each fall called "crush." Once crush meant weeks of real excitement. Across the valleys, you could hear first wagons, then trucks, rolling across vineyards and country lanes at all hours bringing the crop home. Or as grapes headed to a winery across the valley, you could feel the rumble of those heavy-laden vehicles trundling endlessly up and down the Redwood and Napa highways. You would hear the shouting and hollering as baskets were turned out and the fruit fell into the crushers. All day long voices called out to inquire who was picking already, who was crushing, who had filled their tanks, who had waited too long, who had gone too early.

As soon as the grapes were crushed, you would hear a communal wheeze of relief. People walked slower, grinned more: The wine folk knew again that they had beaten the odds, gone to the edge and made the right calls, taken the chances they had to take each year and walked away victorious. Of course, there were many more challenges before the wine was even safer and settled in its barrels for a long rest, when winemakers could truly sigh with relief. But getting through crush was one great and exciting accomplishment. It was like a grand opera opening night every night for weeks.

By now, crush was so diminished that the sound of it was just a quiet murmur hardly audible above the birds and the crickets. The once-heady aroma of grape pulp—less like the smell of grapes and more like the smell of wine the moment it was pressed—that pervaded everything at that time of year was now a mere hint, something vaguely fruity in the wind.

Missing crush was like losing critical heartbeats in the rhythm of a community.

That wineries continued to close down was an economic tragedy, but not all was lost, as often the vineyards continued to operate. Even if a winery's door had been padlocked, its owners could well be doing something else with the land: selling fresh-juice grapes, planting prunes or fruit trees on some proportion of vineyard land to make sure a small income was coming in. And if the revenue turned out to be just enough to pay the taxes, that alone would have been heartily welcomed. Some wine tanks in the wine counties were now standing empty, dried-up hollow ghosts; others were kept full of water so the redwood they were made of would not shrink and if Prohibition should ever end and the Eighteenth Amendment was repealed, they would be ready as soon as needed.

Chapter Nine

The Reign of the Bludgeon and of Force

Grape growers were hesitant but hopeful that the Wicker-sham Commission, President Hoover's inquiry into the state of the country's law enforcement, might bring them good news. Ever since Hoover had appointed George Woodward Wickersham, former Attorney General of the United States, to head what was more formally called the National Commission on Law Observance and Enforcement, in May 1929, the wine folk of Napa and Sonoma had hoped against hope that something good might come of it. There had been rumors for some months that the commission might recommend the nation start some prelimi-nary discussions to end Prohibition, the repeal of the Eighteenth Amendment.[1] But a preliminary report in spring of 1930 offered nothing fresh. President Hoover was merely moved to send Congress some vapid recommendations for consider-ation: that the federal courts should be reorganized to eliminate congestion and that the nation should focus more on the detection and prosecution of Prohibi-tion violators.

The wine folk were not shocked at how anodyne these suggestions were. Hoover had done little to help them so far.

However, in early February 1930, both Wets and Drys across the country were surprised to hear that the House Judiciary Committee would allow the discussion of some possible initiatives that might lead to repeal, the end of Prohibition, or to some modification of Prohibition. The chairman of the committee, Representative George S. Graham of Pennsylvania, said *TIME* magazine, had decided to give the floor to some Wet ideas after anti-Prohibitionists said they planned to hold their own mock, and very public, hearing if Graham would not allow them to participate in discussions. Though there was a huge majority of Drys in his committee, and he would have known how unpopular any discussion of Wet perspective would have been to them, it appeared from Graham's comments that he thought it might be time to consider that changes were needed to the country's Dry laws.

Graham stunned his colleagues on Capitol Hill when he said:

> I wouldn't want to restore the old condition but I do believe we could frame and fashion a new system of control that would not be Prohibition and would make the law enforceable and practical. What a sorry state this country is in today! Revenues have fallen off. Crimes have multiplied. We are under the reign of the bludgeon and of force. The very church, its bishops and ministers, cheer all sorts of pain and shootings, it applauds force. Have we lost the right of conscience?[2]

Graham was right, force still held sway in Wine Country: It had become the terrible lingua franca between citizens and enforcements agents that now ran like a toxin throughout every strata of society in Napa and Sonoma.

In early January 1930, Robert D. Freeman, a federal Prohibition agent, along with a fellow agent, Henry Jones, set off to the home of Mr. and Mrs. John South, well-off ranchers living in the tiny enclave of Yountville, reported the *St. Helena Star*. Freeman and his colleague had in their possession, said the local district attorney, a search warrant that charged the couple with selling liquor. The two agents arrived in Yountville at around noon. When they rang the doorbell at the South home, Mr. South opened the door. The agents were shown into the house, which they proceeded to search for evidence. They found a bottle of port, a bottle of claret, two pints of brandy, and a bottle of bitters. When Jones put the bottles on the table and went into another room to search further, Mr. South rushed to the sink, the agents said, and started to pour the liquid from one of the bottles down the sink. Agent Freeman ran to Mr. South and they started wrestling for the bottle. Mr. South somehow reached for a gun from a low shelf and shot Freeman in the right arm and chest. Freeman was seriously wounded by the buckshot. Freeman's colleague ran to help him. Suddenly Mrs. South entered the fray holding a shotgun. She screamed to the agents that if they hit her husband, she would shoot them.

Mr. and Mrs. South were charged with assaulting a federal agent and unlawful possession of alcohol, and were taken from their very comfortable family home to Sacramento to appear before the federal court.[3]

Their bail had been enormous: $40,000 for each of them. The federal court charged that it was exorbitant. Eventually Mr. South's bail was reduced to $10,000, Mrs. South's, to $3,000. The couple was charged with shooting and wounding Freeman. However, they both swore they had no idea that the men were Prohibition agents. They thought violent criminals in search of liquor had invaded their home. And they declared, in their defense, that they had not been shown a search warrant and that at no time had the officers identified themselves.[4]

Crime grew darker and more frightening to locals as crime syndicates and gangsters, jubilant with the success they had enjoyed so far with bootlegging, took more and more advantage of the lonely wooded hills in Wine Country, so convenient to their best market, San Francisco, with its seemingly bottomless yearning for booze.

In April, the two wine counties are perhaps at their loveliest. Evening walks are perfumed with the smell of orange and lemon blossoms, and the first roses of the summer add their perfume to the air as they tumble over picket fences and climb up the walls and fences of family farms. Lilacs, white and mauve, wave in the warm spring breezes. Everyone is planting vegetable gardens. Fruit trees are still in blossom: pears, persimmons, plums, cherries: the little towns dotted throughout the hills and valleys look like they have been decorated with pink and white spun candy. And orchards appear to be frothed with millions of yards of delicate white lace. Though evenings are still cool, the afternoons are warm.

It was on one such lovely, gentle April afternoon that Prohibition officers crept up through the pines and waving grass and the sound of crickets to a massive still some eight miles northwest of Napa city. One Napa resident and nine others from Oakland, some miles to the south, operated it: the sure sign of a syndicate. The still was capable of producing 50 gallons of alcohol daily. All 10 men were arrested, and bail of $2,500 was set for each of them, reported the local newspapers. Upon investigating the backgrounds of the accused, police declared that one of them was Joseph Gallia, probably the man who had wrecked a wine-laden roadster in northern Napa the previous year and disappeared; his colleague in crime that day, Faustino Abate, was killed in the accident and lay dead in the car as Gallia took off into hiding.[5] It was an illustration to local inhabitants of how ruthless the criminals were who were now doing business all around them.

People worried about being out late or in remote places, fearing even chance contact with men of this sort.

Two months later, Sheriff J. P. Steckter received a tip about a still operating in the hills near the Napa–Sonoma county line. He put together a team with W. Gaffney and two deputies, and they headed some lonely miles up some rough and rarely traveled trail. As the officers approached the suspect ranch, they came up against a heavily padlocked gate. "A guard armed with a double-barreled shotgun was on duty." He was surprised, immediately taken into custody, and handcuffed when he attempted to resist arrest, reported the *St. Helena Star.*

Suddenly the police officers saw two other men race from the ranch house and dive headlong into the dry brush. The officers leapt after them, searching for any trace of their passage, to no avail. Eventually the officers said the duo must have bolted over the crest of a hill to an automobile concealed for emergencies. The still they left behind could pump out 250 gallons of alcohol a day using 40,000 pounds of sugar.[6]

These well-organized operations had a constant supply of ingredients brought up through the hills. In the dead of night, a constant supply of booze headed back down to points south.

Later in the summer, the grape growers were warned of more trouble. California's grape industry was facing collapse. The Depression, it was said, had reduced buying power throughout the country, and the growers were to expect that the demand for grapes would be very disappointing.

It was more poignant then that by September 1930, the grape harvest was expected to be large. Though delayed by a cool summer—a circumstance usually seen as fortuitous because winemakers in many cities did not like to make wine in warm weather and sales were often better later in fall—growers had a dreadful feeling a later harvest was not going to help them. Prices were horrifyingly low. The new federally funded cooperative Grape Control Board had fixed the lowest price for grape sales at $17.50 per ton, with $1.50 per ton to be deducted for the stabilization fee to buy up the surplus crop to prevent market glutting, reported the *Sonoma Index-Tribune.* Only a few years earlier, Napa and Sonoma grapes had sold for over $100 a ton.[7]

If they wished to participate in the new control program, growers had to sign up with the board. They would be told how much tonnage would be allotted to them, where they had to appear to sign contracts for delivery of that tonnage, and when and where to deliver their grapes. All these rules grated on the entrepreneurial spirits of Napa and Sonoma, but sign-ups were increasing as growers recognized that the markets were uncontrollable because of the country's economic condition and because the unmanaged surpluses of the last few years had hurt all of them. The new control program promised stability, at least.

Marketing programs designed to manipulate emotions were getting the message out to grape-growing folk throughout California that it was necessary that 85 percent of producers sign up to participate if the project was going to work. In one promotion, that appeared in the *Grower* in July 1930 and aimed straight at the heartstrings, a photo of what is obviously meant to be a humble farming family—a mother, father, and small daughter in rolled-up dungarees—stare thoughtfully out across a lush vineyard. The copy is designed so the "thoughts" of the father appear under a huge headline that reads:

> What Shall I Do?
> "It is all so muddled—I almost wish I could chuck the whole business, move away and start over. But where would I go: what would I do.
> "I can't sell my land now—and who would ever buy it if this drive fails? I must think of my family, my children. They deserve better things. . . .
> "Shall I sign this growers' contract? Or is it merely putting myself into another and deeper hole? That can't be. The Federal Government is behind it. The wisest farm experts in the whole nation say it's a good thing. The new organization will be headed by the finest men.
> "And it promises relief from one thing we have all been blind to—something we couldn't solve before—a way to take care of the surplus grape crop. . . .
> "I'm afraid not to sign. If we lose the sympathy of the government there'll be no chance left for us. If I stay 'outside' I'm afraid I'll find my crop is part of the surplus—not salable at any livable price.
> "And so I think I'll sign. Yes, I will sign. I'll get Jim and Old Man Johnson to go along with it, too. And if this Government plan doesn't work, no one can say we growers didn't do our part."[8]

By October, the eastern markets showed some small signs of improvement and the juice-grape harvest was in full swing. Grape growers were heartened by better-than-expected demand for Zinfandel; prices reached $25 per ton and more. Advertisements in newspapers throughout the East, including many foreign-language papers, were responsible for a more buoyant air at the markets by providing a detailed, renewed assurance by Prohibition authorities that making 200 gallons of homemade wine was absolutely legal.[9]

Amid the good news, some bad. In November came a report from New York that racketeers in that city were warring over California wine grapes. The Unione

Siciliana mob was asking Italians in New York to buy wine grapes only from its dealers, and the gangsters had ordered Italian winemakers to sell their wines at bargain prices—between $1 and $2 a gallon—to offset a takeover of the market by Irish and Jewish interests known as the Broadway Mob. Squads of Unione "henchmen were sent to do guard duty over their principal distribution centers," which included Washington Market in Manhattan, Mott Haven Yards in the Bronx, and Sunnyside Yards in Queens. The *New York Daily Mirror* estimated that close to $3 million—though it did not say whether this was an annual sum—was being extorted from buyers and sellers of wine grapes. And it added that threats of violence to anyone muscling in on what it termed the "foreign racketeers" wine-grape interests had been made.[10] None of this made wine-grape sales any more profitable to the growers in Napa and Sonoma.

While there were hassles in grape markets far away, the country's economic troubles came closer to Healdsburg when a national disaster agency announced a campaign in that little city to raise $500 to help alleviate starvation in other parts of the country.

However, that news was countered with boisterous celebrations when, riding a huge wave of popularity, James Rolph Jr., the former mayor of San Francisco, an avowed and very public Wet, was voted the new governor of California. Supporters in the wine industry were jubilant when he carried every one of California's 58 counties. It was a wish fulfilled for Napa and Sonoma. Rolph had campaigned on a future of good education, good roads, and a strong economy—all of which voters obviously wanted to hear. And his assurances about the importance of agriculture to California, along with his well-known personal partiality for wine, were read by the wine industry to believe that he would do everything he could to counter the Prohibition forces in the state.

But even that good news to the wine industry was tempered by tougher words from the markets. Unfortunately, by the end of the season, the eastern juice markets were declared a disaster again. The season had looked rosy earlier, as prices and demand improved slightly as the harvest went to market. Heavy shipments at the end of the season flooded the market and brought heartbreak at the end of another year of struggle in the vineyards of the two wine counties.

The *Grower* said it had witnessed a perfect lesson in how to extinguish a market in the quickest possible manner. Despite knowing that the buying power of consumers across the country was well below the average of the past two seasons, the shippers had, with a "lack of sound business judgment," deployed such a high volume of grapes that there was no possibility of profit. The journal reminded both grape growers and shippers that the Grape Control Board had time and again warned about the danger of sending too many grapes to market and had asked growers to use caution when making decisions about how much they would send. Shipping records had been broken, and the markets collapsed under the mountain of grapes sent East.

Clearly a voluntary system was not going to work, said the *Grower* at the beginning of December 1930: "as the situation now stands one man with a hundred cars of grapes can break up a voluntary arrangement and cause losses of millions of dollars."[11]

Grape growers were chastened but desperate. They had all tried to get their grapes to market faster than anyone else. Although they understood the problems, they found it impossible to hold back their grapes when everyone else was sending theirs. It was a desperate battle, neighbor against neighbor in some cases, to get grapes to market as early as possible.

The San Francisco market had fared a little better than the eastern ones. Prices had not been as gloomy as elsewhere. More than 2,700 railcars of grapes had arrived at Drumm Street and the equivalent of another 500 cars had arrived by truck.

Every day during September and October, sellers opened 30 to 50 cars full of grapes. Hundreds of consumers all looking to buy the grapes they would need to make the year's "grape juice" visited. Crowds increased on Saturdays and Sundays, especially with Italian buyers who came down the precipitous hills from their homes in the nearby Telegraph Hill and North Beach districts.[12]

At the beginning of 1931, the *California Grape Grower* forecast "difficult marketing conditions for the next several years. A considerable acreage of grapes in California has already been removed or abandoned and indications point toward a further decrease in acreage." The previous year, about one-fifth of the entire California crop was estimated to have been left on the vines unharvested.[13] A special committee of the California Grape Control Board reported that some drastic action must be taken.

Another of the committee's conclusions hardly needed a study: it was clear to everyone in the grape business that hundreds of thousands of tons of grapes were being grown that could never be sold: there was a surplus of 630,000 tons of table, wine and raisin grapes being grown. "A program of vine pulling was urged," reported the *Healdsburg Tribune* in February 1931.

The lack of demand for grapes was translating into precipitous drops in the price of grape ranches. The committee's investigations had revealed some sobering information about the indebtedness of California's grape growers. These were once a thrifty group of people who had worked arduously to acquire their land.

Now it appeared that more than 85 percent of the vineyards in the state were mortgaged to financial institutions for amounts equal to or greater than their sale value. The indirect results of Prohibition had initiated a cruel implosion of equity in the landholdings of many of California's winemakers and grape growers. The only way to return value to that land, said the committee, was to remove surplus vineyards.[14]

Even the president of the Bank of America, Arnold J. Mount, an investor in grape-growing mortgages, voiced complete support of the plan to pull vines.[15] While much of the attention about over-planting was aimed on the vast acreages turned to juice-grape vines during the early 1920s in the Central Valley, it is interesting to note that while there were 93,500 bearing acres of wine grapes in 1920, the United States National Agricultural Service reports that while there was a Prohibition high of 188,000 acres in 1930, that number had only dropped back to 178,400 by 1933. But what is even more telling is that while in 1920, ranchers were making on average $75 per ton for grapes, by now, 1931, they were getting $19 per ton on average, and next year, 1932, the return would fall to $12 per ton. It was a nasty tumble.[16]

But amid the dark news, many wine folk had some genuine festivities to share in. Only a couple of months ago, they had cheered as James Rolph Jr., was elected California's twenty-seventh governor. Now it was time for his inauguration and spirits were raised again, this time to carnival level. In early January 1931, the state capital, Sacramento, was full of exuberant, jolly visitors from around the state all decked out in their Sunday best to celebrate the elections of family and friends.[17]

An orchestra played "Smiles" and a governor's salute of 17 guns was fired by army cannon. During the afternoon, a military parade was held, and at night, the inaugural ball.[18] While Rolph did not specifically mention Prohibition in his inaugural address, which specifically mentioned water and irrigation, oil and gas development, transportation and education, among other things, he did say: "Upon the success of our agriculture depends the welfare of our labor and the prosperity of nearly every California industry and nearly every person within our state. The farm problem must be solved and solved promptly. To that purpose I shall put my shoulder to the wheel."[19]

The state's wine industry read "change for the better for vineyards" between the lines. But any such changes had to take backseat on the governor's schedule to the growing legions of California's desperate and poor. The Depression was filling the roads of California with both desperate families and anguished individuals looking for work. Only days after the fun and backslapping of Governor Rolph's introduction to Sacramento, 500 unemployed men and women shouted outside his windows demanding that he meet with a select committee representing them. The place was put under police guard. Rolph refused to meet with the committee. And a standoff lasted for about an hour, until the group disbanded.[20] A few weeks later, 90 miles away from the capital of the state, 1,000 unemployed men battled police over food problems at a charity restaurant in San Francisco. The riot had lasted half an hour and "resulted in five arrests, the beating of several policemen and the severe clubbing of a rioter." The *Tribune Service* story that ran in the *Healdsburg Tribune* did not fail to mention that the restaurant was just around the corner from "communist headquarters" at Third and Harrison streets.[21]

In January 1931, the little city of Healdsburg adopted two projects for the relief of unemployment in that city—an extension to city reservoirs and the removal of the smokestack on city premises. The work could be done for $200 and would employ one or more men.[22] Shoes were also being collected for families who could not afford them, so children did not have to go to school barefoot.[23]

The economy made lives precarious: One morning an aged itinerant vineyard worker had knocked at the door of a ranch house in Sonoma County and asked for something to eat, reported the *Healdsburg Tribune.* He looked in dire need of sustenance but was told that breakfast was over, although he could have a cup of coffee. The man entered the house and sat down on a chair to wait for the coffee. Before it could be served to him, he fell dead. Police later found a rough bed in the freight shed at the Lytton railroad station. No marks of identification were found on either the man's worn clothes or bedding. Police were hoping to find someone who knew him and described him as five foot four inches in height, weighing 130 pounds, with a full beard.[24]

Charities operating from the Healdsburg Chamber of Commerce were giving aid to a half dozen families, one with four children two of whom who had no underclothing. A supply had been donated, and now the children were able to attend school in comfort.[25]

As the economy got worse in Napa and Sonoma, crime seemed to get worse as well. Thieves had spent a couple of nights siphoning port out of the Scatena winery north of Geyserville. They were moving wine from large puncheons into 50-gallon barrels and loading them onto two trucks, the side of one of trucks was emblazoned with the words "Empire Moving Van and Storage Company of San Francisco." The first night the operation had been a success, and their haul had been worth about $5,000. They came back a few days later for a second night of siphoning. That night was not so profitable; agents caught them at work and arrested them. Officers said the gang kept Scatena and his son, now living in San Francisco, under surveillance there so that the raids could be timed when they were not be near the winery.[26]

Only a few days after that in January 1931, there had been a particularly vicious case for federal and Sonoma County authorities to solve. They were looking for the source of poisoned liquor that had killed 12 persons since New Year's Day in Central California, said the *Healdsburg Tribune*, including one young woman and her parents who had attended the same party in Salinas. Police finally arrested three men in Sonoma County and seized 165 gallons of booze. The men had confessed to handling the liquor, and Lee Wilson, a retired Petaluma hotel and billiard parlor operator was arrested as its owner.

Police discovered that on several occasions, Wilson had been the victim of hijackers who had stolen liquor from him. He was said to have told friends he was going to "fix" those responsible for stealing his stock. Police had heard a rumor that he had added wood alcohol to the booze.

Three men confessed to hijacking the liquor. One, William F. Peters, a Petaluma taxicab operator, had given some to his family in Salinas, not knowing it was poisoned. Peters admitted he had given his brother Fred the alcohol, "but I didn't think it was the liquor that killed the wife. There were other people at the party and they haven't died. Fred himself wasn't sick, although he did go to the hospital for a day or so."[27]

Prohibition agents were also having difficulties with the law.

At the trial of Antone Providenty, who had been charged with resisting a federal officer during a Lowell Valley liquor raid, the court heard Providenty, a 21-year-old truck driver, testify that Officer Martin J. Buckley had failed to identify himself as an agent when he stopped his truck. Providenty also claimed that Buckley's car was weaving on the road as it approached his truck. When Buckley stopped and tried to get out of the car, he almost fell on the ground. Providenty said he ran over and tried to help Buckley up but Buckley struck him over the head with a revolver. Buckley meanwhile said that Providenty attacked him. Buckley then fired over Providenty's head, fatally wounding Ugilino Prasso, a suspected booze maker. Providenty said it was only when they raced Prasso to a doctor's office in Sonoma that Buckley identified himself as a Prohibition officer, reported the *Healdsburg Tribune.*

Buckley was drunk when he first met up with Providenty, said the young truck driver, and was still drunk when they arrived at the doctor's office. Providenty said Buckley had walked up and down the room, first laughing and then crying. He was thrown out of the physician's office twice. Buckley called his wife in San Francisco, Providenty said, and was heard saying to her "I'm in wrong. I have shot a man and if I get out of this mess, I am going to give up my badge."

Emmet Mullen, deputy sheriff of Sonoma County, also testified that Buckley was intoxicated in the doctor's office. Gus Morgue, another Prohibition agent who worked with Buckley, agreed that Buckley had been drinking the night of the shooting.[28]

Prohibition crime continued to infect every part of the wine industry from one end of the country to the other. The *Grower* was growing concerned by the news of racketeering in New York and other major cities. It reported that bootleggers and racketeers in those major wine-grape markets were profiting even more from the glut of grapes that had been devastating grape growers' returns for the last five or six bad years. "A carload of grapes must be sold and unloaded quickly to prevent deterioration and spoilage," explained the journal. "Racketeers seize this opportunity to prevent the unloading of cars, threaten legitimate buyers and terrorize distributors." The condition of the grapes worsens, prices drop precipitously, then a bootlegger buys grapes for "almost nothing, converts it to strong 'commercial' wine by fortifying it with the 'renatured' bad alcohol which the racketeer knows so well how to get. The result is loss to the producer and consumer of a legitimate product" and a "profit to an outlaw."[29]

While Napa and Sonoma could understand tough gang activities in faraway New York, they were disheartened to hear that their beautiful part of the world was no longer the relatively safe, idyllic rural paradise it had once been.

In a case that also terrified the two wine counties, authorities were investigating the untimely death of Mrs. Ivy Chord, 36, who had been the chief dietitian at the Veterans' Home at Yountville. It was suspected from the first that poisoned liquor was involved.

At the same time, the police were continuing to looking into the deaths of three other people: Two had died at the institution during the same week under similar circumstances, and the other, an ex-resident of the home, had been visiting them. District Attorney Wallace C. Rutherford said, in a story in the *Healdsburg Tribune,* that two residents of the home, Anthony Storm, 51, and James Farrell, 60, along with Robert Baer had died after they had drunk whiskey purchased by Baer.

Sheriff Steckter was searching for a female bootlegger, whose name was known to the police and who had been operating in Napa County. Mrs. Chord, the dead woman, was the wife of Ray Chord, also an employee of the Veterans' Home. She had obtained the liquor from the bootlegger two days prior, her husband told authorities. After she drank the liquor, she was stricken blind, Chord said, and that night she was taken to Victory Hospital at Napa, where she died early the next morning. Chord had also become ill from the liquor but recovered.[30]

When a further investigation into the deaths led to the son of a San Francisco police officer, as the suspected liquor source for the bootlegger, local winemakers became even more disillusioned about the government and its laws. That people who sold dangerous forms of booze were now making money when they could not, added insult to injury.[31] An autopsy performed by the county coroner a few days later showed that Mrs. Chord had consumed large amounts of denatured alcohol. It was suspected that the other three deaths were caused by alcohol from the same source.[32]

The wine families were horrified that people who wanted an alcoholic beverage were now driven to drink poison. It made no sense to them at all.

While this wave of crime had been washing through every corner of the wine counties, grape growers and winemakers had also been living with the dire news from Washington that the Wickersham Commission had recommended that the Dry laws should remain as they were.

Most Americans were as stunned as the wine industry by the committee's conclusions given the evidence it had heard.

The commission had been brutal in its comments on the effects of Prohibition. Its conclusion did not jibe with its findings. Corruption was everywhere, the commission said, to no one's surprise—from street level to the highest reaches of Prohibition bureaucracy; it flourished in police departments everywhere across the country; the connection between corrupt local politicians and gangs and the organized liquor traffic was chilling.

Special-interest Dry groups had completely hijacked the country's court system, said the commission's report. Often state and federal prosecutors were appointed and elected under the pressure of organizations concerned only with Prohibition, as if nothing else were to be considered. And, perhaps worse, judges were appraised solely by their zeal in liquor prosecutions. Obsessive organizations dictated appointments and sought to direct the course of administering the law, added the report.

The margin of profit in illegal alcohol, especially in illicit distilling and bootlegging, made lavish expenditures for corruption possible. And it put great temptation in the way of everyone engaged in law enforcement or administration. In fact, Prohibition directly financed organized crime, declared the commission.

Since the Senate Judiciary Committee had reported on the revolving door of senior Prohibition staff in 1926, nothing had changed. In the succeeding three years, there had been 91 changes of district administrators in 27 districts. In some districts, the average length of service was a mere six months. The report said that no organization could reasonably function efficiently with changes of that magnitude or the quality of staff it had had for so many years. It reminded the nation that back in 1927, when Bureau of Prohibition staff had at last been required to take civil service examinations, a shocking 59 percent of them had failed.

Enforcement agents continued to be dismissed in large numbers for bribery, extortion, theft, violation of the national Prohibition Act, falsification of records, conspiracy, forgery, perjury, and a long list of other causes.[33]

The report could not have described a worse—moral or financial—burden for a nation to carry.

The United Press quoted a high-level source in the government who claimed that President Hoover had intervened at the last moment to have the report altered and had dictated the commission's conclusions.[34]

The Senate soon made the same charges against the president. Wickersham refused to explain the fact that the report may have contained material that recommended an immediate revision of the Dry laws. Although only 1 of the 11 commission members would not sign the findings, 6 of the 11 commissioners, a majority of 1, called for a change in the laws. Five favored a further trial for Prohibition. Two of those who voted with the change team, believed outright Repeal of Prohibition would have been the best recommendation.[35]

In Wine Country, life changed not a whit due to the Wickersham Commission's conclusions. Crime continued, sometimes merrily, on its way. The Sonoma

County jail in Santa Rosa was often referred to as a vacation resort; when children whose fathers had been incarcerated during Prohibition—and there were many of them—were asked by busybodies where their dad was, they had been trained to answer, "He's away on vacation."

Alfredo Barsotti's time there probably was not as cruel a trial as one might expect. Barsotti was one of the owners of the Riverside Villa, a vacation hideaway on the Russian River near Healdsburg that offered dances, boating, and swimming along with a "well-stocked bootleg liquor bar and private dining and sleeping rooms," says Holly Hoods, Healdsburg Museum Research curator, in a story for the *Russian River Recorder*. The Villa catered to "wealthy clientele from San Francisco with deep pockets. Parties were rowdy, raucous and frequent." The resort was popular, adds Hoods, with "men trysting with women" who were not their wives. It was suspected that many of the women who frequented the upstairs bedrooms of the Villa were call girls.

Barsotti, adds Hoods, "an affluent San Francisco haberdasher and unrepentant bootlegger" was incarcerated as "head man in the distillery" when federal Prohibition officers raided a "$70,000 bootlegging operation on the ranch of Calvin Foote, a former constable and justice of the peace."[36] The still was one of the most elaborate ever found in the county, opined the local newspaper, the *Healdsburg Enterprise*. The fact that Barsotti's fellows in crime were from out of the county suggested that they were partners in a crime syndicate.

At the Santa Rosa jail, the accommodations were more like rooms than cells. Sheriff Harry L. Patteson discovered that Barsotti liked to cook and named him head cook for the jailhouse. Since Barsotti needed supplies each day, including fresh ingredients, Patteson let him out each afternoon to go shopping, related Lou Colombano in a 2008 interview. Barsotti used to drive up some 15 miles to Dry Creek Valley each afternoon and share a few glasses of wine with old friends before he gathered up the makings of that night's dinner and headed back to the jailhouse. Barsotti needed a car to get to market, said Lou Colombano, so Sheriff Patteson gave him the use of a car he had probably seized in an illegal liquor raid.[37] Gene Cuneo remembers that when his own father was incarcerated near the end of Prohibition for distilling brandy and bootlegging, he and his mother would go down to Santa Rosa a few times each week to visit. His father was "staying" on the third floor of the jail which was almost entirely set aside for bootleggers, he remembers. He'd help his mother take his father proper

Italian food and drink. On each visit, they delivered two bottles of brandy—from the illegal stock kept out back of their grape ranch—one for Gene's father and one to be tucked into the drawer of Sheriff Patteson's desk as they made their way upstairs.[38]

After the disappointing conclusions of the Wickersham Commission's examination of Prohibition had been digested, the lives of the grape growers got no better. Even worse, 1931 brought drought conditions, a terrible heat, and insect infestations. Grape growers sent their smallest crop to market since 1921. Juice grapes had, unfortunately, matured early before consumers were ready to contemplate making wine.

To add to that litany of woe, the grape crop had arrived to markets buffeted by an economic depression more severe than in many years. Again sales and profits were disastrous, said the *Grower*. Juice grapes sold at the lowest prices on record in New York.[39] The Red Cross was aiding "hunger belt" victims across the country from Maryland to Texas. People remembered with bitterness and anger just how many jobs and how much tax revenue had been lost with Prohibition. And the costs of maintaining Prohibition had grown to ever more shocking heights. In February 1932, the federal government reported that it cost $101,000,000 a year ($1.5 billion in 2008 dollars) to maintain Dry laws, that astounding total including not only the cost of the Prohibition Bureau but the expenditures of courts and jails, the Coast Guard, and ongoing legislative expenses.[40] Prohibition was starting to look like a wicked and foolhardy venture by those politicians who didn't care if citizens starved or went without work, or if the country's economy continued to shrink into oblivion.

The most astute politicians had seemed to sense some time ago how tough the mood of many voters had become on the issue of Prohibition. By the beginning of election year, 1932, it was now agreed by most of them that it would be a crucial issue come November. And they would have to weigh carefully the interests of their Wet and Dry constituents.

In January, John J. Raskob, chairman of the Democratic National Committee, canvassed Democratic leaders on party issues and concluded from their comments: "I have no doubt that the Democratic platform will contain a Prohibition plank." He revealed a poll of Democratic contributors showing a 91 percent majority in favor of change.[41]

On top of California's economic problems, the weather had been brutal. On January 15, 1932, snow fell in the city of Los Angeles for the first time in 54 years.[42] The heaviest snowstorm in 15 years had hit the wine counties. Most unusually, it had been accompanied by thunder and lightning. Two to three inches of snow cut power and pulled down telephone wires.[43]

Soon the Republicans were hinting at a Wet plank in their platform too. President Hoover's campaign initiative was that each state be allowed to handle the liquor problem as it saw fit, with the federal government managing those states that still wanted to maintain Prohibition.

At the end of summer and looking ahead to the election that fall, the *Sonoma Index-Tribune* expressed the wishes of the wine counties to have light wine reinstated immediately after the election: "It would mean the survival of business and activity akin to the days when Sonoma Valley vineyards and the homes built by the owners were the show places of the country."

The newspaper recounted the damage of the Eighteenth Amendment and the Volstead Act that had left many vineyards in disrepair and winery owners in economic distress: "It is not a partisan issue. Both parties are responsible for the destruction of these vineyards." They could start to correct the damage in Congress at the end of the year, the paper said. December action would give winemakers and grape growers in Sonoma Valley an opportunity to prune and cultivate their vines in preparation for the next year's harvest. It would be a "long and slow process" to change the law, the paper admitted, but Congress could give the wine-grape industry a "break after these 12 years of disaster."[44]

Winemakers in Napa and Sonoma now felt the country recognized Prohibition's time had run out. Perhaps it was just a matter of money; the Depression was hastening its demise. Not all politicians would allow that it had been a huge mistake. But the country was hurting for jobs and if liquor, beer and wine were permitted and saloons and bars and hotels were allowed to re-open their drinking places, it would bring lots of new work. All three levels of government were starved for the massive tax revenues that would return. The wine industry could not yet foretell the timing, but it sensed relief was on the way. And Sonoma and Napa were not going to wait to see what December would bring. Many winemakers in the two counties who hadn't been regularly making wine through Prohibition under sacramental or medicinal licensing, decided to make wine that harvest of 1932 anyway, so sure they were that the law would change. It just had to happen soon, they believed. And they set to set to cleaning tanks, steaming them, picking fruit, and embarking on "crush." The sounds and smells alone were intoxicating.

In early November, just before the election, President Hoover started west on a final intensive campaign offensive and would close his campaign with a dash home to California. "The improved condition of the country," he announced, "affords me the deep satisfaction of coming home to vote."[45]

Wet forces were imploring voters in California to repeal the Wright Act on Election Day. If national repeal occurred and state voters did not repeal the Wright Act, Prohibition would still stand in California.

The state's wine industry knew that the repeal of the Wright Act could be as important a part of the election as was their vote for president. It was buoyed when, in October 1932, the pastor emeritus of the First Presbyterian Church in San Francisco, Dr. William Kirk Guthrie, came on their radios and spoke to the moral imperative of voting out Prohibition law. Guthrie made a strong argument in his talk, reported the *California Grape Grower,* for voting away Dry laws and Dry politicians.

> Some people have tried to scare us by telling us that if we give up Prohibition and repeal the Wright Act, which was passed to try and make Prohibition effective, we shall be deluged with drunkenness and all manner of crime. Friends, we are not kept from evil by the laws we pass. What saves us is not our laws or our lawmakers but our own sense of right. The reason that Prohibition has been such a ghastly failure is because it has outraged the country's sense of right.
>
> Innocent people have been murdered; armed thugs invested with authority have broken into our houses and outraged our liberties. Your agents have solicited people to drink and to buy liquor that they might drag them off to jail and you have soothed yourself with the old sophistry that the end justified the means. You have corrupted the peace officers of the country till all law has fallen into disrepute. You have built up an army of bandits which it will take years to get rid of, and worse of all, you have made drunkenness fashionable.[46]

On November 8, 1932, 10,000 Californians jammed the Oakland train station and cheered wildly as the president's official train arrived. Oakland city officials stood around excitedly as they waited to offer their official greetings to the country's chief executive.

When President Hoover was escorted to the platform, the crowd cheered in welcome. He announced, "I believe I am entitled to another chance as president of the United States because of the steady recovery our country has witnessed during the past several months." A special boat took him across the bay to San Francisco's grand Ferry Building[47] where he was met by a reception committee and escorted to the city hall. School children were massed in the civic center, reported the *Healdsburg Tribune,* and overlooking them, on a city hall balcony the mayor extended a welcome to the president. Then Hoover was to head by car to another civic reception in his home town of Palo Alto, 35 miles south.

Notwithstanding the hero's welcome in San Francisco, however, neither the country nor California thought Hoover should have another chance. In California, it was all over early in the evening when, with only 80 percent of the votes counted, Franklin D. Roosevelt was winning. Eventually the Democrats polled 1.3 million votes in California, the Republicans, 847,000.[48]

The city of Sonoma had voted 335 to 165.

In Napa County, the precinct of Agua Caliente East had voted 172 to 42 in favor of Roosevelt; Vineburg, 202 to 70.

Healdsburg had voted in larger numbers that in any election in recent years and it, too, gave Roosevelt a decisive lead over Hoover: Roosevelt 550, Hoover, 356.

Hoover had done nothing for the wine folk of Napa and Sonoma. So many were glad to see him go.

To add to the joy of winemakers and grape growers, California had also voted down the Wright Act. It seemed 1.45 million Californians, were at last more than ready to have that particular piece of state Prohibition legislation off the books.

The day after the election, there was electricity wherever people met up in the little towns and cities of the two wine counties. People congratulated each other in the streets and in shops. The results of the election remained almost impossible to believe. The entire West Coast—Washington, Oregon, and California—had held referendums on Prohibition, as did Arizona, Colorado, Louisiana, Michigan, New Jersey, and North Dakota. Wets won by significant margins everywhere.

Roosevelt's tremendous victory proved decisively that Prohibition in the United States was doomed. The Democrats would have 313 seats in the House of

Representatives, the Republicans, 117. In the Senate, the Democrats would have 59 seats, the Republicans, 36.

Majorities like that in both the Senate and House could ensure that Roosevelt's plans for the end of Prohibition would soon prevail.

Thanksgiving 1932 was the headiest, happiest one in Wine Country in 13 years—the toasts around family dinner tables that day were jubilant.

Chapter Ten

The Worst and Most Cruel Experiences

fter Franklin Roosevelt's election in the fall of 1932, California's winemakers held their breath in anticipation.

Roosevelt had vowed to clean up the mess that was Prohibition. By now it had lasted nearly 13 years, and citizens wondered whether Roosevelt would be a man of his word. Beyond that, they were worried about how long it might take to steer the changes through Congress, through state legislatures, and then out to the streets and the vineyards. They knew now from experience how convoluted and time-consuming legislative change could be and were not surprised when murmurs from Washington indicated that a ratification of the Twenty-first Amendment that would repeal the Eighteenth Amendment through state conventions could take up to seven years.

As some of those winemakers wandered through their vineyards during that fall of 1932, they must have wondered what they would be doing with the harvest from those vines next year. Some winemakers, like Louis Foppiano, had courageously decided to crush that year. "As soon as it looked certain, we steamed and soaked our tanks and got ready," he explained.[1] Foppiano had an especial interest in seeing his wine tanks full again—six years had passed since up to 140,000 gallons of his wine had been poured into a ditch under the supervision of Prohibition agents. Lou had been 14 when his father had died, leaving his mother to manage a vineyard and a winery. He was now just turning 23 and he felt a huge responsibility toward his mother and two sisters to get the winery open for business again.[2]

To survive the tough years, his family had planted prune trees between the rows of vines, he recounted, but he added, "Let's not talk about prunes. There's nothing worse than picking prunes. But we never did pull out the vines." The prunes had helped carry the family through Prohibition, "but when Repeal came we pulled those trees right out of the ground."[3]

Foppiano had been able to fill up wine tanks from the 1932 crush as the election campaign was under way, thinking that by so doing he could ensure a vintage was ready to be released in 1933 if Prohibition should be over. Other winemakers throughout Napa and Sonoma debated crush, too: If they waited to make wine in the fall of 1933, they reasoned, it would not be ready till 1934—and it would mean an entire year where wines might possibly be legal again and they would be left without a product to sell.

Anxiety about juice-grape markets in the East that fall had made the decision easy for many of them: Why send the grapes there, they reasoned, when there was little if any profit to be made? The wine of 1932 would have a shelf life of some years. Even if the government took its sweet time to repeal Prohibition, it should be over long before the wine would age too much to sell. And with Roosevelt in the White House, it would not take that long, many believed now.

If repeal was a possibility, it made no matter to bootleggers that fall.

Milt Brandt, who after Prohibition went on to be a much admired community builder and businessman in the county of Sonoma, remembered in a personal memoir that is part of the collection of the Healdsburg Museum that towards the end of 1932 his rancher father returned to their house and informed his wife and two children that they would be moving into Healdsburg almost immediately. The children were shocked. Dad must have lost the house to the bank, they thought; in the Brandt household, as in many others in Wine Country during those difficult economic times, that possibility was often discussed. But no, the bank had not repossessed their home, his father explained. He had rented their house and ranch to a "businessman" for a year.

A few days later, Milt's father came home for supper and showed the family a $500 bill. There was much laughing and shouting: Milt and his sister, Dorothy, had never seen anything "larger than a twenty, and very few of them," he said. His money was rent payment for the farm, including the use of their fruit-dehydrating building. A bootlegging operation needed somewhere like the Brandt homestead safe in the country to produce liquor and it wanted to include the dehydrator in the deal, as the building was an ideal spot to house a huge still. It was perfect because it sat very close to the river, and a large supply of running water was required to run a still.

To Milt and his sister, that year in town was a very happy time. They could visit with school friends anytime they wanted without having to wait for a parent to find the time to drive them into town. And maybe even better, there were none of the heavy-lifting farm chores such as getting the wood for the cooking stove so their mother could cook meals not only for the family but for the ranch hands as well—in town wood was delivered.

After the year was over and the family moved back to the farmhouse, Milt remembered one day seeing three carloads of Treasury men drive up "in their soft-top sedans. They jumped out and scattered out toward the dehydrator building with their riot guns and a couple of Thompson submachine guns on the ready." To have precipitated such a storming by so many agents, armed with such serious firepower, the bootleggers who had rented the Brandt place, must have been running a still of vast size with great success. But by then, the place had been cleaned up, all the equipment, bags of sugar, cans, and barrels had long gone, and there was nothing for the agents to attack or seize.

Milt's father was worried, but eventually the agents left without making arrests. Brandt's family's experience was all part of the Sonoma "see no evil, hear no evil, speak no evil" philosophy, though perhaps the conclusion of the maxim in Wine Country was, "see no evil . . . and maybe there'll be some good in it for you."

Sometime very soon after the visit by the armed Treasury agents, Milt's father took his children down the road a bit, along a pretty winding road that followed the twists and turns of the Russian River, to see where neighbor Botch Foppiano's still had been raided.

"Before we even arrived at the site you could smell the results of the raid," Milt recollected. The still, which had been located in an enviable position under a grove of trees next to a prune orchard and tucked between two streams of a river on a lonely dead-end road, had been really "worked over." Bits of the still had been thrown everywhere. Neighbors eventually gathered up the least damaged pieces and kept them for Botch in their barns to keep just in case they might come in handy sometime.[4]

As 1933 wound down, it was clear the year would be as difficult for many in the Wine Counties as it had been at the beginning. At the beginning of December, a shoving match in Sonoma County, reported by the *Sonoma Index Tribune,* showed just how desperate vineyard owners and workers had become.

A number of grape pickers at the Madrone vineyard had complained that they had not been paid for their work, and an ugly confrontation ensued. Constable John Mohr arrived at Madrone armed with a warrant for the arrest of Arthur Katzakian, a member of the family leasing and working the vineyard. Mohr, jostled and pushed by Katzakian and his brother, was forced to serve the warrant with his revolver drawn.

Arthur Katzakian simmered down and later agreed to accompany the constable to Sonoma where he appeared before a justice of the peace, on charges of failure to pay wages preferred by H. McFarland, one of his group of workmen.

The total amount of the wages thought to be due from the Katzakian brothers was $130. Katzakian claimed there were simply no funds to pay them. The revenue from grapes had dropped precipitously in the last few months. Everyone in the industry had expected the year to go better—but precious little revenue had come back to the vineyards for their crops and bills could no longer be paid.[5]

Eventually, at the trial, Katzakian produced a statement from the Pacific Fruit Exchange that explained that the fruit company had agreed to acquire all the grapes from the vineyard in return for giving the Katzakians $125 for their personal expenses and $500 to pay for help. The Katzakians had exhausted the workmen's fund and had even used some of their personal funds to pay the men when grape prices had dropped. The jury, sensing the hopelessness of the case, voted to acquit Katzakian. He had operated in good faith. Everything was stacked against the vineyard owners and their workers.[6]

Before Christmas, California governor James Rolph, decided to release any prisoners still incarcerated on alcohol violations under the state's now-defunct Wright Act. He had even prepared some rather grand pardon certificates complete with huge red state seals.[7]

The December weather leading up to the Christmas holidays had been brutal—one of the longest cold spells (with temperatures ranging between 14 and 18 degrees Fahrenheit) that anyone could remember. To Wine Country residents, this was near Arctic weather. The countryside was released from the icy grip when a downpour dumped more than two inches of rain across the hills and valleys, filling the rivers to the brim with wild water: This was more like the start of a Wine Country winter—mild and wet. It boded well for good irrigation that summer and a healthy crop of grapes to follow. That storm finally broke the cold snap, letting residents go about their holiday shopping without mufflers and mittens and extra knits under their biggest coats. One advertiser in local papers had tempted customers through the cold snap with winter cruises to Hawaii—$90 for a first-class one-way trip from the port of San Francisco to Maui.[8]

In late December, a California grape industry delegation consisting of E. M. Sheehan, Edmund A. Rossi, and W. L. St. Amant had testified, along with Congressman Clarence Lea, before the House Ways and Means Committee, to plead for the immediate legalization of wine. The group had said it would welcome legislation to allow light or low-alcohol wine to be made. The men called for California's financial and industrial leaders to press the state's case for wine wherever they could with their contacts in Washington.[9]

President-elect Roosevelt's Inaugural would not happen till Saturday, March 4, 1933, but he had made his wishes clear and there was no way now that Prohibition would survive. Congress got on with the job. By February 16, 1933, Senator Joseph T. Robinson, the Democratic majority leader, proposed some ideas to make repeal happen. The party promised Prohibition would be ended by a majority vote of state conventions from 36 out of the 48 states that would ratify a Twenty-first Amendment which would, to all effects, cancel out the Eighteenth Amendment. A hush fell over the Senate as the historic question on whether the resolution for repeal should pass. A roll call was taken and at last the votes were tallied. there were 63 yeas and 23 nays. More than two-thirds of the senators present had said yes: the resolution was passed.

The Senate suddenly became a place of cheering, shouting, and back-slapping. For some noisy minutes, the Wets celebrated very audibly.[10] Two days later, the Senate resolution was presented to the House. After quick minutes of discussion, the House voted 289 to 121 in favor of the resolution for repeal.

It was a giant step.

Next, the resolution was to be sent to the states, where citizens would be asked to vote on the issue: the Democrats had declared this would be a referendum by the people. After that vote, conventions would follow that would sign off for each state.

It was as if a dam had suddenly burst, crumbled, and been born away downstream on powerful waters. For so many years, nothing had happened; Wets could not get their voices heard in Congress, then suddenly the action among legislators was fast and furious. Winemakers watched as the question about repeal was sent out to the states and the machinery for the state votes was initiated.

For the interim period until repeal, 3.2 percent alcohol wine was to be legalized. The wine industry had been hoping for light wine to be legalized which was defined as wine containing 10 percent alcohol. That was not to occur, but both 3.2 percent wine and beer were made possible on March 13 when President Roosevelt delivered a firm message to Congress encouraging the legalization of beer "and other beverages of such alcoholic content as is permissible under the Constitution." The House promptly passed this resolution 316 to 97, and the Senate adopted it with a vote of 43 to 30. Beer and wine with an alcohol content of not more than 3.2 percent were legal as of April 7, 1933.[11]

The reactions in Wine Country to 3.2 percent wine were surprisingly mixed. Some people in the wine industry thought it a tragic development. These products would not be wines at all, complained the *California Grape Grower*, stating that the lowest alcoholic content in any wines worthy of the name is about 8 percent. So-called wines below that say, at 6 or 7 percent, said the *Grower*, would be extremely acidic and unpleasant to drink; the best wines had somewhere between 10 and 14 percent alcohol.[12] It was expected that carbonated water would be an important ingredient in the new 3.2 percent products.

But others in Wine Country were overjoyed. At last, there was reason to be happy again, they said, to get up each day and walk through their beloved vineyards, knowing that there were no more padlocks on their wineries. The doors could be flung open after 14 long years. Even if they were making what they considered more of a soft-drink than a wine, they'd need to fill their tanks with real wine again as that would be the starting point for the new products. Now, too, there would be income for their vineyards and their families, with no fear of a jail sentence or a large fine.

Sonoma and Napa prayed that the period of 3.2 percent wines would be short. And they cheered when their own congressman, Clarence Lea, introduced a new 10 percent light wine bill in the House. Lea was responding to the loud demands of grape growers throughout the state, especially those of Italian background, who thought that the 3.2 product was nothing more than legalized "mouth wash," though some of them would bend and make light wines, if necessary, they said.[13]

Beer got off to a fast start. At the beginning of April, 800 people stood in the rain outside the White House as a man hopped out of a fancy new beer truck and delivered two cases of beer to the president. On the truck a huge banner declared "President Roosevelt, the first real beer is yours." One beer industry journal reported that more than a million barrels of beer were sold in the first 24 hours, and beer sales would later net the government millions of dollars in taxes.[14] Winemakers in northern California salivated at the thought of releasing their products to markets that were obviously so parched.

Roosevelt's words describing the economy of the nation in his inaugural address, "the withered leaves of industrial enterprise lie on every side; farmers find no markets for their produce; the savings of many years in thousands of families are gone,"[15] were grim but they resonated with Americans. It was no wonder that anticipation over repeal and the new jobs it would bring was growing. Already it appeared to be stimulating business across the nation. According to a nationwide survey by the United Press in March 1933, thousands of men had been returning to work and millions of dollars were starting to pour into new enterprises. St. Louis beer-making was said to have resulted in the employment of about 10,000 men with a weekly payroll of $250,000. In Milwaukee, brewers already employed 1,000 men. The New York Ice Machine Corporation of New York had received orders for $100,000 worth of refrigerating equipment. And the Anheuser-Busch Company of St. Louis had ordered 400,000 beer cases and 400,000 gross of bottles—creating much-needed jobs for workers who made containers.[16]

In Sonoma and Napa, some of the early reaction to the promise of repeal was reflected in growing interest in ranch land. Buyers were interested again in investing in fine vineyards in good locations. In April, the Lombarda winery near St. Helena was sold: The purchase included 18 acres of orchard and a home adjacent to the winery property as well a quantity of 1932 vintage wine.[17] Soon more ranch sales in Sonoma County interested the wine community: one of them, the Gladden ranch, which had been in that family for several generations, was sold to a lumber dealer in San Francisco for $20,000. The deal consisted of 50 acres of prime Russian River land.[18]

While repeal continued to work its way through legislatures across the nation, as the states began to elect their convention delegates. Michigan moved fast, says David Kyvig in his book *Repealing National Prohibition*. It voted for its delegates on April 3 and a week later in its state legislature "it ratified the repeal Amendment." The vote was 99 to 1. Other states—"Wisconsin, Rhode Island, New Jersey, Wyoming, New York, Delaware and Illinois" followed rapidly as voters gave 78–89 percent approval to ratification, says Kyvig, and "unanimous convention decisions, except in New Jersey where the results were 202 for repeal, 2 against."[19]

No matter how strong the repeal movement in the nation, Prohibition enforcement did not let up. In Wine Country, agents continued to target stills and bootleggers. At the end of April 1933, someone snitched on Joseph Schalich, a 71-year-old Santa Rosa bonded winery owner, telling Prohibition investigators that wine from his warehouse was being sold through bootleggers. Schalich was arrested and lost 30,000 gallons of wine worth $30,000 as bootleg when the authorities confiscated it. He also had to pay a $1,000 fine after he was formally charged with the crime of selling five gallons of wine for $7.50. Finally, he was made to forfeit his $3,500 government bond that permitted him to run a winery.[20]

While the winemakers and grape growers of Sonoma and Napa were delighted with the news of the many state convention elections on the road to repeal, they realized that their state was lagging behind. Grape growers were impatient for California to weigh in on the issue and were starting to feel annoyed by what they believed was political foot-dragging in Sacramento, where some Drys from the south, they worried, still seemed to want to slow down the repeal process.

With more and more states scheduling their elections for repeal of the Eighteenth amendment—the wine industry felt it was time for California to make its move. At the beginning of May 1933, Governor Rolph responded to pleas by representatives of the grape growers of northern California and area legislators to get on the job. The governor held a press conference on May 3, 1933, after a meeting with state Senator Herbert W. Slater and Enrico Prati, now president of the Sonoma County Grape Growers' association who had gone to Sacramento to jump-start Rolph's managing of the repeal process. Assemblyman Ernest Crowley attended to support Napa County. Rolph said he would move immediately to introduce a bill in the legislature for a special repeal election. The election was tentatively set for June 27.[21]

California had some catching up to do, not only in its legislature but also with the sale of low alcohol wines. In April, 3.2 percent wines had made their debut in the country; surprisingly, the first low-alcohol wines were not produced in California but were the product of a New York company, H. T. Dewey & Sons of Fulton Street, New York, who had sold very a popular grape juice for years. The Dewey folk been experimenting for some time with low-alcohol wines and were pleased with the results. On the first day of sale, there was a mob scene at their store, reported the *California Grape Grower*. Consumers had been rationed to two bottles each, the company was not able to close the doors till late in the evening, and it had to turn down as many orders as it had been able to fill. Californians noted with some disdain that the company's new light claret and sparkling Burgundy had a distinct Concord grape flavor, which West Coast palates sneered at— and they were not cheap, selling at $1.50 a bottle.[22]

Horatio F. Stoll had tasted some of the low-alcohol wines that California producers were about to launch, carbonated red and white wine "drinks" that met with mixed response. "Some have proved a great surprise," he said. "They were crystal clear, with beautiful color, plenty of body and pleasing favor, with enough of a vinous taste to make them real wine beverages. Others were mediocre and still others poor, with little color and so much sweetening and dilution that the flavor of the grape was lost and all one got was the impression of a soda pop." Stoll warned that the weaker products should not be put on the market. He was worried, as were some winemakers, that consumers trying this wine for the first time who had a negative initial impression might not come back to try "real" wines after repeal.[23]

The product that the great Asti winery in northern California was putting out reminded wine lovers how much was lost in comparison to a glass of real wine from the past. The Asti wine moved the *Sonoma Index-Tribune* to write: "it is to weep" to realize what a great winery is forced to do. The paper declared the new 3.2 percent products to be spurious imitations of the real thing. The product, the paper declared, while palatable, appeared to contain little wine and too much water and carbonation.[24]

The industry consoled itself that at least this was a legal market, however distasteful to real wine lovers. And while winemakers must have held their noses as they tasted some of their own new products, they were overjoyed that their wineries' doors were open again and that there was increased zeal in getting vines back in order and equipment refurbished.

In May, the Massoni-Scatena winery, a family operation in Healdsburg, announced that it, too, was in the 3.2 percent wine business. It would be opening a new bottling plant to produce 400 cases of light product daily, each case containing twenty-four 12-ounce bottles. The new beverage was to be called "Sparkling Clarette." The company explained its wine would be reduced to the legal 3.2 alcoholic content by a special process. Tasters believed that process involved much dilution of the product rather than clever chemistry. To make the new product, the winery estimated it would use approximately 2,000 gallons of wine each week. William Massoni said with the Clarette sales and with sales to other bonded wineries for the medicinal trade, the winery hoped to dispose of about 250,000 gallons of the wine it had stored in the company's Healdsburg plant.[25]

The news that light beer and wines were now available encouraged even more tourists to flock to Sonoma and Napa during the summer. The Redwood and Napa highways were lined with cars each weekend, headed not only to the area's many resorts but also to the summer cottages owned by so many San Franciscans. Others camped or rented newfangled auto camp cottages. Every weekend that summer brought thousands of pleasure seekers to the two wine counties. Swimming, canoeing, boating, fishing, riding, and all kinds of other summer sports kept visitors busy, and the evening's longtime favorite entertainment—dancing and socializing—seemed even more pleasurable now that people could be served a glass of wine at the table with a meal instead of having to sneak out to a car for a tipple.[26]

Two weeks before California was to vote on the election of delegates to the state repeal convention reported the *Sonoma Index-Tribune*, Sophus Federspiel, the president of the state's Grape Growers League, reminded citizens that the end of Prohibition would bring more economic benefit to California than to any other state in the country.

Speaking on behalf of 27,000 grape growers, he appealed publicly to civic, agricultural, and industrial groups to help "get out the vote" in June. Federspiel reminded voters that the revival of the grape industry would do more than any one other thing to restore a prosperous good life to California.

The Golden State, he continued, would be saying good-bye to abandoned vineyards, grape ranch foreclosures, and bankrupt wineries. The fortunes of not only the 90,000 members of grape growers' families who depended on grapes would blossom from the legislation; those who made bottles, barrels, sold lumber, ran trucking companies, and resorts, hotels, and restaurants would also benefit.

Federspiel closed his appeal with the plea for Californians to vote for repeal by an overwhelming margin; doing so would not only help the state move ahead quickly, but would serve as an example to other states that had yet to vote.[27]

At the special repeal election scheduled for June 27, Californians were to choose from 22 names on the ballot. Each congressional district in the state would nominate one candidate who favored ratification and one who opposed. From this field the voters would choose the delegates who would meet in Sacramento to cast their votes. The results of that second vote would be sent to Washington as the state's final decision on Prohibition.

As the date of the vote grew nearer, emotions were volatile. What was at stake was crucial for the two wine counties. The *Sonoma Index Tribune* said, "It has been an acid test of loyalty for these farmers to go on paying taxes and interest as foreclosure loomed while the government, through its Prohibition Bureau, supported a vast army of snoopers and parasites," as moonshine from illicit stills flooded the country, and bootleggers and the crime world got rich. "Bring back the price of our grape land," the *Sonoma Index Tribune* demanded; "restore the legal status to the vineyardist and the wine-maker, who has been driven from pillar to post the past thirteen or fourteen years, punished and penalized for a thoroughly discredited and rejected experiment."[28]

Some repealists were worried about the complexity of the ballot. Voters were not going to be asked to put an X next to boxes marked "For Repeal" or "Against Repeal."

Instead, they were to stamp a cross in a circle at the head of either the repeal group of delegates or the Prohibition contingent on the ballot. Since most people did not recognize the names on the ballot, they were told to be very careful to make sure they put their cross in the correct column.[29] Local newspapers explained the voting process clearly and worried about voter confusion when they arrived at the booth. A "yes" or "no" vote would have made for a much clearer choice, but, as the *Sonoma Index Tribune* wrote: "We must accept the ballot as is and make the most of it."[30]

Before the vote there was a crackle in the air in Wine Country, a seeming electric storm of worry and excitement as people talked about little else. Both Wet and Dry leaders were equally confident of victory in California. The Drys believed the vote would be a strong majority to retain Prohibition. The Wets thought the Drys were wrong but were still worried about how southern California would vote.

When the vote was counted, a vast sigh of relief could almost be heard echoing across the vineyards, through the wine valleys, over the hillsides of vines, whistling past the Mayacamas Mountains and circling majestic Mount St. Helena, the highest point in Wine Country. California had voted for the repeal of the Eighteenth Amendment.

Grown men and women leaned on their vines and wiped tears from their eyes. They danced around in circles with their families. Whistles blew. Car horns blasted. They slapped each other on the back in the streets and shook hands with strangers.

By a majority that exceeded most predictions, California voted, and sent notice to its legislature that the voters supported repeal. The state had voted 965,000 for repeal, 305,000 to retain Prohibition. Southern California, long considered a Prohibition stronghold, had broken tradition to contribute generously to the repeal majority. Even the two driest counties in the state, Riverside and Orange, both close to Los Angeles, had voted Wet—though Riverside just squeaked into repeal territory with 7,927 votes against Prohibition and 7,014 to retain it.

At the other end of the spectrum, San Francisco, the Golden State's Wet heart, had voted for the end of Prohibition by 16 to 1: 127,665 votes to 8,975. That city celebrated as much as the two wine counties, and its restaurants were thronged with people singing and drinking and shouting. In Napa County, the vote was 5 to 1 in favor of repeal: 5,800 votes to 1,008, in Sonoma 13,317 to 2492.[31]

The *Sonoma Index-Tribune* warned the wine industry not to get too excited too soon; there was still a perilous journey between the state vote and a final decision in Washington on the repeal of the Eighteenth Amendment, with support of 36 of the 48 states in the Union needed. However, the paper declared that it looked as if the deal Sonoma had been waiting for was more than likely "after one of the worst and most cruel experiences to which a thrifty and prosperous rural community was ever subjected at the hands of its own neighbors and countrymen and all in the name of reform and a smug morality."[32]

Next California's secretary of state, Frank Jordan, called for the final vote of the 22 California delegates elected in the special election for Monday, July 24, in Sacramento.

By the end of June, California and 15 other states—Michigan, Wisconsin, Rhode Island, Wyoming, New Jersey, New York, Delaware, Nevada, Illinois, Indiana, Massachusetts, Iowa, Connecticut, New Hampshire, and West Virginia—had voted for repeal although not all states had completed state conventions.

California's wine industry had now launched more 3.2 percent products. Some were dubbed "Burgundy" or "Sauternes," though with their carbonation they would not have resembled those wines in any way. The new products—"La Conquesta," a sparkling wine from Shewan-Jones in Lodi; the "Sonnie Boy" brand products from B. Cribari & Sons of San Jose; and Mission Dry Corporation's carbonated and sweetened "California Burgundy Wine Beverage" with its elaborate gilt label—all made for unusual drinking for wine lovers, reported the *Grower*. [33]

Plucky Congressman Lea was still battling in Washington on behalf of California for light—10 percent—wine. He appeared before the House Ways and Means Committee imploring them to have sympathy for the working folk of California. "The laboring people of California are very much interested in securing this legislation. A very large percentage of all the money spent on the production of grapes and wine is for the labor cost."

He was further impassioned when he spoke about the 300 or 400 wineries he believed would soon be rehabilitated throughout the state. "That means labor for masons. It means labor for carpenters. The container industry will be benefited." But Congress was busy with other things; Lea's pleas may have been heard but they had no effect.[34]

The federal government had decided it would close down the Prohibition Bureau: It had never served its purpose properly, had brought shame and embarrassment to the government, and Washington seemed content to kill it dead. At midnight, Friday, June 30, 1933, all Prohibition agents in Sonoma were to be relieved of their jobs on orders from headquarters. Twenty-four agents plus a deputy administrator would be turning in their axes and guns and closing out their files.

In keeping with its reputation in Wine Country, the Bureau was mean-spirited to the end. As a last good-bye that final evening, just an hour or two before they were made obsolete, the local agents raided a popular roadhouse near Windsor dubbed, rather grandly, The Windsor Castle, though its design owed nothing to British architecture, with its Spanish-style roof and a large Dutch windmill leaning out from its second floor. The soon-to-be unemployed agents seized a small quantity of liquor and arrested the chef, Guido Converso, who had been left in charge that evening.

The unlucky Converso was taken to the county jail in Santa Rosa, fingerprinted and photographed, and then taken before U.S. Commissioner J. Harold McAlpine for arraignment on a charge of liquor possession. Bail was fixed at $750.[35]

Even the current Prohibition director, the ruddy and chubby Alfred Vernon Dalrymple—the last of the five men who had headed the Prohibition Bureau over the past 13 years—had now accepted the inevitable. The "professional" Dry conceded: "There's no use to kid ourselves and there isn't any use in delaying the start of liquor manufacture. It will mean putting hundreds of thousands of men back to work and it will mean hundreds of thousands of dollars of new business."[36]

As summer progressed in Wine Country, more and more wineries buzzed with activity. Some were slower to start up again, and others did not have the heart or the resources to get back in the wine business immediately.

Sam Sebastiani from Sebastiani wines in Sonoma said he was confident prosperity was ahead for Sonoma, reported the *Sonoma Index-Tribune,* as repeal was moving closer each day. He was already bottling sparkling wines and "orders were piling up." The Pagani winery, formerly the Chauvet winery, said it would crush that season for the first time since Prohibition. Arthur Kunde's Wildwood Vineyard, near Kenwood, was considering crushing again this harvest. Kunde had sold grapes throughout Prohibition, but it was his Cabernets that had helped build his name. The legendary Rhine Farm of the Bundschus had suffered during Prohibition: Walter Bundschu's wife, Sadie, had been one of very few Prohibitionists with a winery. The Bundschus had left the wine business entirely, although they had sold grapes to the wine-juice grape market. Luckily, buyers were plentiful concluded E. M. Sheehan, director of the Grape Growers League of California, who said investors from the East with $25 million in capital wanted to invest in California vineyards. "One Eastern syndicate has made $10,000,000 available to acquire vineyards and wineries," he said in a story reported in the *Sonoma-Index Tribune.*[37]

On Monday, July 24, California's 22 delegates arrived in scorching-hot Sacramento for the final vote in the state on repeal. They were called to order by Secretary of State Frank Jordan, who had always opposed Prohibition. The small group proceeded to enact the final chapter of Prohibition in California, said the *Grower.*

Delegate Byron C. Hanna of Los Angeles gave a speech that included the words: "California has long been the principal grape growing and wine making state in the United States, and at the time of the adoption of the Eighteenth Amendment grape growing was one of the most profitable industries in our com-

monwealth." He went on at great length to list the indignities and the losses that
Prohibition had brought to the state.

After various formalities, the delegates voted. Everyone in the room held their
breath when the vote was read out. The Wets had no need to worry. It was unanimous; all 22 delegates had voted for repeal of the Eighteenth Amendment of the
Constitution of the United States.

Later in the day, Jordan sent the certified documents to Washington, and
California became the fourteenth state to give formal ratification of the repeal of
Prohibition.[38]

By the middle of August 1933, it became clear that the harvest was not going to
be a huge one. Many ranchers decided to send very few grapes to the eastern markets. The profit is in the wine, not in the grape, and there was no good reason to
send good wine grapes off to an uncertain future in eastern markets. In July 1933,
before that year's harvest, there were already an estimated 22 million gallons of
wine in storage in California: 12 million gallons of dry wines and 10 million of
sweet wines, such as Sherry, port, and Madeira. Eleven of the 12 million gallons
of dry wine were held northern California; they included 16 different wines, such
as 5 million gallons of claret, 2.7 million gallons of Riesling, and 1 million gallons
of Zinfandel.[39]

In the summer of 1933, there had been 25 million gallons of wine in the entire United States. Wines from New York, Ohio, Louisiana, Wisconsin, and
Rhode Island made up about 3 million gallons. That California's share was nearly
90 percent of the total revealed the absolute dominance of the domestic wine market of that state.[40]

On August 10, the federal Prohibition Bureau passed out of existence as a
separate organization. It was now to be part of a newly formed Division of Investigation of the Department of Justice with J. Edgar Hoover as its head.[41]

By the end of August, two-thirds of the necessary states had voted for repeal
when Arizona, Missouri, and Washington completed their votes.

At the same time, harvest was about to get under way—a little later than normal—and the first grapes had reached $35 per ton, according to the Picetti Broth-
ers, owners of the once-famous Glaister Vineyard and winery. Carl Bundschu,
brother of Walter Bundschu of Gundlach Bundschu, had been hired by the widow

Niebaum (the wife of the founder of the winery, Captain Niebaum) and was now running one of Napa County's famous wineries, Inglenook. He had already toured Sonoma Valley vineyards and had bought some grapes for about $35 a ton. Sam Sebastiani was expected to have the largest crush in southern Sonoma and was also expected to buy grapes from throughout Sonoma and from adjacent wine counties to supplement his own. He was to add about 300,000 gallons of wine to his cellars.[42]

On September 28, 1933 a story in the *Healdsburg Enterprise,* quoted Carl F. Wente, vice president of the Bank of America, who said he had just made a business tour of northern California and had found that "rehabilitation of wineries in anticipation of the repeal of the Eighteenth Amendment has stimulated business to a marked extent in Napa, Sonoma and Mendocino counties." He reported that in one day alone $3,000 of new payroll checks was handled by the St. Helena branch of his bank.[43]

By the end of September, crush was well under way at the wineries. It was thought that this harvest would produce 25 to 30 million gallons of wines: 17 million gallons in old cooperage that was empty or had been reconditioned and the remaining 8 million gallons in new cooperage. At the end of the vintage, California wineries were expected to have cellared 50 million gallons of wine, including that stored from previous years.[44]

During September, Colorado, Idaho, Maine, Maryland, Minnesota, New Mexico, and Vermont had voted yes for repeal. On October 3, Virginia had also voted yes for repeal. Now only four states were needed to finalize the repeal process.[45] The wine counties counted down with great anticipation as one state after another voted to end Prohibition.

One of the most tragic results of the nastiest of Prohibition practices shocked the Wine Country in October when one of Santa Rosa's star athletes was blinded by poisoned liquor. That it had happened so close to repeal made the event particularly heartbreaking. Ralph "Nellie" Holm, 24, reported the *Press Democrat,* was a handsome young athlete who had been a popular student at Santa Rosa High School and had gone on to more sports success at the University of California. He had been discovered late one afternoon by his father, just sitting in his car near the family home. When his father looked into why he was sitting still in a parked car, he discovered that his son had gone blind. Holm had been visiting friends all afternoon, drinking whiskey. When he started to drive home, he began to lose his sight. By the time he got close to home, he couldn't see anything. It was some time later, his father found him in the car, unable to walk to the house. Holm was the second young Santa Rosa man to have been blinded that year from drinking poisoned alcohol. Hugh Roberts, 23, had become blind only months earlier, after drinking whiskey at a beach party. Eventually he recovered part of his sight, but his family was suing the proprietor of a Tomales bootlegging parlor for $50,000.

Holm's father took him to the hospital immediately. The poisoned liquor had left him in critical condition. Holm was totally blind for more than 24 hours, though later it was reported, he could distinguish light from dark, but in one eye only. Doctors believed his symptoms indicated wood alcohol poisoning but no one else at the party he'd been at had been harmed by the alcohol that they'd been drinking, which had been bought from a bootlegger. Holm would not identify the friend who had given him the liquor.[46]

As the repeal votes rolled into Washington from around the United States, the Drys had faith and hope that all was not lost to them. Dr. F. Scott McBride, the national superintendent of the Anti-Saloon League, who had taken over after Wayne Wheeler had died in 1927, said that if repeal did occur, he believed the nation would be repulsed and that before long voters would beg for Dry laws to be reinstituted.[47] Folk in the wine valleys just guffawed rudely at the thought. But McBride's words were only a momentary distraction from a brutal fight that was occurring, this time among the growers themselves.

Growers had seen the price of grapes climb steadily as harvest progressed. They had soon realized there was a very strong demand for the small harvest that year and before long they were expected to get $45 and $50 a ton for their grapes. At the beginning of October, the Miller Fruit Company in Healdsburg purchased 1,000 tons of wine grapes from J. B. Foppiano at $40 a ton. The grapes, mostly Zinfandel, with some Carignane and Petite Sirah, said the *Press Democrat,* were to be crushed at the Foppiano winery.[48] Growers watching the sale were pleased at the $40 deal. But soon those prices plummeted.

Some of the largest winery owners in Napa and Sonoma had decided that instead of buying local wine grapes for $40 and up per ton, it would be to their advantage to import cheaper fruit from California's Central Valley. Soon hundreds of tons of valley grapes were brought into Sonoma for as low as $10 or $12.50 per ton.[49] This brought howls of outrage and shouts accusing the large wineries of being greedy. There also was anger that the superior grapes of northern California would be mixed with less desirable valley grapes, and the wine made from them could still be labeled Napa or Sonoma wines.

An enraged band of Sonoma grape growers gathered, said the *Press Democrat,* to formulate a plan to fight these purchases and to protect what they called "the county's reputation for high quality wine." The group said they would fight in state and federal courts any attempt to make wines from imported grapes that were sold as Sonoma wines.[50]

As more and more states voted for repeal, wineries got busier. In November 1933, a *Healdsburg Enterprise* story reported that an estimated $5 million had been spent during the past six months on the rehabilitation of wineries in preparation for repeal—a better way to spend funds than on profit to bootlegging crime syndicates.[51]

While the battle over Central Valley grapes continued, more states had been voting on repeal: Soon the requisite 36 states out of 48 had voted for the end of Prohibition. Although South Carolina had voted Dry, the states of Kentucky, Ohio, Pennsylvania, and Utah were the last of the 36 Wet elections needed. Although not all votes had been counted by November 9 the Eighteenth Amendment appeared to have been voted out of the constitution yesterday." Wine Country newspapers plastered the story with huge headlines across their front pages: the version in the *Sonoma Index-Tribune* read "REPEAL GOES OVER THE TOP" in huge type usually reserved for the outbreak of a major war.

It was finally done; Prohibition was dead.

Repeal would become effective early in December when the four final states signed off completely on repeal by the voting of their delegates. December 5 would be the date of the last convention. On that day Prohibition would constitutionally be concluded, but for all intents and purposes, it was over already.[52]

There was not much time to relive the past. There was lots to be done. Some got to work. Others hit the town. The *Press Democrat* reported on November 8, that San Francisco watering holes had already thrown open their long-barred doors, restaurants sold mixed drinks, beer parlors were packed, and the streets were filled with partygoers going from one drinking spot to another. Thousands of cars full of excited partygoers created a traffic jam downtown. Cocktails were selling for 25 cents a glass.[53]

Sonoma's Italian Club celebrated repeal almost immediately at its club rooms on First Street East, in the city of Sonoma. F. Mosso, club president, acted as master of ceremonies and chef. Along with traditional chestnuts, both roasted and boiled, fine red wines made before World War I had been hauled out of members' cellars: One can only imagine the splendor of those aged wines, the treasured, hidden vintages from winemaking family cellars. The celebration concluded with a farewell toast to Old Man Prohibition, saluted with fine old California brandy that had been made 20 years earlier, reported the *Sonoma Index-Tribune.*[54]

The American market was officially open for Sonoma and Napa wines again, reported the *Sonoma Index-Tribune.* At recent count, there were 137 wineries and 11 brandy distilleries in northern California. Napa had 39 wineries, Sonoma, 69. And the largest winery of them all with a capacity of 3,250,000 gallons was the Italian Swiss Colony at Asti in Sonoma County.

St. Helena, a town of 2,000 in the center of Napa County had 16 wineries around it. Healdsburg was next, followed by Santa Rosa with 12.

The brand new Wine Producer's Association, representing 110 California wineries that controlled 80 percent of the wine in the state, declared that wine drinkers everywhere should buy California wine. It said it would launch a nationwide marketing campaign to let the public know why American wines should be the favorite of the nation.

Good American wine had not been available to consumers for years. The association said its responsibility was to ensure that the younger generation brought up on "synthetic gin and moonshine" was educated to appreciate the great wines of California.[55]

Like many other wineries, the giant Italian Swiss Colony winery was preparing to have wine ready for the moment repeal occurred. But before the official date arrived, the winery turned November 24 into a great celebration. In his book, *Legacy of a Village: The Italian Swiss Colony Winery and the People of Asti, California,* Jack W. Florence relates a memory of that day of a Pathé News cameramen heading up to the winery in the gentle hills north of Geyserville and newspaper reporters arriving. It was a tremendous photo op. Guests were welcomed warmly: there was wine, there were banners. Barrels of wine were rolled onto a train that had arrived on Asti's own spur line. Ida Prati, daughter of Angela and Edoardo Seghesio and wife of Asti's superintendent, Enrico Prati, cracked a bottle of champagne over the train's steam engine. Steam whistles blew, crowds cheered, girls from Cloverdale High School participated by wearing Italian-Swiss costumes in red, white, and green. Forty-five thousand gallons of wine were shipped that day in 12 refrigerator cars[56] on a train labeled "California Wine on its Way."[57]

Lou Colombano was at the winery at Asti that day with his father, who had bootlegged wine and grappa during Prohibition. In an interview in September 2008, Colombano recalled that day, when he helped load some of the barrels onto railcars. "The barrels were put on the rail car first, then I helped fill them with a hose leading from a wine tank." Twenty-two teams of horses were still at work in the vineyards then. When the hills were very steep, you could only use a horse team; he explained, "A tractor was an impossibility."[58]

Down in the port of San Francisco, the first ships in many years to carry wine back to consumers in the eastern United States were soliciting business. They were advertising "New Ships—New Terminals—Fast Weekly Sailings to New York–Philadelphia."[59]

Just before Prohibition became history, the state of California issued new parameters for the sale of beer, wine, and liquor, listing the "things you can do" and "the things you cannot" starting on December 5, the first day of repeal. The *Healdsburg Enterprise* explained some of the limitations, some of which were risible:

> On the "can do" list: You can drink wine and beer with meals; and you can drink hard liquor over the bar of a private club provided it is your own liquor; and you can purchase as much as five gallons at a time and take this liquor out to the curb, sit down and drink it, or get into your car and drink the liquor or walk down the street with a bottle aloft or stand on the street corner exchanging drinks with a friend or take it to your home, club, office, hotel room, golf course, or any place else *except* a public bar or dining room.

Can't dos included: "You can't be served hard liquor over a public bar, [or] be served cocktails, highballs, liqueurs or other hard liquor in a public dining-room; you can't drink wine in public eating places without a meal."[60] The rules seemed picayune after the endless litany of Prohibition regulations.

Finally the day dawned that so many in the wine counties thought they never would see. On December 5, 1933, at 4:32 P.M. Pacific standard time, 13 years of national Prohibition were legally and constitutionally over.

As the sun was starting to set over the hills in the two wine counties and the dark, leafless grapevines began to cast long shadows through the vineyards, the 21 delegates of Utah's state repeal convention were gathered far away in the House chamber of that state's capitol building. The state's delegates were waiting on the floor of the chamber, while the galleries above were filled with an excited public crowded into their seats by dozens of newspaper and radio reporters and cameramen. When the delegates cast their ballots, Utah became the thirty-sixth state to ratify the Twenty-first Amendment to the Constitution. That was all the ratification process needed to be complete.

The first part of the nation's Twenty-first Amendment would now read: "The eighteenth article of amendment to the Constitution of the United States is hereby repealed."

One of the biggest experiments in social engineering in the United States was over. Driven hard from inception by special interests and politicians, it had finally died, in failure and shame.

When President Franklin D. Roosevelt issued the Repeal Proclamation, he asked the good citizens of United States to help rout all bootleggers, to support the government in its liquor taxation program, to continue to outlaw the saloon, and to promote temperance. His calm, reasonable words were appreciated after the manic propaganda of the past 13 years.[61]

Celebrations in northern California had been so boisterous, so long and so consistent, the rules so relaxed, since the state vote in July that locals swore that the lid would go on when Prohibition was repealed, rather than off. So few daily differences would be seen in Sonoma and Napa after the Proclamation. Like so many other Wine Country towns, for instance, St. Helena had been essentially Wet throughout the Dry years. People were accustomed to drinking what they wanted, mostly when they wanted. But life at the wineries was a very different story. The famous cellar at Beringer had been a madhouse of activity for some weeks as repeal came closer.

On December 5, as soon as word was received from San Francisco that ratification was concluded, a procession of six huge trucks, two with trailers, rolled out of the Beringer winery, turned right through the one main street of St. Helena heading for San Francisco and as far away as Los Angeles. Up the valley at Larkmead, the Salminas were equally busy with a large crew filling orders for their famous vintages.

Wineries like Beaulieu were more than ready for the return of legal wine business. Chaos reigned there and at other wineries as hundreds of excited people glad to be at work were swamped filling orders for delivery on December 5 reported the *St. Helena Star*. A long line of refrigerated railcars was waiting for word to go as soon as repeal was announced.[62] W. L. St. Amant, vice president and general manager of the vineyard, said the company had 1.2 million gallons of wine in storage from previous years and that 450,000 had been added this year in readiness for what was expected to be huge demand. St. Amant said that owner, George de Latour, had recently spent $60,000 on new equipment, including updated machinery, bottles, cartons, labels, caps, and barrels.[63]

In Sonoma County, a $75,000 wine cargo—3,600 cases of wine in four car-loads from the F. B. Vadon winery—had been shipped from Cloverdale. To cele-brate the end of Prohibition and that first train of wine, almost the entire population of the town flocked to the train station to cheer as the "prosperity water" started on its journey to Chicago. The vines on the Vadon ranch were nearly all imported from France and had been carefully cared for during Prohibition so they would be ready for production as soon repeal came.[64]

The newfound freedom galvanized the wine counties. Repeal encouraged es-tablished winemakers with money to spend from other parts of the state to come to northern California's Wine Country. Louis Martini, whose family vineyard had been started in Kingsburg, near Fresno in the Central Valley, admitted he had al-ways "wanted a winery in the dry grape country" and had invested $100,000 in land near St. Helena along with the necessary cooperage and buildings and "22 redwood tanks of 20,000 gallon capacity each."[65]

Under the headline "Hello D-R-Y 1933," the *San Francisco Chronicle* related one of the minor but delightful stories of repeal. Telephone operators at Prohibi-tion headquarters in San Francisco were stymied when they could no longer an-swer "Good morning, Prohibition headquarters." Quickly they changed the greeting. If one called that office after repeal, a voice answered instead with the phone number, "EXbrook-Zero-Five-Eight-Four."[66]

In Rutherford, people were still talking about the day-long repeal celebra-tions hosted by Carl Bundschu at the grand Inglenook Winery. The winery had been built by Captain Gustav Niebaum, who had dreamed for years of building a château in the United States similar to the stately homes of Germany and France.

He completed his château in 1888: a stately gabled stone building, three sto-ries high, its massive walls nearly four feet thick. Although the winery was shut down during Prohibition, grapes were still sold. Now the winery had been re-opened by Niebaum's widow with Bundschu as superintendent. And it was to the Inglenook cellars and Captain Niebaum's old tasting room that prominent officials and citizens from northern California had come to celebrate repeal. Eight worthies had been invited to lunch, including the sheriff of Napa County, the fire chief of Santa Rosa, the mayor of Vineburg, and the editor of the *Santa Rosa Republican*. All afternoon and all through the evening, many other friends had come over to share in the good tidings and toast to a better future, thankful that winemaking was back at Inglenook.[67]

Few of the other winemakers or grape growers in Napa and Sonoma celebrated Prohibition quite in that manner. It was generally a quiet, somber time. Lou Foppiano said, "It was not a big deal by then, we knew it was coming. Nobody got too excited about it."[68]

The Nichelinis, industrious as ever up in their beautiful valley, just got on with the business of winemaking. The family had acquired more vineyard land toward the end of Prohibition and was focused on getting that land planted and improved.[69]

Those in Wine Country who took the time to celebrate the very end of Prohibition that early December in 1933, it seemed, were the exception. Most winemakers and grape growers noted the day with nothing more than a blessing to the Almighty that it was over. Perhaps they enjoyed an extra drink, but likely not even that.

They were tired. They were worn out. They were dispirited from a battle that had gotten too mean and had lasted too long. They felt they had been shamed by their own government as purveyors of poison and misery. They had been brutalized and insulted and treated like criminals. They had lost fortunes in dumped wines, dried-out tanks, and uncared-for vineyards. Yes, some few of them had made money, good money, but the cost had been great. Most of the wine people who had had to break the law only wanted to survive, not a felicitous way of life for decent, rural folk. Their once-welcoming neighborhoods had become mistrustful of government and of strangers.

As Prohibition ended, the winemakers and grape growers knew they faced a long fight to renew their vineyards, to reconnect with business contacts, to catch up on the science of winemaking that had continued unabated in the world's other wine-producing countries, such as Australia. Now countries like that had years of advantage over California. Many winemakers in Napa and Sonoma knew they had to relearn the art and craft of making fine wines again; so many of those talents had been lost in the past 14 years. These American citizens had lost money, lost neighbors, learned that vengeance and cheating were rife in their country—all thanks to their own government.

Prohibition had lasted for nearly 14 years. As far as the winemakers and grape growers of Napa and Sonoma were concerned, the nightmare had continued far too long. As they got back to work without fuss, these thrifty, dutiful, and industrious citizens thought of the waste, the unhappiness, the worry, the anger, the anxiety, the fear, and the losses they had felt in the last few years.

For the grape growers who sold their wine juice grapes and who had been busy during Prohibition, their talents in the vineyard, with their soil and their vines, are still lauded as the basis of so much that came later in making wine that has made Napa and Sonoma great today.

Now, at repeal, there was joy that the craft of winemaking would return to Sonoma and Napa. Although the passion to make wine that had driven those vineyards for so long had not been extinguished during the long night of Prohibition, something had vanished when winemaking was perceived as the work of criminals. Some essential poetry had been lost. At last, winemakers would start to create again, unhindered, unhampered, unafraid of violence and intimidation.

Winemakers are men and women of the sun and the stars and the wind and the rain. Like great seafaring adventurers out on the oceans, they can feel change in the air, heat on its way, rain threatening, a frost looming in a dark night, long before they happen. They are fortune-tellers, every day gambling their knowledge, their intuition, against the risk of elements and climate. Their sense of taste is erotically acute: they can pluck one tiny berry off a vine, chew it for a split second, spit it out, and tell you instantly if that berry is ready to be made into wine or how long it might need to hang on the vine absorbing the goodness of the sun before it is ready to be gathered.

A winemaker is extrasensory. Like a great lover who understands a partner's wishes by the tiniest flutter of an eyelid, a winemaker can recognize the health of an entire vineyard with a glance, the scent on a breeze, the color of a leaf, the way a vine hangs, the way it moves. A winemaker reads these subtleties like a long-experienced inamorata who comprehends every mood, every move, every gesture of a beloved. When you walk with winemakers through their vineyards, they wave their hands across the land as if they are introducing you to someone who keeps them virile and energized and pulsating with pleasure.

Napa and Sonoma were glad to have them back.

Notes

Prologue

1. Richard Paul Hinkle, "Foppiano at the Century Mark," *Wines & Vines*, September 1996.
2. Ibid.
3. "Wine River Flow Stops Noon Today," *Sotoyome Scimitar*, August 17, 1926.
4. "River of Wine Runs On Sunday: Many Take Drink," *Healdsburg Tribune*, August 16, 1926.
5. "Foppiano Tanks Empty Contents in Ditches," *Healdsburg Enterprise*, August 19, 1926.
6. Author interviews with Gene Cuneo, July 5 and August 13, 2006.

Chapter 1

1. "Bone Dry America at once Effective by Senate's Vote," *Press Democrat*, October 29, 1919.
2. Author interviews with Gene Cuneo, July 5 and August 13, 2006.
3. R. L. Nougaret, "Disposition of the 1920 Wine Grape Crop," *California Grape Grower* (*Wines & Vines*), September 1, 1920
4. Ronald L. Miller, "A California Romance in Perspective: The Elopement, Marriage and Ecclesiastical Trial of Henry D. Fitch and Josefa Carrillo," *Journal of San Diego History 19*, no. 2 (1973).
5. Author interviews with Louis J. Foppiano, July 5 and August 13, 2006, and conversations, spring and summer 2008.
6. Jack W. Florence, Sr., *Legacy of a Village: The Italian Swiss Colony Winery and the People of Asti* (Phoenix: Arizona, 1999), p. 69.
7. Ibid., 27
8. Ibid., 41.
9. Ibid., 106.
10. Richard Paul Hinkle, "Seghesio—Slumbering No More," *Wines & Vines*, March 1995.
11. Cuneo interviews.
12. Passalacqua Family History and Genealogy, The Collection of the Healdsburg Museum.
13. Ernest P. Peninou, *History of the Sonoma Viticultural District: The Grape Growers, the Wine Makers and the Vineyards, Vol. 1* (Santa Rosa, CA: Nomis Press, 1998) p. 337.
14. E. O. Essig, Adele Ogden, and Clarence John DuFour, *Fort Ross: California Outpost of Russian Alaska 1812–1841*, (Kingston, Ontario: The Limestone Press, 1991).
15. Ernest P. Peninou, *History of the Sonoma Viticultural District: The Grape Growers, the Wine Makers and the Vineyards, Vol. 1*, (Santa Rosa, CA: Nomis Press, 1998) p.49.
16. "Mission Flowers Found Buried in Adobe Bricks," *Sonoma Index-Tribune*, December 29, 1933.
17. "The Days of Long Ago," *St. Helena Star*, April 6, 1917.

18. "Ships in Port, 1851," The Maritime Heritage Project, www.maritimeheritage.org.
19. Charles L. Sullivan, *A Companion to California Wine: An Encyclopedia of Wine and Winemaking from the Mission Period to the Present,* (Berkeley and Los Angeles, CA: University of California Press, 1998), p. 146.
20. *Appleton's Annual Encyclopedia,* (New York: D. Appleton and Company, 1866) p. 85.
21. Ernest P. Peninou, *History of the Sonoma Viticultural District: The Grape Growers, the Wine Makers and the Vineyards, Vol. 1,* (Santa Rosa, CA: Nomis Press, 1998) p.24.
22. Ibid., 298.
23. Ibid., 297.
24. Ben C. Truman, "The Wines of California: Model Wineries of Napa and Sonoma Counties," *New York Times,* March 13, 1887.
25. Ibid.
26. C. G. Murphy, "History of Grape Growing in California, *Sonoma Index-Tribune,* July 28, 1933.
27. "Twentieth Anniversary of S.F. Fire," *California Grape Grower (Wines & Vines),* April 1, 1926.
28. H.W. Wiley, *American Wines at the Paris Exposition of 1900, U.S. Department of Agriculture,* (Washington: Gov. Printing Office, 1903).
29. "Extinguishing Fire with Wine," *California Grape Grower (Wines & Vines),* April 1, 1926
30. "Antonio Perelli-Minetti, A Life in Wine Making," interview by Ruth Teiser in 1969, Regional Wine History Office, The Bancroft Library, University of California, Berkeley. p. 13, 29, 52.
31. Cuneo interviews.

Chapter 2

1. Author interviews with Toni Nichelini-Irwin, February to August 2008.
2. Horatio F. Stoll, "Now for the 1920 Grape Crop," *California Grape Grower (Wines & Vines)* December 1, 1919.
3. Author interviews with Louis J. Foppiano, March 12 and July 5, 2006, and conversations throughout spring and summer 2008.
4. Herbert Asbury, *The Great Illusion,* (Garden City, New York: Doubleday & Co., 1950) p. 115.
5. Richard F. Hamm, *Shaping the 18th Amendment,* (Chapel Hill, NC: University of North Carolina Press, 1995) p. 241.
6. Jack Florence Jr., *Legacy of a Village: The Italian Swiss Colony Winery and People of Asti, California,* (Phoenix: Raymond Court Press, 1999) p. 146.
7. "What Americans Drink," *World Almanac and Encyclopedia* (New York: The Press Publishing Co., 1920) p. 406.
8. Franklin Hichborn, *Story of the Session of the California Legislature of 1911,* (San Francisco: Press o the James H. Barry Company, 1911), pp. 195–198.
9. Gilman M. Ostrander, *The Prohibition Movement in California 1848–1933,* (Berkeley: University of California Press. 1957) pp. 124–125.
10. Ibid., pp. 128–129.
11. Justin Steuart, *Wayne Wheeler, Dry Boss: An Uncensored Biography of Wayne B. Wheeler* (Westport, CT: Greenwood Press, 1970).
12. Gilman M. Ostrander, *The Prohibition Movement in California 1848–1933,* (Berkeley: University of California Press. 1957) pp. 131–132.
13. "Wine Men Talk it Over," *St. Helena Star,* January 21, 1916.
14. "Don't Misunderstand Proposition #2," *St. Helena Star,* October 13, 1916.
15. "Taft on Prohibition," *St. Helena Star,* August 25, 1916.
16. "Wine Men Talk It Over," *St. Helena Star,* January 21, 1916.
17. "Anti-Prohibition Meeting," *St. Helena Star,* April 14, 1916.

18. "Danger to Wine Industry," *St. Helena Star,* April 28, 1916.
19. "What Prohibition Really Means to the Wine Industry," *St. Helena Star,* September 29, 1916.
20. "Wine Industry Threatened," *St. Helena Star,* August 11, 1916.
21. Gilman M. Ostrander, *The Prohibition Movement in California 1848–1933,* (Berkeley: University of California Press. 1957) pp. 137, 138.
22. "What Prohibition Really Means to the Wine Industry," *St. Helena Star,* September 29, 1916.
23. "Amendments Considered," *St. Helena Star,* October 6, 1916.
24. "Jack Frost Pays Visit," *St. Helena Star,* May 12, 1916.
25. "Vines Recuperating Well," *St. Helena Star,* June 16, 1916.
26. "Napa County Suffers," *St. Helena Star,* July 28, 1916.
27. "Successful Vintage: Wine Making Brought to a Close at Beaulieu Vineyards," *St. Helena Star,* December 15, 1916.
28. James A. Henretta, "Charles Evans Hughes and the Strange Death of Liberal America," *Law and History Review* (Spring 2006), www.historycooperative.org/journals/lhr/24.1/henretta.html, (accessed September 17, 2008).
29. "Result of Election," *St. Helena Star,* November 10, 1916.
30. Gilman M. Ostrander, *The Prohibition Movement in California 1848–1933,* (Berkeley: University of California Press. 1957) p.138–139.
31. Charles A. Fecher, *Mencken: A Study of His Thoughts* (New York: Alfred A. Knopf, 1978), p. 210.
32. "What Should Be Done Under New Wheat Saving Rules?" *St. Helena Star,* April 5, 1918.
33. "Pleads For Wine Growers; Prohibition Would Cost Californians Millions, Kahn Tells Senators," *New York Times,* June 18, 1918.
34. "As Viewed by Phelan," *St. Helena Star,* July 26, 1918
35. "Vineyardists Protest Prohibitory Law," *Healdsburg Tribune,* August 8, 1918.
36. "Prohibition Passes in Senate, 45 To 6; Agricultural Bill with 'Dry' Rider Effective June 30, 1919," *New York Times,* September 7, 1918.
37. "Rain Does Much Damage," *St. Helena Star,* September 20, 1918.
38. "Governor Stephens Re-Elected," *St. Helena Star,* November 8, 1918.
39. "Governor Stephens in Bad," *St. Helena Star,* April 26, 1918.
40. "Governor Stephens Re-Elected," *St. Helena Star,* November 8, 1918.
41. California Proposition 1, Liquor Regulation, Record 75, http://library.uchastings.edu/cgi-bin/starfinder/17987/calprop.txt; California Proposition 22, Prohibition, 1918, Record 89, http://library.uchastings.edu/cgi-bin/starfinder/17987/calprop.txt.
42. "California Vote on Prohibition," *World Almanac and Encyclopedia,* (New York: The Press Publishing Co., 1920) p. 792.
43. "Sonoma 100 Per Cent Joyous," *Sonoma Index-Tribune,* November 16, 1918.
44. "Sonoma Flies Service Flag for Boys Gone to War, *Sonoma Index-Tribune,* July 6, 1918.

Chapter 3

1. "Losses of Allies and Central Powers in the War, compiled by U.S. Central Records, American Expeditionary Forces," *World Almanac and Encyclopedia* (New York: The Press Publishing Co. 1920), p. 685
2. "General Chronology for 1919," *World Almanac and Encyclopedia* (New York: The Press Publishing Co., 1920).
3. Margaret MacMillan, *Paris, 1919* (New York: Random House, 2000), p. 491.
4. *Tax on Pure Fruit-Juice Beverage Act of 1919,* HR. 7840, 66th Cong., 1st sess., *Congressional Record* 58 (July 28, 1919): H 3287.

5.   *Prohibition of Intoxicating Beverages Act of 1919,* HR 6810, 66th Cong., 1st sess., *Congressional Record* 58, part 3, (July 11, 1919): H 2458–2459.

6.   Hugh S. Hersman, Congressional Record Index, 66th Cong., 1st session, *Congressional Record,* p. 9394.

7.   *Prohibition of Intoxicating Beverages Act of 1919,* HR 6810, 66th Cong., 1st sess., *Congressional Record* 58 (July 11, 1919): H 2459.

8.   Joseph Timmons, "Gala City Awaits Hero Sons," and "Ferry Lights Assure Boys They're Here," *San Francisco Examiner,* April 22, 1919.

9.   "Give the Boys Who Served Us a Welcome Home," *Healdsburg Tribune,* November 10, 1919.

10.   *National Prohibition—Veto Message,* HR 6810, 66th Cong., 1st sess., *Congressional Record* 58, part 8, (October 28, 1919): S 7633.

11.   "House, 176 to 55 Overrides Veto of War Prohibition," *New York Times,* October 28, 1919.

12.   "Drys Win: Veto Fails: House Refuses View of President," *Los Angeles Daily Times,* October 28, 1919.

13.   *Prohibition Act of 1919,* HR 6810, 66th Cong., 1st sess., *Congressional Record* 58, part 8, (October 27, 1919), H 7610–7611.

14.   "House, 176 to 55 Overrides Veto of War Prohibition," *New York Times,* ibid.

15.   James D. Phelan, "What Shall We Do To Be Saved? A Statesman's Patriotic Disquisition on the Juice of the Grape," *San Franciscans Magazine* (April 1929), archived on the website of the Virtual Museum of the City of San Francisco, www.sfmuseum.org/hist3/prohibition.html, (accessed November, 16, 2008).

16.   *National Prohibition—Veto Message,* HR 6810, 66th Cong., 1st sess., *Congressional Record* 58, part 8, (October 28, 1919), S 7634.

17.   "President Will Lift Ban with Peace," *Press Democrat,* October 29, 1919.

18.   Charles Sullivan, *A Companion to California Wine: An Encyclopedia of Wine and Winemaking from the Mission Period to the Present,* (Berkeley and Los Angeles: University of California Press, 1998) p. 92.

19.   Jack Jungmeyer, "Epic of the Passing of the Grape," *Sonoma Index-Tribune,* June 21, 1919.

20.   "The Grape Situation," *St. Helena Star,* August 29, 1919.

21.   "The Grape Situation: Vintage is on but Not as in Former Years," *St. Helena Star,* September 12, 1919.

22.   Herbert C. Thompson, "Golden Vineyards: California Grape Growers Find Prohibition Makes Their Business More Profitable Than Ever," *New York Times,* November 30, 1919.

Chapter 4

1.   "Biggest Liquor Haul: 60,000,000 Gallons of Whiskey Go to Uncle Sam Tomorrow," *Washington Post,* January 15, 1920.

2.   "Thefts Reported," Associated Press story printed in the *Press Democrat,* January 15, 1920.

3.   "Toll Liquor's Knell," *Washington Post,* January 17, 1920.

4.   W.F. Heinz, "Prohibition took toll of California wineries in 1920–33," *California Grower (Wines & Vines)* January 1933.

5.   "Federal Stage Set for Dry Law Entry Tomorrow," *New York Times,* January 16, 1920.

6.   "50,000 Gallons of Wine Going into Private Cellars Today," *San Francisco Chronicle,* January 16, 1920.

7.   Millard E. Tydings, *Before and after Prohibition* (New York: Macmillan, 1930), pp.3–4.

8.   John Kobler, *Ardent Spirits* (New York: G. P. Putnam's Sons, 1973) pp. 12–13.

9.   "Toll Liquor's Knell, Home Brew in Demand," *Washington Post,* January 17, 1920.

10.   "'Flu' Kills Four; 390 New Cases Here In One Day," *Chicago Daily Tribune,* January 16, 1920.

11. "1200 Cases of Flu Reported," *Chicago Daily Tribune,* January 17, 1920.
12. "Kentucky Churches Hold Jubilee—Farewells to Alcohol Tame in Larger Cities," *New York Times,* January 17, 1920.
13. "Chicago under Deep Pall," *Los Angeles Daily Times,* January, 17, 1920.
14. "Revelry and Prayer in Rum's Last House," *Los Angeles Daily Times,* January 17, 1920.
15. "John Barleycorn Died Peacefully at the Toll of 12," *New York Times,* January 17, 1920, p. 1.
16. "Merry Revel Marks New York Farewell to John Barleycorn," *Washington Post,* January 17, 1920
17. "Two Libraries Bar Books on Manufacture of Liquor, *Washington Post,* January 16, 1920.
18. "Celebrate Demise of John Barleycorn by 'Sky Funeral," *Atlanta Constitution,* January 16, 1920.
19. "Kentucky Churches Hold Jubilee—Farewells to Alcohol Tame in Larger Cities: Louisville," *New York Times,* January 17, 1920.
20. "Joy, Grief Will Mark End of Rum's Reign in Los Angeles Tonight," *Los Angeles Daily Times,* January 15, 1920.
21. "Liquor Rush to Mexico Clogs Gate at Border," *San Francisco Chronicle,* January 14, 1920.
22. "Final Export from Baltimore," *New York Times,* January 17, 1920.
23. "Wine Washes out Wet Era, Movement of Liquor on Last Day Gigantic," *San Francisco Chronicle,* January 17, 1920.
24. "Whiskey Breath Sleuths to Run Down Drinkers," *San Francisco Chronicle,* January 13, 1920.
25. "Happening in San Francisco—First Day of Prohibition," *San Francisco Chronicle,* January 17, 1920.
26. "Sonoma Wine in Great Demand, Valley Witnesses Remarkable Procession on the Eve of National Prohibition," *Sonoma Index-Tribune,* January 17, 1920.
27. Patsy Strickland, *Korbel History,* (unknown binding) Guerneville, CA, Sonoma Country Wine Library, Healdsburg, CA., 1999.

Chapter 5

1. "Response by Prohibition Commissioner John F. Kramer to a Letter of Inquiry," *California Grape Grower (Wines & Vines)* March 1, 1920.
2. Author conversation with Louis J. Foppiano, April 25, 2008.
3. "Grape Growers Entitled to Fair Prices," *California Grape Grower (Wines & Vines)* July 1, 1920, p.1.
4. "Some Sound Advice worth Following," *California Grape Grower (Wines & Vines)* March 1, 1920, p. 1.
5. "Have Prohibition Laws Made Growers Prosperous?" *California Grape Grower (Wines & Vines)* January 1, 1921, p. 1.
6. "Manufacture of Wine in the Home," *California Grape Grower (Wines & Vines)* November 1, 1920, p.15.
7. www.winepros.org/wine101/grape_profiles/alicante.htm#top, accessed November 20, 2008.
8. "California Grapes Popular in New York," *California Grape Grower (Wines & Vines)* December 1, 1920.
9. "New Country Home," *St. Helena Star,* March 21, 1919.
10. "Here and There," *California Grape Grower (Wines & Vines)* August 1, 1920.
11. Applications for Sacramental Wine, 1919, archives of the Archdiocese of San Francisco.
12. "Louis Kunde Escorts Wine across Continent," *Sonoma Index-Tribune,* March 20, 1920.
13. Author conversation with Foppiano.
14. Rod Smith, *Private Reserve: Beaulieu Vineyard and the Rise of Napa Valley* (Stamford, CT: Daglan Press, 2000) p. 42.
15. Ibid., pp. 81–82.

16. "Will Aid Youth's Directory," *St. Helena Star,* August, 25, 1916.

17. Letter from Xaverian brothers, April 6, 1908, archives of the Archdiocese of San Francisco.

18. Report on Conditions of Rutherford Farm, August 19, 1915, archives of the Archdiocese of San Francisco.

19. Conditions of Farm, St. Joseph's Agricultural Institute, September 1926, archives of the Archdiocese of San Francisco.

20. Notarized letter signed by Father D.O. Crowley, dated March 6, 1920, archives of the Archdiocese of San Francisco.

21. Letter on the Office of the Archbishop letterhead, inscribed with seal, to Mr. G. de Latour from Archbishop of San Francisco, signed Edward J. Hanna, dated March 25, 1920, archives of the Archdiocese of San Francisco.

22. Robert F. McNamara, *Roman Days,* "Archbishop Hanna, Rochesterian," *Rochester History 25,* no. 2 (April 1963): p. 5.

23. Richard Gribble, *An Archbishop for the People: The Life of Edward J. Hanna* (New York: Paulist Press, 2006), p. 150.

24. Ibid., 150.

25. Rod Smith, *Private Reserve: Beaulieu Vineyard and the Rise of Napa Valley* (Stamford, CT: Daglan Press, 2000) p. 40.

26. "Does Not Favor Prohibition," *St. Helena Star,* September 22, 1916.

27. "Does Not Favor Prohibition," *St. Helena Star,* September 22, 1916.

28. Handwritten accounting of purchase price of land sold by Roman Catholic Archbishop to Georges de Latour, February 5, 1923, signed by D. O, Crowley, archive of the Archdiocese of San Francisco.

29. "Crushing in Progress and Shipping Going ahead," *St. Helena Star,* October 3, 1919.

30. "Prospects for Making Wine Seem Very Poor," *St. Helena Star,* August 29, 1919.

31. "Plant Being Erected: J. H. Wheeler To Convert Grape Juice Into Syrup," *St. Helena Star,* December 18, 1919.

32. "Have You Heard of Moonmist?" *California Grape Grower (Wines & Vines)* November 1, 1920.

33. "Forbidden Fruit Grape Syrup, *California Grape Grower (Wines & Vines)* November 1, 1920.

34. M. K. Serailian, Medicinal Properties of Grape Syrup, *California Grape Grower (Wines & Vines),* November 1, 1920.

35. Clarence Grange, "Commercial Dehydration of Grapes in California," *California Grape Grower (Wines & Vines)* March 1, 1920.

36. "Modern Drying Plant," from the *Napa Daily Journal, St. Helena Star,* September 19, 1919.

37. "Beringer Brothers Make Successful Experiment," *St. Helena Star,* October 31, 1919.

38. Charles L. Sullivan, A *Companion to California Wine: An Encyclopedia of Wine and Winemaking from the Mission Period to the Present* (Berkeley: University of California Press, 1998) p. 25.

39. "Beringer Brothers Make Successful Experiment, *St. Helena Star,* October 31, 1919.

40. "Vintage is on but not as in Former Years," *St. Helena Star,* September 12, 1919.

41. Richard Orsi, *Sunset Limited: The Southern Pacific Railroad and the Development of the American West, 1850–1930* (Berkeley: University of California Press, 2007) pp. 328–335.

42. "Refrigerator Car Shortage," from the Produce News, reprinted in the *California Grape Grower (Wines & Vines),* June 1, 1920.

43. "Inquiries for Wine Grapes," *California Grape Grower (Wines & Vines),* February 1, 1920.

44. "Leo G. Altmayer Advertisement," *California Grape Grower (Wines & Vines),* April 1, 1920.

45. "Grapes, Grapes, Grapes," advertisement for Jay H. Twitchell & Co., Chicago, *California Grape Grower (Wines & Vines),* September 1, 1920, p. 13

46. "Sam Sebastiani Buys More Property," *Sonoma Index-Tribune,* November 27, 1920, p. 1

47. Stoll H. F., "Have Prohibition Laws Made Growers Prosperous?" *California Grape Grower (Wines & Vines),* January 1, 1921, p.1

48. "Kramer Sums Up First 'Dry' Year" *New York Times,* January 16, 1921.

49. "Wine Grapes Popular in East," *California Grape Grower (Wines & Vines),* March 1, 1921.

50. "Vine Clad Napa Valley: How the Frosted Vines Have Recovered," *California Grape Grower (Wines & Vines),* June 1, 1921.

51. "California's New Grape Acreage," *California Grape Grower (Wines & Vines),* September 1, 1921.

52. "The San Francisco Grape Market: How the Grapes are Handled," *California Grape Grower (Wines & Vines),* October 1, 1921.

53. Louise Davis interview with George Domenichelli and Alice Senteney Stockham Domenichelli, Wine Library Associates of Sonoma County Oral History Series, 1989, Sonoma County Wine Library, Healdsburg.

54. H. F. Stoll, "Have the Growers Learned Their Lessons," *California Grape Grower (Wines & Vines),* November 1, 1922.

Chapter 6

1. Author interviews with Louis J. Foppiano, March 12 and July 5, 2006.

2. Author interviews with Gene Cuneo, July 5 and August 13, 2006.

3. Author interview with Bob Meyer, June 4, 2008.

4. Author interviews with Cuneo.

5. Author interview with Lou Colombano, June 12, 2008.

6. Author interview with Meyer.

7. Author interview with Lou Colombano.

8. Author interviews with Cuneo.

9. Author interview with Colombano.

10. Laurence F. Schmeckebier, *The Bureau of Prohibition: Its History, Activities and Organisation: Service Monographs of the United States Government* (Baltimore: Lord Baltimore Press, 1929) pp. 173–228.

11. "Government of the City of New York," *1920 Almanac and Encyclopedia,* (New York: The Press Publishing Co.,) p. 868.

12. "Average Monthly Earnings Employees Amer. Railroads—Calendar years," *1920 Almanac and Encyclopedia,* (New York: The Press Publishing Co.,) p. 252.

13. "Tests for Dry Agents," *Napa Daily Journal,* December 18, 1919.

14. Daily report of federal Prohibition agents and inspectors, Treasury Department, U.S. Internal Revenue, Form 1494, dated September 13, 1922.

15. Author interview with Rachel Ann Seghesio, May 1, 2008.

16. *United States v. George Crawford,* 14833 (D. C. Cir. 1922).

17. Ibid.

18. Transcription of Bureau of Internal Revenue interview of George H. Crawford. *United States v. George Crawford,* 14833 (D. C. Cir. 1922).

19. Jack W. Florence, Sr., *Legacy of a Village* (Phoenix: Raymond Court Press, 1999) pp. 69–71.

20. Ibid., 114.

21. Ibid., 157–8.

22. Transcription of Bureau of Internal Revenue interview of George H. Crawford. *United States v. George Crawford,* 14833 (D. C. Cir. 1922).

23. Daniel C. Roper, Treasury Department Commissioner to Supervising Federal Prohibition Agent, San Francisco, March 10, 1920, *United States v. George Crawford,* 14833 (D. C. Cir. 1922).

24. "Dry Agents Indicted on Sonoma Wine Bribe Charge, *Healdsburg Tribune,* March 1, 1923.

25. "Dry Agent Took Ten Thousand Dollars," *Sonoma Index-Tribune,* June 21, 1924.

26. "Winery Man is to Get Back Bribe Coin," *Sonoma Index-Tribune,* December 27, 1924.

27. Letter from Inspectors Bennington and Heintz to William Woods, Jr., Supervisor, re: Destruction of Wine, E. Seghesio, Bonded Winery No. 850, June 27, 1931, Seghesio O71, Special Collections, University of California Library, Davis.

28. Author interviews with Cuneo.

29. "Dry Raiders Seize Sacramental Wine," *New York Times,* September 13, 1922.

30. Ibid.

31. Thomas M. Coffey, *The Long Thirst, Prohibition in America: 1920–1933* (New York: Dell Publishing, 1975), p. 100.

32. "Izzy and Moe Seize "Sacramental' Wine: Purchase 10 Cases After Giving Passwords and Using Marked Bank Notes," *New York Times,* October 13, 1922.

33. General Prohibition Agents Louis F. Gale and John Wear to Divisional Chief, December 18, 1922. Twelfth Division: Beaulieu Vineyard, Papers, University of California Library, Davis.

34. George de Latour to E. C. Yellowley, Federal Prohibition Commissioner, August 15, 1922: Beaulieu Vineyard, Papers, University of California Library, Davis.

35. Prohibition Commissioner Haynes to Federal Prohibition Director, October 17, 1922: Beaulieu Vineyard, Papers, University of California Library, Davis

Chapter 7

1. "Italy Exporting Wine Grapes in Barrels, *California Grape Grower* (*Wines & Vines*), May 1, 1923.

2. "Napa County Shipments," *California Grape Grower* (*Wines & Vines*), Jan 1, 1924.

3. H. F. Stoll, "Trials and Tribulations Of the 1923 Vintage Season, *California Grape Grower* (*Wines & Vines*), November 1, 1923.

4. "Real Facts About Our Grape Industry, *California Grape Grower* (*Wines & Vines*), February 1, 1924.

5. "California's Tremendous Grape Acreage, *California Grape Grower* (*Wines & Vines*), April 1, 1924.

6. H. F. Stoll, "Grafting Thompson Vineyards Over Alicante Bouschet, *California Grape Grower* (*Wines & Vines*), December 1, 1924.

7. "Prohibition Enforcement," *California Grape Grower* (*Wines & Vines*), September 1, 1924.

8. "Presidential Candidates," *California Grape Grower* (*Wines & Vines*), October 1, 1924.

9. "The Philadelphia Grape Market," *California Grape Grower* (*Wines & Vines*), April 1, 1925.

10. "Interesting 1924 Grape Statistics, *California Grape Grower* (*Wines & Vines*), June 1, 1925.

11. "Grape Markets in the South," *California Grape Grower* (*Wines & Vines*), November 1, 1925.

12. "Boston as a Grape Market," *California Grape Grower* (*Wines & Vines*), February 1, 1925.

13. "Chicago as a Grape Market," *California Grape Grower* (*Wines & Vines*), March 1, 1925.

14. "Our Greatest Grape Market, *California Grape Grower* (*Wines & Vines*), January 1, 1925.

15. "Sonoma Wineries May Be Quizzed," *Sotoyome Scimitar,* January 23, 1925.

16. "Twice In The Same Place–$750," *Sotoyome Scimitar,* January 2, 1925.

17. "Napa Justice has Right Idea for Bootleggers," *Sotoyome Scimitar,* March 6, 1925.

18. "Federal Forces Out to Break Wine Bootleggers," *Sotoyome Scimitar,* April 6, 1925.

19. "U.S. Prohi Sleuths Irk Napa County Wine Man Much," *Sotoyome Scimitar,* July 31, 1925.

20. "U.S. Destroyed 9,000 Gallons of Sonoma Wine Monday," *Sotoyome Scimitar,* July 24, 1925.
21. "The Stalker Bill: Increasing Penalties for Prohibition Violations," *California Grape Grower (Wines & Vines),* March 1, 1925.
22. "Coolidge to Press Dry Law Limit," *New York Times,* May 20, 1925.
23. "First Shuffle," *TIME* magazine, August 21, 1933.
24. Laurence F. Schmeckebier, *The Bureau of Prohibition, Its History, Activities and Organization,* (Washington, D. C.: The Brookings Institution, 1929), p. 98.
25. Ibid.
26. "Five Liquor Measures," *California Grape Grower (Wines & Vines),* March 1, 1925.
27. "Two Rabbis Are In Toils For Prohibition Violations," *Sotoyome Scimitar,* May 15, 1925.
28. Letter to Most Reverend E. J. Hannah, March 24, 1925, archives of the Roman Catholic Diocese of San Francisco.
29. "Here Is A Crime—Wine 14 Cents," *Sonoma Index-Tribune,* August 15, 1924.
30. H.F. Stoll, "Vintage Season Proves Disappointing to Growers," *California Grape Grower (Wines & Vines),* November 1, 1925.
31. C.L. Brown, "New York Saturated with California Grapes," *California Grape Grower (Wines & Vines),* January 1, 1926.
32. Acting Assistant. Administrator to Chief Inspector, December 19, 1925: Beaulieu Vineyard, Papers, University of California Library, Davis.
33. Acting Divisional Chief, January 7, 1924: Beaulieu Vineyard, Papers, University of California Library, Davis.
34. "Why Are Wineries Running Full Blast," originally ran in the *San Francisco Examiner,* October 4, 1924, and reprinted in the *Sonoma Index-Tribune,* October 11, 1924.
35. Promotional material for George de Latour's Beaulieu Vineyards, undated, archives of the Roman Catholic Diocese of San Francisco.
36. Author interviews with Gene Cuneo, July 5 and August 13, 2006.
37. "Fog Freezes on Trees, Windshields," *Healdsburg Tribune,* January 13, 1926.
38. "Coast Highway Blocked by Slides," *Healdsburg Tribune,* February 9, 1926.
39. "Special Police Battle in Kearney Street; One Killed, Other Wounded," *San Francisco Chronicle,* January 22, 1926.
40. Author interview with Toni Nichelini-Irwin, February to August, 2008.
41. "Big Liquor Stock Seized in Dry Creek," *Healdsburg Tribune,* January 4, 1926.
42. "Two Healdsburg Resorts Raided By Federal Squad," *Healdsburg Tribune,* February 4, 1926.
43. "Wine Seized at Nardi's 'Mile House'" *Healdsburg Tribune,* February 10, 1926.
44. "Revocation Notice Is Not Yet Entirely Clear," *Sotoyome Scimitar,* November 27, 1925.
45. "200 Gallon Wine Permits Cancelled," *Healdsburg Tribune,* February 9, 1926.
46. "Nullification of Permit Privilege," *California Grape Grower (Wines & Vines),* April 1, 1926, p.6
47. "Prohibition Advances in 1925 Claimed By Wheeler," *San Francisco Chronicle,* January 4, 1926.
48. "Here is Your Opportunity to Express Yourself on Prohibition Law," *Healdsburg Tribune,* March 18, 1926.
49. "Wet Voting is Strongest: Half Million Returns," *Healdsburg Tribune,* March 13, 1926.
50. "Nation's Dry Law Poll over a Million," *Healdsburg Tribune,* March 16, 1926.
51. "Straw Vote on Prohibition, *California Grape Grower (Wines & Vines),* April 1, 1926, p.13
52. "Newspaper Poll Has No Effect Upon Congress," *Healdsburg Tribune,* March 25, 1926.
53. Mabel Walker Willebrandt, *The Inside of Prohibition* (Indianapolis: Bobbs-Merrill Company, 1929), p. 111.
54. Laurence F. Schmeckebier, "Separations for Delinquency, January 1920 to February 1926," *The Bureau of Prohibition,* (Washington, DC: The Brookings Institution, 1929), p. 52.
55. Ibid., 47.

56. Ibid., 51.
57. Author interview with Harvey Rose, March 7, 2008.
58. Dorothy M. Brown, *Mabel Walker Willebrandt: A Study of Power, Loyalty, and Law* (Knoxville: University of Tennessee Press, 1984).
59. Mabel Walker Willebrandt, *The Inside of Prohibition* (Indianapolis: Bobbs-Merrill Company, 1929), p. 121.
60. Laurence F. Schmeckebier, "Separations for Delinquency, January 1920 to February 1926," *The Bureau of Prohibition,* (Washington, DC: The Brookings Institution, 1929), p. 52.
61. "Plans Complete For Hearings In Senate On Booze," *Healdsburg Tribune,* April 3, 1926.
62. "Hearings End," *TIME* magazine, May 3, 1926.
63. Statement by Hon. William Cabell Bruce, Senator for Maryland, 1926 Senate Judiciary Committee Hearings on National Prohibition, U.S. Senate, 69th Congress, April 5–24, 1926.
64. Arrest, Conviction and Seizure Tables to accompany Senator Bruce's Comments, U.S. Senate, 69th Congress, April 5–24, 1926.
65. Statement by Hon. William Cabell Bruce, Senator for Maryland, 1926 Senate Judiciary Committee Hearings on National Prohibition, U.S. Senate, 69th Congress, April 5–24, 1926.
66. Table of Arrests for Drunkenness in some of the Leading Cities of the United States, to accompany Senator Bruce's Comments, U.S. Senate, 69th Congress, April 5–24, 1926.
67. "The New York Market in October," *California Grape Grower (Wines & Vines)*, November 1, 1926,
68. "1926 Alicante Bouschet Deal," *California Grape Grower (Wines & Vines)*, November 1, 1926.
69. "The San Francisco Market, Quality Grapes Bring Good Prices," *California Grape Grower (Wines & Vines)*, October 1, 1926.
70. "The Wright Act Upheld," *California Grape Grower (Wines & Vines)*, December 1, 1926.
71. "Government to Double Alcohol Poison Content and Also Add Benzine," *New York Times,* December 30, 1926

Chapter 8

1. Author conversation with Joe Pelanconi, May 31, 2008, and Joe Pelanconi, *Vino & Biscotti* (Tehama, CA; PWJ Publishing, 2004), pp. 25–26.
2. Inspectors Report on Applications, Treasury Dept, dated November 6, 1923, Pelanconi Winery files–058, Bureau of Alcohol, Tobacco and Firearms Archives: California Wineries Records, D–140, Papers, University of California Library, Davis.
3. James Robb, Acting Divisional Chief to E.C. Yellowley, Chief, January 24, 1924: California Wineries Records, Papers, University of California Library, Davis.
4. E.C. Yellowley, Chief to Major R.A. Haynes, Prohibition Commissioner, April 1, 1924: California Wineries Records, Papers, University of California Library, Davis.
5. Inspectors Report on Applications, Treasury Dept., April 14, 1926: California Wineries Records, Papers, University of California Library, Davis.
6. "Rancher Found Dead, Overcome By Wine Fumes," *Healdsburg Tribune,* October 19, 1926.
7. J. A. Eichwaldt, Prohibition Inspector, to the Prohibition Administrator, May 19, 1927: California Wineries Records, Papers, University of California Library, Davis.
8. D. Pelanconi to Prohibition Director, January 3, 1928: California Wineries Records, Papers, University of California Library, Davis.
9. F. H. Driscoll, Chief Inspector to Edward R. Bohner, Prohibition Administrator, February 17, 1928: California Wineries Records, Papers, University of California Library, Davis.
10. "Mike Teldeschi: Vineyardist of Dry Creek Valley, An Oral History," interview by Carole Hicke, 1995, copyright Winegrowers of Dry Creek Valley, p. 7.

11. Author interview with Holly Hoods, Research Curator, Healdsburg Museum, June 9, 2008.
12. Ibid.
13. "New Radio Sets Will Entertain Resort Guests," *Sonoma Index-Tribune*, June 15, 1928.
14. "River Sheikhs and Rum Hounds Beware," *Sonoma Index-Tribune*, February 25, 1928.
15. "Plan of Strict Enforcement is now to Prevail," *Sonoma Index-Tribune*, June 15, 1928.
16. H. F. Stoll, "Raisin Growers Bring Disaster to Grape Industry, *California Grape Grower (Wines & Vines)*, September 1, 1928.
17. "Sam Sebastiani Buys Lodi Wine Plant," *Sonoma Index-Tribune*, March 9, 1928.
18. "Owner Of Big Local Winery Says Arrest Is Mistake," *Sonoma Index-Tribune*, October 19, 1928.
19. "Sam Sebastiani Is Exonerated in Wine Case," *Sonoma Index-Tribune*, November 16, 1928.
20. H. F. Stoll, "Poor Demand for California's Wine Grapes," *California Grape Grower (Wines & Vines)*, October 1, 1928.
21. "All The Grapes You Wanted for Only $4 a Ton," *Sonoma Index-Tribune*, December 21, 1928.
22. "R. Spreckels Favors Smith, Gives Reasons," *Sonoma Index-Tribune*, September 14, 1928.
23. Gilman M. Ostrander, *The Prohibition Movement in California, 1848–1933* (Berkeley: University of California Press, 1957) p. 167.
24. "County Officers Nap Five Bay City Liquor Runners," *Healdsburg Enterprise*, March 7, 1929.
25. "Five Sentenced to Prison for Rum Running," *Healdsburg Enterprise*, March 28, 1929.
26. Author interviews with Harry Bosworth, February and August 2008.
27. Author interview with Harvey Rose, February 27, 2008.
28. Author interview with Mary Perotti Decia, July 2008.
29. William F. Heintz, "*Grapes and Wine in California's Alexander Valley*," November 1979, p. 142–3.
30. "We Used Everything but the Squeal: 1920s–30s Ranch Life In Geyserville, An Oral History With Luke and Gus Tedeschi," interview by Jim Meyers, edited by Holly Hoods, *Russian River Recorder* (Winter 2000), p. 10.
31. "Octopus Grabs Man Hunting Abalones," *Healdsburg Enterprise*, April 25, 1929.
32. "Remmel Griffith Bags 200-lb Bear on Pine Mountain," *Healdsburg Enterprise*, August 8, 1929.
33. "Fire Chief Hooks Trout 17 Inches Long," *Healdsburg Enterprise*, August 8, 1929.
34. Author interviews with Louis J. Foppiano, March 12 and July 5, 2006.
35. Ibid.
36. Author interview with Walter Murray, March 31, 2008.
37. "Farm Relief is Outlined for Grape Growers," *Sonoma Index-Tribune*, March 14, 1930.
38. "Mrs. Doran's Drinks," *TIME* magazine, December 9, 1929.
39. "The Prohibition Chief and His Mirage," *Sonoma Index-Tribune*, September 13, 1929.
40. "New York Grape Market during October," *California Grape Grower (Wines & Vines)*, November 1929.
41. "Never Trust a Stranger, Advice of a Prohi Agent," *Sonoma Index-Tribune*, November 15, 1929.
42. "Prohibition took toll on California Wineries 1920–33," *California Grower (Wines & Vines)*, January 1933.

Chapter 9

1. "To Improve Enforcement of Prohibition," *California Grape Grower (Wines & Vines)*, February 1, 1930.
2. "Turning Tide," *TIME* magazine, February 10, 1930.
3. "Dry Officer Shot in Raid," *St. Helena Star*, January 3, 1930.
4. "South Case Continued," *St. Helena Star*, January 17, 1930.

5.   "Large Still Uncovered," *Napa Register* reprinted in *St. Helena Star*, April 18, 1930.

6.   "Huge Still is Uncovered," *Napa Journal* reprinted in *St. Helena Star*, June 20, 1930.

7.   "Board Sets Grape Price At $17.50 Ton," *Sonoma Index-Tribune*, September 12, 1930.

8.   "What Shall I Do?," *The California Grower, (Wines & Vines)* July 1, 1930.

9.   "Sonoma Grape Demand Is Better," *Sonoma Index-Tribune*, October 3, 1930.

10. "New York 'Racketeers' In War Over California Wine," from *New York Daily News*, used with permission and reprinted in the *Sotoyome Scimitar*, November 13, 1930.

11. C.L. Brown, "Three Major Grape Problems," *California Grape Grower* (*Wines & Vines*), December 1, 1930.

12. "The San Francisco Grape Market," *California Grape Grower* (*Wines & Vines*), December 1, 1930.

13. "The Grape Outlook for 1931," *California Grape Grower* (*Wines & Vines*), February 1, 1931.

14. "Surplus in 1931 Again In Prospect," *Healdsburg Tribune*, February 13, 1931.

15. "Tear Up Vines Advises Banker," *Healdsburg Tribune*, February 18, 1931.

16. California Wine Grapes, 1920–2007, California Historic Commodity Data, Revised in 2008, United States Department of Agriculture, National Agricultural Statistics Service, California Field Office. p.1,
       www. nass.usda.gov.statistics_by_state/California/historical_data/grapes-W.pdf.

17. "Big Whoopee Opens James Rolph Term," United Press story reprinted in *Healdsburg Tribune*, January 5, 1931.

18. "Inaugural Ceremony Of Color Held," United Press story reprinted in *Healdsburg Tribune*, January 6, 1931

19. Governor James Rolph Inaugural Address, presented January 6, 1931, www.californiagovernors.ca.gov/h/documents/inaugural_27.html, accessed November 26, 2008

20. "Mob Refuses to Hear Rolph," United Press story reprinted in *Healdsburg Tribune*, January 8, 1931.

21. "Thousand Riot on S.F. Street," *Tribune Service* story reprinted in *Healdsburg Tribune*, February 2, 1931.

22. "Addition to Reservoir to Help Jobless," *Healdsburg Tribune*, January 6, 1931.

23. "Shoes On Hand for Children," *Healdsburg Tribune*, January 7, 1931.

24. "Aged Itinerant Dies As Food Is Proffered," *Healdsburg Tribune*, January 12, 1931.

25. "Prompt Aid by Local Charity," *Healdsburg Tribune*, January 10, 1931.

26. "Hijackers of Geyserville Wine Seized," *Healdsburg Tribune*, January 9, 1931.

27. "Poison Booze Supply Found at Penngrove," *Healdsburg Tribune*, January 12, 1931.

28. "2 Claim That Dry Agent in Raid 'Drunk,'" *Healdsburg Tribune*, January 28, 1931.

29. "The Story of Fruit Industries, Ltd.," *California Grape Grower* (*Wines & Vines*), February 1, 1931.

30. "Poison Liquor Hits Vets Home," United Press reprinted in *Healdsburg Tribune*, February 20, 1931.

31. "Booze Source Is Traced In Napa Deaths," United Press reprinted in *Healdsburg Tribune*, February 21, 1931.

32. "Poison Alcohol in Woman's Stomach," United Press reprinted in *Healdsburg Tribune*, February 25, 1931.

33. *Report on the Enforcement of the Prohibition Laws of the United States, National Commission on Law Observance and Enforcement,* The Wickersham Commission Report on Alcohol Prohibition, Conclusions and Recommendations, signed by commission, January 7, 1931, sent to President Hoover, January 15, 1931

34. "Hoover Hit in Dry Report," United Press story, printed in *Healdsburg Tribune*, January 21, 1931.

35. "Wicker Shambles," *TIME* magazine, February 2, 1931.
36. Holly Hoods, "From Respectable to Roaring: "The Storied Past of the Riverside Villa," *Russian River Recorder,* no. 95, (Winter 2007).
37. Author interview with Lou V. Colombano, June 5, 2008.
38. Author interview with Gene Cuneo, July 5 and August 13, July 5 and August 13, 2006
39. "The New York Grape Market In September," *California Grape Grower (Wines & Vines),* October 1, 1931.
40. "Enforcement of Laws Cost Held At $101,612,362," United Press reprinted in *Healdsburg Tribune,* February 8, 1932.
41. "Raskob to Back Home Rule Plan For Prohibition," United Press reprinted in *Healdsburg Tribune,* January 6, 1932.
42. "Los Angeles Covered By Snowfall," United Press reprinted in *Healdsburg Tribune,* January 15, 1932.
43. "Snow Blocks Highways in North State, *Healdsburg Tribune,* January 15, 1932.
44. "Revitalise Sonoma Valley Vineyards," *Sonoma Index-Tribune,* August 19, 1932.
45. "Hoover on Westward Swing," United Press reprinted in *Healdsburg Tribune,* November 3, 1932.
46. "Repeal the Wright Act," *California Grape Grower (Wines & Vines),* November 1, 1932.
47. "Throngs Cheer Chief Executive in California, United Press reprinted in *Healdsburg Tribune,* November 8, 1932.
48. http://clerk.house.gov/member_info/electioninfo/1932election.pdf

Chapter 10

1. Richard Paul Hinkle, "Foppiano at the Century Mark," *Wines & Vines* (September 1996).
2. Author conversations with Louis J. Foppiano, spring and summer, 2008
3. Richard Paul Hinkle, "Foppiano at the Century Mark," *Wines & Vines* (September 1996).
4. Milt Brand, memoir, undated, part of the collection of the Healdsburg Museum.
5. "Near Riot at Vineyard Over Failure to Pay Wages," *Sonoma Index-Tribune,* December 2, 1932.
6. "Vineyard Lessee Found Not Guilty Of Criminal Charge," *Sonoma Index-Tribune,* December 9, 1932.
7. "California's Dry Law Prisoners Freed," *Healdsburg Tribune,* December 20, 1932.
8. "Matson Line, Hawaii cruise Advertisement," *Sonoma Index-Tribune,* December 16, 1932.
9. "Grape Growers League Heads Issue Statement on Wine Modification," *Healdsburg Tribune,* December 27, 1932.
10. "Twenty First Amendment," *TIME* magazine, February 27, 1933.
11. H. F. Stoll, "Beer But Not 'Light Wines' Legalised," *California Grape Grower (Wines & Vines),* April, 1933, p. 3.
12. H. F. Stoll, "Beer But Not 'Light Wines' Legalised," *California Grape Grower (Wines & Vines),* April, 1933, p. 3.
13. "Lea Ready to Move For Real Wine," *Healdsburg Enterprise,* March 23, 1933.
14. David E. Kyvig, *Repealing National Prohibition* (Chicago: University of Chicago Press, 1979), (2nd edition: Kent: OH: Kent State University Press, 2000) p. 177.
15. First Inaugural Address of President Franklin D. Roosevelt, Saturday, March 4, 1933, http://avalon.law.yale.edu/20th_century/froos1.asp, (accessed December 1, 2008).
16. "Wave of Activity Sweeps United States: Thousands of Men Return to Work," United Press reprinted in the *Healdsburg Enterprise,* March 30, 1933.
17. "Winery of Late A. Forni is Sold," *Healdsburg Enterprise,* April 6, 1933.
18. "Two Sales of Ranches are Reported here," *Healdsburg Enterprise,* May 18, 1933.

19.   David E. Kyvig, *Repealing National Prohibition* (Chicago: University of Chicago Press, 1979), (2nd edition: Kent: OH: Kent State University Press, 2000) p. 178.

20.   "Prohis Get Wine Stock And Vintner," *Healdsburg Enterprise,* April 27, 1933.

21.   "Rolph Aids Special Vote On Repeal," *Healdsburg Enterprise,* May 4, 1933

22.   H. F. Stoll, "3.2 Percent Wines Make Their Appearance," *California Grape Grower (Wines & Vines)*, May 1, 1933, p. 1.

23.   Ibid.

24.   C. G. Murphy, "Casual Corner," *Sonoma Index-Tribune,* May 5, 1933.

25.   "Local Winery to Enter 3.2 Beverage Trade," *Healdsburg Enterprise,* May 11, 1933.

26.   "Resort Areas Entertain Big Crowds here," *Healdsburg Enterprise,* June 1, 1933.

27.   "Grape Growers Ask New Deal for Big Industry," *Sonoma Index-Tribune,* June 16, 1933.

28.   "Give Grape Growers a New Deal On April 27th," *Sonoma Index-Tribune,* June 16, 1933.

29.   "The Coming Election and Its Problems," *Sonoma Index-Tribune,* June 23, 1933.

30.   Ibid.

31.   H. F. Stoll, "Repeal at an Early Date now Assured," *California Grape Grower (Wines & Vines)*, July 1933.

32.   "Sonoma Valley's Future Brightens with Repeal Vote," *Sonoma Index-Tribune,* July 7, 1933.

33.   "Some New Wine Beverages," *California Grape Grower (Wines & Vines)*, July 1933, p. 13.

34.   "Lea's Pleas for 10 Percent Wine," *California Grape Grower (Wines & Vines)*, July 1933.

35.   "Windsor Castle Raided: Final Prohi Gesture," *Healdsburg Enterprise,* July 6, 1933.

36.   "'Repeal by Christmas,'" *TIME* magazine, July 31, 1933.

37.   "Sales During Week Indicate Vineyard Rise," *Sonoma Index-Tribune,* July 21, 1933.

38.   H. F. Stoll, "California's Convention Ratifies Repeal Amendments," *California Grape Grower (Wines & Vines)*, August 1933.

39.   H. F. Stoll, "Distribution of the 1933 Wine Grape Crop," *California Grape Grower (Wines & Vines)*, September 1933.

40.   "California's Wine Production," *California Grape Grower (Wines & Vines)*, October 1933.

41.   "Dry Enforcement Bureau Passes, *California Grape Grower (Wines & Vines)*, September 1933.

42.   "$35 per Ton Is Being Offered To Vineyardists," *Sonoma Index-Tribune,* September 29, 1933.

43.   "Activities in Wineries Bring Stimulated Business In North Bay Area, Banker Declares," *Healdsburg Enterprise,* September 28, 1933.

44.   "California's Wine Production," *California Grape Grower (Wines & Vines)*, October 1933.

45.   "Progress of Prohibition," *California Grape Grower (Wines & Vines)*, October 1933.

46.   "Poison Rum Blinds S.R. Youth, Ralph Holm Loses Sight After Party," *The Press Democrat,* October 4, 1933.

47.   Clarence P. Stewart, "Twenty-Nine States will be Dry as ever when Eighteenth Amendment is Repealed," *Press Democrat,* October 7, 1933.

48.   "Grapes Bought at $40 A Ton," *The Press Democrat,* October 1, 1933.

49.   "Importation of Cheap Grapes Here Bared," *The Press Democrat,* October 17, 1933.

50.   Grape Men Map Fight To Guard Old Name of Sonoma County Wines, *The Press Democrat,* October 26, 1933.

51.   "Wine Industry Puts 20,000 to Work in Plants," *Healdsburg Enterprise,* November 9, 1933.

52.   "Repeal Goes Over the Top," *Sonoma Index-Tribune,* November 10, 1933.

53.   "'Hard Liquor' Sold in Cafes, 'Speaks' Thrown Open in S.F.," *Press Democrat,* November 8, 1933.

54.   "Local Italian Club Celebrates Repeal of 18th Amendment," *Sonoma Index-Tribune,* November 10, 1933.

55.   "Sonoma County Heads the List with 69 Wineries, *Sonoma Index-Tribune,* November 10, 1933.

56. Jack Florence, *Legacy of a Village: The Italian Swiss Colony and People of Asti, California* (Phoenix: Raymond Court Press, 1999), p. 167.
57. "First Train of Wine Leaves Asti Winery," *Healdsburg Enterprise,* November 23, 1933.
58. Author conversation with Lou Colombano, September 17, 2008.
59. "Wine Given Special Handling and Storage," *California Grape Grower (Wines & Vines),* December 1933, p. 11.
60. "'Cans' and 'Can'ts' after Repeal are outlined by Law Experts," United Press reprinted in *Healdsburg Enterprise,* December 7, 1933.
61. "Sonoma Wine Men Rejoicing Over Change," *Sonoma Index-Tribune,* December 8, 1933.
62. "Great Activity at Wineries in Napa Valley Greets End of Prohibition," *St. Helena Star,* December 8, 1933.
63. "Beaulieu Wine Plant is Ready for New Boom," *San Francisco Chronicle,* December 6, 1933.
64. "$75,000 Wine Cargo Shipped at Cloverdale," *Press Democrat,* December 7, 1933.
65. "Martini Puts Winery in Dry Grape Country," *San Francisco Chronicle,* December 6, 1933.
66. "Hello, D-R-Y 1933," *San Francisco Chronicle,* December 6, 1933.
67. Dr. S.W. Shear, "The Wine-Grape Situation," *California Grape Grower (Wines & Vines),* November 1933.
68. Author interview with Louis J. Foppiano, September 14, 2008.
69. Author interview with Toni Nichelini-Irwin, September 12, 2008.

Bibliography

Allsop, Kenneth. *The Bootleggers and Their Era.* Garden City, N. Y.: Doubleday Company Inc., 1961.

Allsop, Kenneth. *The Bootleggers: The Story of Chicago's Prohibition Era,* New Rochelle, N.Y.: Arlington House, 1961.

Asbury, Herbert. *The Barbary Coast.* Garden City, NY : Garden City Publishing Company, Inc., 1933.

Asbury, Herbert. *The Great Illusion: An Informal History of Prohibition.* Garden City, NJ.: Doubleday & Company, 1950.

Bean, Walton. *California: An Interpretive History.* New York: McGraw-Hill, Inc, 1968.

Behr, Edward. *Prohibition: Thirteen Years that Changed America.* New York: Arcade Publishing, 1996.

Bowden, Carlos Jr. *Italians of the Bay Area: Images of America.* Charleston, SC, Chicago: Arcadia Publishing, 2006.

Brown, Dorothy M. *Mabel Walker Willebrandt: A Study of Power, Loyalty, and Law.* Knoxville: University of Tennessee Press, 1984.

Buti, Bruno. *Jackass Brandy.* Cloverdale, CA: Buti Publications, 1994.

Cashman, Sean Dennis. *Prohibition: The Lie of the Land.* New York: The Free Press, Macmillan Publishing, Co. Inc., 1981.

Clar, C. Raymond. *Out of the River Mist.* Palo Alto: River Mist Distributors, 1984.

Clark, Norman H. *Deliver Us from Evil: An Interpretation of American Prohibition.* New York: W.W. Norton & Company, 1976.

Clark, Norman H. *The Dry Years: Prohibition and Social Change in Washington.* Seattle: University of Washington Press, 1988.

Coffey, Thomas M. *The Long Thirst, Prohibition in America:* 1920–1933. New York: Laurel Edition, Dell Publishing, 1975.

Conaway, James. *Napa.* Boston: Houghton, Mifflin Company, 1990.

Conaway, James. *The Far Side of Eden: New Money, Old Land, and the Battle for Napa Valley.* Boston: Houghton Mifflin Company, 2002.

Coodley, Lauren. *Napa: The Transformation of an American Town.* Charleston, SC: Arcadia Publishing, 2004.

de Groot, Roy Andries. *The Wines of California: The Pacific Northwest & New York,* New York: Summit Books, 1982.

Dobyns, Fletcher. *The Amazing Story of Repeal: An Expose of the Power of Propaganda.* Chicago: Willett, Clark & Company, 1940.

Duis, Perry R. *The Saloon: Public Drinking in Chicago and Boston 1880–1920.* Urbana: University of Illinois Press, 1983.

Durham, David L. *Place-Names of California's Old Wine Country.* Clovis, CA: Quill Driver Books/Word Dancer Press, Inc., 2000.

Engelmann, Larry. *Intemperance: The Lost War Against Liquor.* New York: The Free Press, 1979.

Essig, E. O. Adele Ogden, Clarence John Dufour. *Fort Ross: California Outpost of Russian Alaska 1812–1841.* Kingston, Ontario: The Limestone Press, 1991.

Fisher, Irving. *Prohibition at its Worst.* New York: Alcohol Information Committee, 1927.

Fleming, Thomas. *The Illusion of Victory: America in World War I.* New York: Basic Books, 2003.

Florence, Jack. W. Sr. *Legacy of a Village: The Italian Swiss Colony Winery and People of Asti, California.* Geyserville, CA: Raymond Court Press, 1999.

Florence, Jack W., Sr. *A Noble Heritage: The Wines and Vineyards of Dry Creek Valley, Healdsburg.* Wine Growers of Dry Creek Valley, 1993.

Gaffey, James P. *Citizen of No Mean City: Archbishop Patrick Riordan of San Francisco (1841–1914).* Wilmington, NC: A Consortium Book, 1976.

Gribble, Richard. *An Archbishop for the People: The Life of Edward J. Hanna.* New York and Mahwah, NJ: Paulist Press, 2006.

Hagedorn, Ann. *Savage Peace: Hope and Fear in America, 1919.* New York: Simon & Schuster, 2007.

Hamm, Richard F. *Shaping the 18th Amendment: Temperance Reform, Legal Culture, and the Polity, 1880–1920.* Chapel Hill: University of North Carolina Press, 1995.

Hawkes, Ellen. *Blood & Wine: The Unauthorized Story of the Gallo Wine Empire.* New York: Simon & Schuster, 1993.

Haynes, Irene. *Ghost Wineries of Napa Valley.* San Francisco: The Wine Appreciation Guild, 1995.

Haynes, Roy A. and President Warren Harding. *Prohibition Inside Out.* Garden City, NJ: Doubleday, Page & Company, 1923.

Healdsburg Museum and Historical Society. *Healdsburg: Images of America,* Charleston, SC: Arcadia Publishing, 2005.

Heintz, William F. *California's Napa Valley: One Hundred Sixty Years of Wine Making.* San Francisco: Scottwall Associates, 1999.

Heintz, William F. *Wine Country: A History of Napa Valley The Early Years: 1838–1920.* Santa Barbara: Capra Press, 1990.

Heinzel, Hermann. *Birds of Napa County.* Berkeley, CA: Heyday Books, 2006.

Howell, Patton, editor, with Mary Ann McComber, Ruth Berggren, Donald McComber;, Lawrence Barker, and Joan Howell. *Napa Valley.* San Francisco: Saybrook Publishing Co., Inc., 2000.

Issler, Anne Roller. *Stevenson at Silverado.* Fresno, CA: Valley Publishers, 1974.

Jacobs Altman, Linda. *The Decade that Roared: America during Prohibition.* New York: Twenty-First Century Books, 1997.

Johnson, Paul. *A History of the American People.* London: Phoenix Giant, Orion Books, 1998.

Kennedy, David M. *Freedom From Fear, The American People in Depression and War, 1929–1945.* New York: Oxford University Press, 1999.

Kernberger, David and Kathleen Kerberger, *Mark Strong's Napa Valley 1886–1929,* Napa, CA: Schieck Printing, 1978.

Kerr, K. Austin. *Organized for Prohibition: A New History of the Anti-Saloon League.* New Haven: Yale University Press, 1985.

Kobler, John. *Ardent Spirits: The Rise and Fall of Prohibition.* New York: G.P. Putnam's Sons, 1973.

Kruckeberg, Arthur R. *Introduction to California Soils and Plants,* Berkeley, Los Angeles: University of California Press, 2006.

Kyvig, David E. *Repealing National Prohibition,* Chicago: University of Chicago Press, 1979, 2nd edition, Kent: OH: Kent State University Press, 2000.

Kyvig, David E. *Daily Life in the United States 1920–1940: How Americans Lived Through the Roaring Twenties and the Great Depression.* Chicago: Ivan R. Dee, Publisher, 2002.

Laube, James. *Wine Spectator's California Wine.* New York: Wine Spectator Press, 1995.

LeBaron, Gaye and Mitchell, Joanne. *Santa Rosa: A Twentieth Century Town.* Santa Rosa, CA: Historia, 1993.

Lerner, Michael A. *Dry Manhattan: Prohibition in New York City.* Cambridge, MA: Harvard University Press, 2007.

London, Jack. *The Valley of the Moon.* Berkeley, Los Angeles and London: University of California Press, 1999.

Lukacs, Paul. *American Vintage: The Rise of American Wine.* New York: W. W. Norton & Company, 2000.

MacMillan, Margaret. *Paris 1919.* New York: Random House, 2001.

Mathes, Valerie Sherer and Diane Moll Smith. *Sonoma Valley: Images of America.* Charleston, SC.: Arcadia Publishing, 2004.

Maxwell-Long, Thomas. *Napa County Wineries: Images of America,* Chicago: Arcadia Publishing, 2002.

Maxwell-Long, Thomas; *Sonoma County Wineries: Images of America,* Chicago: Arcadia Publishing, 2001.

Merz, Charles. *The Dry Decade.* Seattle: University of Washington Press, 1969.

Murray, Robert K. *The Harding Era.* Minneapolis: University of Minnesota Press, 1969.

Napa Valley Museum and Weber, Lin. *Napa Valley Wine Country.* Charleston, SC: Arcadia Publishing, 2004.

Nishi, Dennis, *Prohibition.* Farmington Hills, MI: Greenhaven Press, 2003.

Olson, James S. *Historical Dictionary of the 1920s: From World War I to the New Deal, 1919–1933.* Westport, CN: Greenwood Press, 1988.

Oppel, Frank. *Tales of California.* Secaucus, NJ: Castle Books, 1989

Orsi, Richard J. *Sunset Limited: The Southern Pacific Railroad and the Development of the American West, 1850–1930.* Berkeley: University of California Press, 2005.

Osbourne, Katharine D., *Robert Louis Stevenson in California,* Chicago: A.C. McClurg & Co., 1911.

Ostrander, Gilman. *The Prohibition Movement in California, 1848–1933.* Berkeley: University of California Press, 1957.

Parker, Reny. *Wildflowers of Northern California's Wine Country & North Coast Ranges.* Cloverdale, CA: New Creek Ranch Press, 2007.

Parrish, Michael E., Anxious Decades: America in Prosperity and Depression: 1920–1941, New York: W. W. Norton & Company, 1992.

Pegram, Thomas R. *Battling Demon Rum: The Struggle for a Dry America, 1800–1933.* Chicago: Ivan R. Dee, 1998.

Pelanconi, Joe. *Vino & Biscotti: Italy to Sonoma County and Back.* Tehama, CA: PWJ Publishing, 2004.

Peninou, Ernest P. *History of the Sonoma Viticultural District, Volume 1.* Santa Rosa, CA: Nomis Press, 1998.

Pinney, Thomas. *A History of Wine in America. From Prohibition to the Present. Berkeley and Los Angeles:* Berkeley: University of California Press, 2005.

Powers, Madelon. *Faces Along the Bar: Lore and Order in the Workingman's Saloon, 1870–1920.* Chicago: The University of Chicago Press, 1998.

Prchal, Dolly. *Josephine Marlin Tychson: The First Woman Winemaker in California 3.* no. 4 (1986). Napa CA: Napa County Historical Society.

Ray, Barbara F., *Windsor: Images of America,* Charleston, SC: Arcadia Publishing, 2004.

Richards, Leonard L. *The California Gold Rush and the Coming of the Civil War.* New York: Alfred A. Knopf, 2007.

Rose, Kenneth D. *American Women and the Repeal of Prohibition.* New York and London: New York University Press, 1996.

Russack, Benjamin. *Wine Country: A Literary Companion.* Berkeley: Heyday Books, 1998.

Schlesinger, Arthur M., Jr. *The Age of Roosevelt: The Crisis of the Old Order 1919–1933.* Boston: Houghton Mifflin Company, 1957.

Schmeckebier, Laurence F. *The Bureau of Prohibition: Its History, Activities and Organization.* Washington, DC: The Brookings Institution, 1929.

Sinclair, Andrew. *Era of Excess: A Social History of the Prohibition Movement.* New York: Harper & Row, 1964.

Smith, Rod. *Private Reserve: Beaulieu Vineyard and the Rise of Napa Valley.* Stamford, CN: Daglan Press, 2000.

Sparks, Drew and Sally, Kellman. *A Salon at Larkmead: A Charmed Life in the Napa Valley.* Berkeley: Ten Speed Press, 2000.

Starr, Kevin. *Americans and the California Dream, 1850–1915.* New York: Oxford University Press, 1973.

Starr, Kevin. *Endangered Dreams: The Great Depression in California.* New York: Oxford University Press, 1996.

Steuart, Justin. *Wayne Wheeler: Dry Boss.* Westport: Greenwood Press, Westport, 1970, orig. publisher, New York: Revell Co., 1928.

Stevenson, Robert Louis, *An Inland Voyage and the Tale of the Silverado Squatters,* Charleston, SC: BiblioBazaar, 2006.

Street, Richard Steven. *Beasts of the Field: A Narrative History of California Farmworkers, 1769–1913.* Stanford, CA: Stanford University Press, 2004.

Sullivan, Charles L. *Napa Wine: A History.* San Francisco: The Wine Appreciation Guild, 1994.

Sullivan, Charles L. *A Companion to California Wine: An Encyclopedia of Wine and Winemaking from the Mission Period to the Present.* Berkeley and Los Angeles: University of California Press, 1998.

Sullivan, Charles L. *Zinfandel: A History of a Grape and Its Wine.* Berkeley and Los Angeles: University of California Press, 2003.

The World, 1920 Almanac and Encyclopedia, New York: Press Publishing Company, 1919.

Tydings, Millard E. *Before and After Prohibition.* New York: Macmillan Company, 1930.

Watkins, T. H. *The Great Depression: America in the 1930s.* Boston: Little Brown and Company, 1993.

Watkins, T. H. *The Hungry Years: A Narrative History of the Great Depression in America.* New York: Henry Holt and Company, 1999.

Weber, Lin. *Roots of the Present: Napa Valley 1900 to 1950.* St. Helena, CA: Wine Ventures Publishing, 2001.

Weber, Lin. *Old Napa Valley: The History to 1900.* St. Helena, CA: Wine Ventures Publishing, 1998.

Wichels, John. *Railroads in Napa County, Why They Came and Why They Failed.* Napa, CA: Napa County Historical Society, 1979.

Willebrandt, Mabel Walker. *The Inside of Prohibition,* Indianapolis: The Bobbs Company, 1929.

Wilson, Edmund. *The American Earthquake: A Documentary of the Jazz Age, the Great Depression, and the New Deal.* Garden City, NJ: Doubleday Anchor Books, 1958.

Zee, John van der. *Welcome Iron Steed, Healdsburg's Railroad Days.* Healdsburg: Healdsburg Arts Council, 1998.

Index